CASE STUDIES IN THE
NEUROPSYCHOLOGY OF VISION

Case studies in the neuropsychology of vision

edited by
Glyn W. Humphreys
University of Birmingham, UK

Psychology Press
a member of the Taylor & Francis group

Psychology Press Ltd, Publishers
27 Church Road
Hove
East Sussex, BN3 2FA
UK

British Library Cataloguing in Publication Data

A catalogue record for this book is available from the British Library

ISBN 0-86377-895-X (hbk)
ISBN 0-86377-896-8 (pbk)

Cover design by Stephen Kent. Illustrations taken from
the "Foreshortened View Task" from *BORB* (*Birmingham
Object Recognition Battery*), M. Jane Riddoch & Glyn W.
Humphreys, © 1993 Psychology Press Ltd.

Typeset by Graphicraft Limited, Hong Kong
Printed and bound in the UK by Biddles Ltd, Guildford and King's Lynn

Contents

List of contributors

Marlene Behrmann, Department of Psychology, Carnegie Mellon University, Pittsburgh, PA 15213-3890, USA

Alan Cowey, Department of Experimental Psychology, University of Oxford, South Parks Road, Oxford, OX1 3UD, UK

Jules Davidoff, Department of Psychology, Goldsmiths' College, University of London, London SE14 6NW, UK

Edward H.F. De Haan, Psychological Laboratory, Utrecht University, Heidelberglaan 2, 3584 CS Utrecht, The Netherlands

Martha J. Farah, Department of Psychology, University of Pennsylvania, 3815 Walnut St, Philadelphia, PA 19104-6196, USA

Emer M.E. Forde, Psychology Institute, University of Aston, Aston Triangle, Birmingham B4 7ET, UK

Charlie A. Heywood, Department of Psychology, Science Laboratories, University of Durham, South Road, Durham, DH1 3LE, UK

Glyn W. Humphreys, Cognitive Science Research Centre, School of Psychology, University of Birmingham, Edgbaston, Birmingham, B15 2TT, UK

Morris Moscovitch, Department of Psychology, Erindale College, University of Toronto, Canada; and Rotman Research Institute, Baycrest Centre for Geriatric Care, Toronto, Canada

M. Jane Riddoch, Cognitive Science Research Centre, School of Psychology, University of Birmingham, Edgbaston, Birmingham, B15 2TT, UK

Elizabeth K. Warrington, National Hospital, Queen Square, London WC1N 3BG, UK

Gordon Winocur, Department of Psychology, Erindale College, University of Toronto, Canada; and Rotman Research Institute, Baycrest Centre for Geriatric Care, Toronto, Canada; and Department of Psychology, Trent University, Trent, Canada

Josef Zihl, Max-Planck-Institut für Psychiatrie, Kraepelinstrasse 10, 80804 Munich, Germany

General background

Disorders of vision, consequent on selective brain lesion, have been known since the beginnings of modern neurology. Indeed, many of the classic accounts that have dominated thinking up to the present day stem from that time—an example being Lissauer's (1890) classification of the visual agnosias (see Humphreys, Farah, this volume). Throughout this period, much of the research has been undertaken on single patients who have presented with unusual, and informative, clinical deficits. Case studies have formed the bedrock on which the neuropsychology of vision has been built.

There are several reasons for the dominance of case studies in this field. One is the paucity of patients. Disorders of vision are associated with damage to posterior brain regions, and disorders of object perception and recognition—highlighted in this book—are linked with lesions of inferior ventral (occipito-temporal) areas. These regions are not close to the major blood supplies to the brain, and so are less likely than some brain regions to be the victim of some common causes of brain insult, such as haemorrhages. In addition, many frank disorders of object perception and recognition occur only following bilateral damage (since the neural systems involved are bilaterally represented). Only a minority of patients will suffer bilateral damage to the critical areas.

Although interesting single case studies in this field have long been reported, it can be argued that it was not until the early 1980s that neuropsychological research in vision began to be linked to detailed theoretical accounts of visual processing. The work of Elizabeth Warrington in the late 1970s was crucial in this respect. She showed that patients could achieve high-level perceptual representations of objects (e.g. they might be able to match pictures of objects shown from different views) and yet still fail to recognise the objects. She also demonstrated that there could be selective problems in deriving high-level perceptual representations, so that patients were impaired at matching objects across views though many other visual-perceptual abilities remained intact (see Chapter 4). This research influenced theorists such as David Marr (1982), who used evidence of high-level perceptual abilities in the absence of recognition to argue for a bottom-up approach to object processing. The emergent theories have since played an important part in constraining accounts of how perception and recognition break down, with the theories in turn being embellished to accommodate subsequent neuropsychological data.

This book contains seven chapters that deal with disorders of visual perception and object recognition, and that relate the disorders to contemporary accounts of object processing (Chapters 4–10). The chapters highlight many of the recent single case studies that have helped to advance our understanding of object perception and recognition. The cases range from patients with disorders of early stages of visual processing (Humphreys) through to those with deficits in memory access and retrieval (Riddoch, de Haan). The chapters also cover disorders that affect different kinds of objects to different degrees. Forde, for example, reviews evidence on patients whose problems are restricted to certain classes of object—most usually, a deficit for living things (animals, birds, insects, also fruits and vegetables) relative to nonliving things. These differences may reflect disorders at different levels of the object-processing system in different patients, with at least some problems due to impairments of particular types of stored knowledge. Farah, in the final chapter, discusses her idea that agnosias for objects, words and faces (the latter typically being termed alexia and prosopagnosia) can be due to impairments to certain forms of perceptual description. Impairments to the coding of wholistic perceptual descriptions will affect faces and some objects; impairments to the coding of partonomic descriptions will affect words and some objects. This interesting proposal leads to testable predictions concerning the relations between agnosias for different stimuli.

On at least some accounts, stored visual knowledge about objects is not only used on-line during object recognition, but it is also interrogated off-line when we have to answer questions about the visual properties of objects from their name. This notion, of off-line interrogation of perceptual knowledge stores, can be used to explain some aspects of category-specific deficits found in patients (Forde). The proposal is examined in some detail in Behrmann's chapter, which reviews evidence for imagery processes being intact in agnosia. At least in cases where the agnosia seems due to relatively early perceptual impairments, some degree of dissociation can be observed (see also Humphreys). Exactly which processes overlap, and which are distinguished, in imagery and perception is an old question that is beginning to be addressed through these neuropsychological studies.

Other old questions being addressed by neuropsychologists concern whether visual information can be used for action even when the particular objects involved cannot be recognised, and whether patients can process information to a certain level without being conscious of doing so. The question of the relations between recognition and action is considered in the chapter by Riddoch. She argues that some learned actions can be initiated by direct association with stored visual knowledge even when a patient fails to retrieve full semantic information about the object and its associations. She suggests that this dissociation between recognition and action can be seen in the syndrome "optic aphasia". The question of unconscious processing of information is dealt with by de Haan, who reviews evidence of unconscious face processing in prosopagnosia. Such work demonstrates that information can be processed covertly, when brain damage limits explicit access to outputs from perceptual processing.

The book begins, however, with chapters dealing with visual disorders affecting perceptual modules for colour and motion. Since the early neuropsychological case studies of vision, patients have been documented not only with disorders of object recognition, but also with central deficits affecting the processing of even the basic dimensions of vision—colour, motion, even texture (Battelli, Casco & Sartori, 1997). Studies of these patients have been important for understanding how the brain processes elementary properties of the visual world, since evidence of selective breakdowns suggest that such properties are processed independently. Disorders of motion perception are reviewed by Heywood and Zihl and disorders of colour perception are considered by Heywood and Cowey.

Overall I hope that the chapters in the book illustrate the worth of single-case analyses in this field, and how insights from neuropsychological impairments can help shed light on the complex process of vision.

GLYN W. HUMPHREYS

REFERENCES

Battelli, L., Casco, C., & Sartori, G. (1997). Dissociation between contour-based and texture-based shape perception: A single case study. *Visual Cognition, 4*, 275–310.

Lissauer, H. (1890). Ein Fall von seelenblindheit nebst einem Beitrage zur Theorie derselben. *Archiv für Psychiatrie und Nervenkrankheiten, 21*, 222–270.

Marr, D. (1982). *Vision*. San Fransisco: W.H. Freeman.

CHAPTER ONE

Motion blindness

C.A. Heywood
Department of Psychology, Science Laboratories,
University of Durham, UK

J. Zihl
Max-Planck-Institute für Psychiatrie, Munich, Germany

INTRODUCTION

It is no longer disputed that one of the, albeit rare, consequences of brain damage is a remarkably selective impairment of vision. This contrasts with the scepticism that met earlier reports in the latter years of the last century of selective sparing, or disruption, of the ability to perceive motion or colour. Such disturbances were at odds with prevailing opinions about cortical organisation (see Zeki, 1990a, 1991, for reviews). The view was trenchantly held that the visual image on the retina, encoding the many attributes of the visual scene, was transmitted to, and passively analysed by, a single region of visual cortex residing in the occipital lobe. It was argued that if a single region were responsible for processing the many attributes of the visual scene then damage to this region should compromise the perception of all of them. Selective disturbance, or sparing, of a single attribute could not readily be explained in this scheme of things. Recent acceptance of the existence of selective disorders stems partly from substantial advances in our understanding, derived chiefly from animal studies, of the anatomy and physiology of the visual pathways in the brain. These studies have been supplemented by conclusions drawn from careful behavioural assessment of single neurological cases who have sustained brain damage.

The discovery of an impressive patchwork of cortical visual areas that lies in the extrastriate cortex of the monkey has led to the suggestion that each is relatively specialised for the processing of a particular visual attribute (see Chapter 2). The homologous, or analogous, regions in the human brain are now beginning

1

to be identified and it is a simple step to conclude that the destruction of a single area will result in the disturbance of a single function. However, the problems with this apparently straightforward view are manifold (Cowey, 1994). First, some 30 areas have now been identified in the macaque monkey and we would perhaps be hard pressed to readily identify an equivalent number of visual attributes, e.g. colour, motion, form and depth. Certainly, one cannot easily infer the role of an individual area on the basis of the response properties of its neurons. The regional variation in receptive field properties of cells is not so clear as to provide an unerring indicator of the role of an area in visual processing. Second, only a small number of apparently selective disorders, e.g. impairments in the perception of colour, motion, form, space and depth, have, as yet, been identified in neurological patients. Third, and more alarmingly, surgical removal of a single visual area in the monkey has rarely, if ever, resulted in a deficit that parallels any of the clinical findings.

However, all is not lost. Selective disorders could reveal themselves in many guises and may not be revealed by tasks which merely require simple discriminations within a particular visual dimension. For example, impairments of colour memory, colour naming or colour constancy may exist without loss of colour discrimination (see Chapter 2). The difficulty may thus stem from establishing, and adequately specifying, the behavioural deficit. It is becoming clear that what can readily be viewed as a single visual dimension, e.g. orientation, direction, wavelength or disparity, can each be used to define a particular visual attribute. For example, a shape can be perceived, among other things, on the basis of chromatic, luminance or velocity differences between figure and ground. In principle, it is then possible for a deficit in the perception of form defined by one dimension to exist with a spared ability to perceive form defined by another. Such fractionation of disorders has become possible as perceptual tests become more sophisticated. Similarly, the fact that cortical areas cannot readily be distinguished on the basis of the proportion of cells responding to particular visual dimensions may reflect the crudity in the way in which receptive fields are characterised. The use of comparatively impoverished stimuli to test receptive field properties may conceal real differences among apparently similar populations. Thus, cells in area V1 respond to the direction of the component parts of a moving pattern while cells in area MT respond to the global pattern motion (Movshon, Adelson, Gizzi, & Newsome, 1985) and to the relative motion of a stimulus against its background (Allman, Miezin, & McGuinness, 1985).

Notwithstanding these difficulties, it is with one of the most striking disorders that considerable strides have been made in understanding its relation to the organisation and function of the primate visual system. The discovery of a region of the monkey brain, cortical area V5 (also known as MT), provided strong evidence that the visual cortex of the monkey brain is functionally specialised (Zeki, 1974). Neurones in this region are finely tuned to the direction of visual motion and it was promptly referred to as "the motion area". Thereafter, the case of a patient with a relatively selective and profound deficit in the perception of visual motion was reported (Zihl, von Cramon, & Mai, 1983).

THE CASE OF L.M.

In May 1980 a 43 year-old female patient, L.M., arrived at the Neuropsychological Unit of the Max-Planck-Institute for Psychiatry in Munich, Germany. She had sustained brain damage in October 1978 when she had suddenly lost consciousness and was admitted to hospital. L.M. reported that looking at objects in motion made her feel quite unwell. The explanation she gave sounded rather odd. She claimed that she no longer saw movement; objects which should move, as she well remembered, now appeared as "restless" or "jumping around". Although she could see objects at different locations and distances, she was unable to find out what happened to them between these locations. She was sure that objects did not move, but appeared as "jumping from one position to the next, but nothing is in between". Because of these difficulties she avoided streets, busy places, supermarkets and cafés. Traffic had become very frightening; she could still identify cars without any difficulty but could not tell whether they were moving or stationary. The only way for her to establish this was to wait until the car became either conspicuously bigger or smaller. However, this turned out to be very complicated, especially when there were other cars in the vicinity. As a consequence, she no longer risked crossing the street except at pedestrian crossings. When people walked nearby, she usually waited until they passed, because the "restlessness" they produced by their walking irritated her so much that she had to interrupt her walking to find a "resting point for my eyes". Furthermore, she reported substantial difficulty in pouring fluids into a cup or glass, because the tea, coffee or orange juice appeared "frozen like a glacier". She could not see the fluid rising, and therefore, couldn't establish when to stop pouring. In addition, she felt very irritated when looking at people while they were speaking: their lips appear to "hop up and down", so she had to look away so as not to become confused. "To my friends, this behavior appears very strange if not unkind; they believe that I am no longer interested in their conversation because I am always looking absent-minded. But it is the only way to listen to them without being disturbed". For this reason she had decided no longer to meet her friends.

The patient quite accurately described her difficulties, and attributed them correctly to her illness. However, her difficulties were initially not assumed to be exclusively caused by brain damage, but were attributed, at least in part, to agoraphobia. The original diagnosis was made in the absence of any convincing alternative to explain her striking behaviour, especially in the first weeks and months, which presented a severe handicap in her daily activities. For example, she was unable to wash and dress herself, but had no obvious motor or somatosensory deficits; she had difficulty in understanding language, but had no aphasia; she could not perform activities like using a vacuum cleaner or preparing a plain meal, but had no apraxia. All her activities were extremely slow and cautious.

In contrast to these functional impairments, she seemed to have normal intellectual abilities, including memory and planning. Apparently no expert believed the patient's report, probably partly because no similar case could be found in the neurological and neuropsychological literature. On the contrary, well-known authorities, such as Holmes, Critchley and later Teuber, had generally refused to accept clinical reports on selective impairments of individual visual functions (for a detailed review, see Zeki, 1993). Admittedly, in contrast to the body of evidence for the existence of achromatopsia, the selective loss of colour vision (Zeki, 1990a), the evidence for selectively impaired movement vision was not strong before the report of patient L.M. (Zeki, 1991). The only case with impaired movement vision after acquired brain damage that had been examined in detail was reported by Goldstein and Gelb (1918) (case Schn . . .). However, these authors interpreted their case as a special type of apperceptive visual agnosia ("visual form agnosia"). Accordingly, Goldstein and Gelb considered the loss of movement vision in the same patient as just one symptom of the impairment in (actively) constructing a Gestalt. Poppelreuter (1923) doubted the "pureness" and specificity of visual form agnosia in this case, because the patient showed additional visual deficits, among them a concentric loss of form vision in the region of the extrafoveal visual field, which could explain his difficulties with the identification of moving visual objects. In addition, Jung, who in 1949 published a detailed re-examination on the same patient, put the existence of visual agnosia in this case in doubt, because he was unable to find evidence for a "form or movement blindness". Jung recognised the scientific value of single-case studies, but stressed the importance of "elaborated" examinations in such studies. This view was later adopted by Shallice (1977), who pointed out that detailed experimental analysis of single cases can sometimes contribute much more to the understanding of brain organisation than group studies of patients with multiple defects which are difficult to compare. This argument is particularly forceful since cases with selective functional deficits caused by brain damage are extremely rare. No doubt this is because, as Campbell pointed out at the beginning of the century (1905), ". . . it is almost impossible for nature to restrict a damaging lesion to the cortex, and to the cortex only, in question."

BEHAVIOURAL CONSEQUENCES OF L.M.'S MOVEMENT VISION DISORDER

When L.M. was first tested, some 18 months after brain damage had occurred, she was severely handicapped. At that time she lived alone because her husband had died about three years earlier. Before her illness, she had been running a small electrical retail business. Although she showed considerable improvement

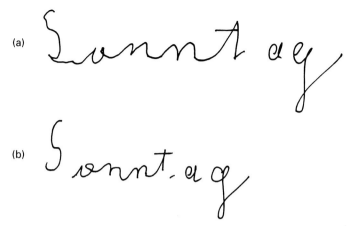

FIG. 1.1   L.M. was asked to write "Sonntag" (a) with eyes open and (b) with eyes closed. She was substantially less hesitant with her eyes closed, reflected in the time taken to perform the task: eyes open, 26s; eyes closed 4s.

during her stay in the rehabilitation centre, she was judged as totally disabled in her daily life. In August 1980, Dr Mai and one of us (J.Z.) provided regular practice for L.M. with daily activities like crossing streets, using buses and the tube, shopping in supermarkets, walking in the presence of other pedestrians, cooking, cleaning the apartment, active participation in discussions (starting with only two people), and writing. Of course, understandably L.M. was often very frightened and developed an exaggerated caution, and sometimes showed clear symptoms of distress. The "treatment" lasted for about three years, but since then L.M. copes quite well with her difficulties. She has adjusted success-fully to the demands of daily life, lives independently in her own apartment, and has an active social life. She has become proficient at avoiding distressing situ-ations but is nevertheless better at coping with them. Accordingly, she organises her daily activities such that she arranges shopping when the supermarket is nearly empty, uses public transport outside rush hours, and never invites more than four people at once to have tea or coffee with her. Of course, her friends are acquainted with her problem and understand the peculiar nature of her behaviour in certain situations.

Despite L.M.'s very efficient adaptation, the degree of the impairment of her movement vision has not changed essentially (Zihl, von Cramer, Mai, & Schmid, 1991). She still shows severe impairments in conditions where she would need the ability to see movement. For example she still has difficulty in guiding her moving hand visually. Figure 1.1 shows an example. When L.M. was asked to write a word with her eyes closed, she performed much better and faster than when asked to write the same word with her eyes open. In the latter condition she had to stop several times because "my fingers and my hand are somehow restless, and this disturbs me." A similar problem exists with walking; L.M. tries to avoid looking at her feet because their movements would distract her. In town she feels safe when walking along the walls of houses; otherwise she is unsure if an approaching person is likely to collide with her. "Sometimes I do not even know whether a person is approaching me or is receding." When using the bus or tube, she avoids looking out of the window.

Moving stimuli persist in being highly disturbing and unpleasant to L.M. Even after countless hours of testing and intensive practice with moving displays, she finds the experience uncomfortable. Regular breaks are required to avoid such discomfort as much as possible. Usually, after about 30min of testing, she no longer looks at moving stimuli and experiences a strong feeling of nausea and unpleasantness which she has difficulty in describing. She would comment "To me, everything becomes restless, and so I have no idea where to look at and what to do to find out which response would be the correct one." This experience, which has not essentially changed over the past 15 years, is in clear contrast to patients with achromatopsia, who report their surroundings as "pale" or "drained of colour", but the absence of colours does not seem to cause similar discomfort.

NEUROPSYCHOLOGICAL ASSESSMENT

L.M. had been admitted into hospital in a state of stupor on the 7 October 1978. Examination did not reveal any focal neurological symptoms. On panarteriography the cortical veins in the temporoparietal region were not filled, and a superior sagittal sinus thrombosis was diagnosed. In the next weeks the patient's health status improved considerably, and she could eventually be transferred to a rehabilitation centre. There, she undertook systematic regular practice with daily activities and was, in addition, treated for agoraphobia.

When L.M. was first seen by one of us (J.Z.) in May 1980, about 19 months had elapsed since her admission. She still showed general slowing and tended to fatigue easily; after about 20–30min of testing she felt exhausted. Detailed neurological and neuropsychological examination did not reveal any motor or somatosensory deficits. No apraxic symptoms were present. Verbal and nonverbal memory performance was in the lower normal range; topographical memory was normal. She showed mild anomia which involved all modalities equally. She had difficulties in copying and drawing from memory (Grüsser & Landis, 1991, pp. 372–3) and with writing. When asked for an explanation for these difficulties, she complained that she felt disturbed by tracking the trajectory of her own right hand. This visuomotor disturbance was more or less unchanged even ten years later (Rizzo, Navrot, & Zihl, 1995). Visual fields were full for light, colour and form targets, and there were no signs of visual neglect or impaired simultaneous vision. Visual acuity, spatial and temporal contrast sensitivity, colour vision, discrimination of greys and form perception were normal.

Visual identification and recognition of objects, faces and places were preserved. The patient exhibited full stereopsis although stereoacuity was reduced (best value: 150s of arc). She could correctly locate targets in space using eye and hand movements. At the time of testing it became clear that, in contrast to the patient reported by Goldstein and Gelb (1918), L.M. did not exhibit visual deficts which might have explained her difficulties with movement vision. However, one further issue remained to be resolved. As mentioned above, all activities were markedly slowed in L.M.; for example, when she was tested for the first time in May 1980, her simple visual reaction time was about four- to five-fold higher (1294ms on average) than that of an age-matched female control subject. It could therefore be argue that her difficulties in detecting moving objects in time was a result of extreme cognitive and motor slowing. Intensive practice was given to L.M., and after nearly 22 hours of training her visual reaction time dropped down to 280ms in the foveal region (normal subject: 228ms), and to 330ms in the peripheral visual field at 45° eccentricity (normal subject: 255ms). There was, in contrast, no similar reduction in the time required to detect a slowly moving target, or to discriminate a moving target from a stationary one. Furthermore, although the patient reported that practice had enabled her to "see things and people earlier", and she could now get "a much quicker overview", her difficulties with "all moving things" remained essentially unchanged. We next tested whether impaired temporal resolution might explain her deficit in movement vision, because she might have difficulty in distinguishing discrete visual impressions. We thus measured critical flicker fusion (CFF) foveally and at peripheral visual field locations, but could find no evidence of an impairment. In addition, she had no difficulties in correctly reporting the order or presentation of two visual stimuli, and did not require longer interstimuli intervals than the control subject, indicating that the basic "temporal processing units" were not altered (Zihl et al., 1983). We began to speculate that L.M. might indeed suffer from a selective loss of movement vision. In fact, it turned out that L.M. was the first case to show unequivocally that movement vision can be selectively impaired after brain damage.

The ensuing report (Zihl et al., 1983) of a selective case of "motion blindness" was accepted uncritically by comparison with the controversy that accompanied the first reports of cases of achromatopsia (see Zeki, 1990a), a condition consistent with the existence of an extrastriate area playing a special role in the visual processing of colour. The lack of controversy, no doubt, was the result of an acceptance of the notion of functional specialisation of visual cortex that had arisen from earlier studies, identifying an area outside the striate cortex in monkeys apparently specialised for the analysis of visual motion (Dubner & Zeki, 1971; Zeki, 1974).

Deficits in motion perception have now been reported in a number of patients (Thurston, Leigh, Crawford, Thompson, & Kennard, 1988; Vaina, 1989; Vaina, Lemay, Bienfang, Choi, & Nakayama, 1990; Beckers & Hömberg, 1992;

Morrow & Sharpe, 1993; Plant & Nakayama, 1993; Plant, Laxer, Barbaro, Schiffman, & Nakayama, 1993). Nevertheless L.M. remains the most extensively studied case. The term "akinetopsia" has been coined by Zeki (1991) to refer to the "motion blindness" of patients such as L.M. The impairment is impressively selective but, given the ubiquitous role of motion in primate vision (Nakayama, 1985), it is unsurprising that L.M. displays a number of motion-related deficits.

CEREBRAL AKINETOPSIA

On formal tests, L.M.'s movement vision is severely impaired although the perception of motion in the tactile and auditory modalities is unaffected. One very effective way of establishing the capacity of the motion system is by testing with a class of visual stimuli known as random dot cinematograms. These are composed of a random display of elements which lack an overall conspicuous form. When some of the dots are spatially displaced during sequential frames of the display, the normal observer effortlessly perceives smooth visual motion. By varying the parameters of the display, such as the density, distributions of direction and distance of the displaced elements, exposure duration and interstimulus interval, the limits of motion vision can be characterised. The displays have the particular advantage that the observer is unable to detemine which element in the second exposure corresponds to which element in the second. It is therefore impossible to infer motion from the change in location of individual elements. Processes that extract such motion have been termed "short-range" (Braddick, 1974), in contrast to longer-range processes that extract motion information from displays that contain small numbers of clearly defined elements. The minimum (D_{min}) and maximum (D_{max}) spatial displacement to reliably discriminate direction is frequently used to describe these short-range processes. Hess, Baker, and Zihl (1989) demonstrated a considerable degree of residual function in L.M.'s short-range processes. A D_{max} of 0.37° compares favourably with 0.8° for the normal observer. However, a D_{min} of 0.09° is considerably greater than the 0.007° measured in the normal observer.

When L.M. was tested with conventional grating stimuli to assess spatiotemporal contrast sensitivity it was established that there was no perception of motion above 14deg s^{-1} and she was unable to detect reliably the direction of a drifting, suprathreshold grating above a velocity of about 8deg s^{-1}. She was never better than 85% correct for velocities as low as 2deg s^{-1}. She was unable to discriminate velocity above 10deg s^{-1}. All this points to a deficit which is selective for visual motion.

However, there is a distinction between an ability to *detect* moving stimuli and an ability to *discriminate* the properties of the motion, i.e. direction or velocity (Hess et al., 1989). The minimum contrast required by normal observers to detect the presence of a grating is comparable to that needed to discriminate its direction of motion. Even at low velocities, L.M. required a twenty-fold increase in contrast, compared with a normal observer, to correctly judge the direction of motion. This was true at all spatial frequencies. However, her contrast threshold for detecting the presence of a grating did not show such a large elevation. Although L.M. showed an impairment in the discrimination of spatial frequency and contrast for suprathreshold gratings, she was considerably more impaired at the discrimination of temporal frequency or velocity. Her deficit was not, therefore, in the *detection* of motion but in making judgements of the attributes of stimulus motion.

How can we account for such a pattern of impairments? The response properties of neurons in visual pathways, up to and including striate cortex, suggest they act as spatial and temporal filters, i.e. they are tuned to the spatial and temporal properties of visual stimuli. Motion vision requires the comparison of the output of a number of such filters and the impairment in L.M. can be characterised as a failure to reliably perform the necessary comparison (Hess et al., 1989). The amplitudes and latencies of visual evoked potentials to reversing chequerboards are reportedly normal in L.M. and her mildly affected contrast sensitivity points to the integrity of early visual processes up to and including striate cortex. This suggests that more anterior regions are implicated, a conclusion that has been confirmed by the results of neuroimaging.

In contrast to reports on cerebral achromatopsia, where it was already known that the crucial location of the brain damage typically comprises the lingual and fusiform gyri, nothing was known regarding the location of the brain lesion which might be responsible for loss of movement vision. CT scanning of L.M. in 1980 (Zihl et al., 1983) revealed a bilateral lesion affecting the lateral temporo-occipital cortex and the underlying white matter. The lesion sites in the two hemispheres were approximately symmetrical, the right-sided lesion was, however, larger than the left-sided one. A magnetic resonance scan a decade later (Zihl et al., 1991) demonstrated severe bilateral damage to the middle temporal gyrus and the adjacent portion of the occipital gyri, and confirmed the earlier subcortical damage affecting the lateral occipital and occipito-parietal white matter. Recent advances in imaging techniques with the living brain have resulted in identification of the location of presumptive area MT in people. Positron emission tomography (Watson, Myers, Frackowiak, Hajnal, Woods, & Mazziotta, 1993) and the more recent technique of functional magnetic resonance imaging (Sereno, Dale, Reppas, Kwong, Belliveau, Brady, Rosen, & Tootell, 1995) have revealed an area in lateral prestriate cortex at the junction of the occipital and temporal lobes. Stimuli which activate this region in the human brain are consistent with the response properties of cells in area MT of the monkey, suggesting a close functional resemblance (Tootell, Reppas, Kwong, Malach, Born, Brady, Rosen, Belliveau, 1995).

In the decade since the case of L.M. was first reported substantial advances have been made in our knowledge of the organisation of primate vision.

Cortical area MT

Cortical area MT, an area first identified in the owl monkey, resides in the middle of the temporal lobe. An area located in the posterior bank and floor of the caudal superior temporal sulcus of the macaque monkey, labelled cortical area V5, has also been described. This area possesses properties that are closely akin to those of MT and they are probably homologous. They both contain heavily myelinated axons, share similar connectivity to other cortical visual areas and contain neurons that are directionally selective. The term MT is now commonly used to refer to both areas. Moreover, the strikingly high proportion of cells that preferentially respond to the direction of stimulus motion suggest that this area plays a central role in the processing of movement in the visual field and it is unsurprising that it has been dubbed the "motion area".

This description should not conceal the many perceptual roles that motion plays in primate vision. For example, the relative speed and direction of motion of an object moving against its backround enables the visual system to segment figure from ground. When different velocities are present in the same retinal location, resulting in "shearing" motion, the visual system assigns the different velocities to different depth planes. In addition, motion serves an efferent role for the maintenance of posture and in allowing primates to navigate successfully through the world without mishap. The ubiquity of motion is reflected in the several classes of cells in the visual pathways which respond to different properties of motion. It may be deduced that the cells that are selective to direction of stimulus motion, and those that are tuned to stimulus velocity play a role in motion perception. However, for some cells, directional selectivity can be contingent on velocity, while for others, direction selectivity can be radically affected by the motion of a textured background. Thus, while these cells show no direction sensitivity to the motion of an isolated, single stimulus, introduction of a textured moving background results in strong selectivity. Perhaps these latter cells play a role in the perception of motion in depth or motion segregation.

The "motion area", area MT, is chiefly associated with the M-channel of visual processing, which, along with its companion P-channel, underlies the functional segregation in the visual pathways of primates (for reviews see Livingstone & Hubel, 1987a,b; Zeki & Shipp, 1988; Schiller, Logothetis, & Charles, 1990; Zeki, 1990a,b). Both pathways originate in discrete populations of retinal ganglion cells, and remain segregated up to primary and secondary visual cortical areas. The P-channel projects ventrally into the temporal lobe and is associated with the processing of colour and form (see Chapter 2). The dorsal pathway, or M-channel, arises from the $P\alpha$ retinal ganglion cells, which project, via the magnocellular layers of the dorsal lateral geniculate nucleus (dLGN), to layer IVCα and to layer IVB of area V1. Cells in layer 4B innervate cortical areas MT (V5), V3 and V3A, both directly and via cells in the thick stripes of area V2. The high luminance contrast gain together with the orientation and direction selectivity of cells in the M-channel, in the absence of wavelength selectivity, is consistent with its proposed role in conveying motion and form information to areas in the parietal lobes.

Neurones in MT are not selective for colour but are selective for binocular disparity and direction and speed of motion (Maunsell & Van Essen, 1983a,b). The cells are active during perceptual decisions which depend on these properties (Salzman & Newsome, 1994). Their large receptive fields, some 8–10 times larger in linear dimensions than cells in V1 of comparable eccentricity, are retinotopically organised and have silent suppressive surrounds which are also selective for the direction of stimulus motion (Allman et al., 1985; Tanaka, Hikosaka, Saito, Yukie, Fukuda, and Iwai, 1986). Thus, cells respond optimally to the relative motion of a stimulus against its background. Furthermore, cells in MT respond to more complex characteristics of motion than those in area V1. Cells in the latter respond to the component parts of a complex pattern. In MT, cells respond to the vector sum of the motion of the component parts and thus code global pattern motion (Movshon et al., 1985).

One difficulty that the visual system faces is the inherent ambiguity resulting from the limited field of view that is available to a single neuron through its receptive field. This is known as the *aperture problem*. If an infinitely long edge moves through a receptive field then the velocity of the edge, when viewed through a restricted window, is indistinguishable from that produced by combinations of many different speeds and directions. In each case the motion would be perceived as being orthogonal to the border. A local measurement of motion, made through a single aperture, is not sufficient to yield information about the direction of object motion. The correct motion of an object could be derived from the integration of information from a set of directionally selective neurons (see Fig. 1.2). Clearly, under normal circumstances observers do not make errors that are characteristic of a single neuron, where speed and direction are confounded. To establish the true motion of an object from several ambiguous local measurements requires integration of the responses of a set of directionally selective neurons. Area MT receives directionally selective inputs from V1 and V2 and the receptive field size of MT neurons make MT a likely candidate as the site for such integration.

These neuronal properties presumably reflect a role for MT in the processing of the moving image. The key question is whether "motion blindness" can be accounted for by the destruction of the human counterpart of area MT. The question can be readily addressed by a careful assessment of the effects of partial or total removal of cortical area MT in the macaque monkey.

Motion blindness and MT

Early studies on monkeys demonstrated that neither contrast sensitivity nor the ability to saccade to a moving target were impaired by lesions to MT. However,

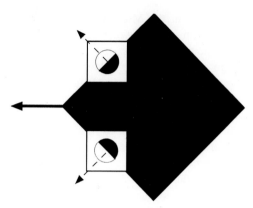

FIG. 1.2   An illustration of the aperture problem. The figure shows a diamond moving to the left. The local movement of the diamond, viewed through apertures, is orthogonal to the component diagonals and is represented by dotted lines. To establish the true direction of motion the visual system must integrate local information derived from component parts. The vector sum of the speed and direction of the component diagonals, shown here as a solid arrow, represents the true motion of the diamond. After M.J. Morgan (1984). Computational vision. In J. Nicholson and H. Beloff (Eds), *Psychology survey 5* (pp. 95–128). Leicester, UK: British Psychological Society.

pursuit eye movements to a moving target were slowed (Newsome, Wurtz, Dursteler, & Mikami, 1985), perhaps paralleling L.M.'s underestimation of target speed. The ability to detect structure-from-motion and shearing motion (Siegel & Andersen, 1986) have been shown to be substantially impaired. Perhaps the most compelling parallel between the vision of L.M. and monkeys with bilateral MT ablation has been reported by Newsome and Paré (1988). Normal observers have no difficulty in detecting the direction of motion of a small proportion of dots that move coherently in an otherwise random dot display (see Fig. 1.3). Removal of MT results in a gross impairment in this ability even when the proportion of correlated dots is considerably increased. L.M.'s threshold, as measured by the minimum coherence required for consistently accurate judgement of direction of motion, is comparable with that of the monkey lacking MT (Baker, Hess, & Zihl, 1991).

However, while L.M.'s impairments have been long-lasting, impairments in monkeys are generally short-lived and followed by rapid recovery to essentially normal levels of performance. There are several possible reasons for the brevity of these latter deficits. Small neurotoxic lesions produced by ibotenic acid largely spare the white matter while destroying cells in MT. L.M.'s lesions are the result of a cerebrovascular accident. They are bilateral and invade territory which surrounds the location of the putative human MT area. These are presumably areas MST FST and LIP, known to process motion. Cerebrovascular accidents result in additional white-matter damage. The extent of the deficit is graded in proportion to the extent of the lesion (Pasternak & Merrigan, 1994).

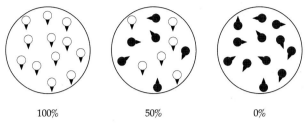

100%   50%   0%

FIG. 1.3   The figure shows three displays. In each, individual random dots are represented by small circles with the attached arrows indicating their direction of motion. On the left, all dots are moving in the same direction (100% motion coherence), on the right, direction of motion of the dots is random (0% motion coherence). In the centre, only half the dots have the same direction of motion, the direction of the remainder is random (50% motion coherence). Under appropriate conditions normal observers can reliably detect direction of motion for dot displays with 2–5% coherence. After R. Sekuler & R. Blake (1990). *Perception* (2 edn). New York: McGraw-Hill.

One study which examined the effects of total MT ablation (Cowey and Marcar, 1992) demonstrated deficits in the perception of motion of small targets that were permanent. While the permanence of the deficit can be explained by the completeness of the removal, it is plausible that such lesions unavoidably damage adjacent cortex, notably MST and FST. However, the weight of evidence does not favour this interpretation, since damage to these regions alone does not result in equivalent impairments on at least some tasks that are severely disrupted following complete removal of MT, namely the detection of kinetic boundaries between a moving and a stationary random dot field or random dot fields moving in opposite directions (Marcar & Cowey, 1992).

The perceptual deficits in L.M. are clearly more severe than those in the monkey without MT, even when MST and FST are also compromised. This may well reflect the extent of damage in L.M., since other patients with less substantial damage, but nevertheless including presumptive area MT, show a pattern of perceptual deficits more closely resembling those following MT ablation in the monkey (Vaina, 1989; Vaina et al., 1990). However, while L.M.'s deficits are quantitatively different from those of the monkey, qualitatively there are impressive parallels, i.e. a reduced sensitivity to motion and subjective velocity. However, despite the convenient shorthand of "motion-blindness", L.M. does retain rudimentary movement vision. Direction of motion of high contrast stimuli, moving at an optimal speed of 4.5deg s^{-1}, can be discriminated, at least for cardinal directions (Shipp, de Jong, Zihl, Frackowiak, & Zeki, 1994) and speed can be discriminated below ~6deg s^{-1}. Presumably, such residual motion vision relies on the motion-processing capacities of surviving cortical areas. While Hess et al. (1989) have already drawn attention to the possibility that area V1 may well contribute to L.M.'s residual motion vision, it remains plausible that other regions may contribute. This is reflected in surprising dissociations that have been reported between different aspects of motion processing, suggesting that several varieties of the disorder may exist. For example, despite the severity of L.M.'s disorder, she is able to perceive higher-order motion normally. Thus, when a moving pattern of dots, created by attaching small lights to the joints of an actor filmed in the dark, defines "biological motion" such as running, squatting and jumping (so-called Johansson figures), L.M. has no difficulty in readily identifying the action.

CONCLUSIONS

The case of L.M. has proved informative and has begun to provide answers to the thorny question of what role the many cortical visual areas play in vision. Her case has illustrated the degree of specificity of impairment that can result from brain damage. Moreover, her deficits bear more than a passing resemblance to those seen in monkeys following bilateral removal of area MT. The similarity should not, however, conceal real differences. An explanation for the more substantial and permanent nature of impairments in L.M. needs to be addressed. While the more extensive nature of the brain lesion may account for such differences, the sparing of some aspects of higher- and lower-order motion vision in L.M. must be the result of, as yet, unidentified regions that remain intact.

Such studies of single neurological cases have clearly contributed to the widespread acceptance of the notion of functional specialisation in visual cortex. However, such studies have posed as many questions as they have sought to address. The challenge will be to hone behavioural tasks and other techniques to reveal further the processes underlying our visual capacities.

REFERENCES

Allman, J., Miezin, F., & McGuinness, E. (1985). Direction and velocity-specific responses from beyond the classical receptive field in the middle temporal area (MT). *Perception, 14*, 105–26.

Baker, C.L., Hess, R.F., & Zihl, J. (1991). Residual motion perception in a "motion-blind" patient, assessed with limited-lifetime random dot stimuli. *Journal of Neuroscience, 11*, 454–61.

Beckers, G., & Hömberg, V. (1992). Cerebral visual motion blindness: transitory akinetopsia induced by transcranial magnetic stimulation of human area V5. *Proceedings of the Royal Society (London) Series B, 249*, 173–8.

Braddick, O. (1974). A short-range process in apparent motion. *Vision Research, 14*, 519–27.

Campbell, W. (1905). *Histological studies on the localisation of cerebral function.* Cambridge, UK: Cambridge University Press.

Cowey, A. (1994). Cortical visual areas and the neurobiology of higher visual processes. In M.J. Farah, & G. Ratcliff (Eds), *The neuropsychology of high-level vision* (pp. 3–31). Hillsdale, New Jersey: Lawrence Erlbaum.

Cowey, A., & Marcar, V.L. (1992). The effect of removing superior temporal cortical motion areas in the macaque monkey: I. Motion discrimination using simple dots. *European Journal of Neuroscience, 4*, 1219–27.

Dubner, R., & Zeki, S.M. (1971). Response properties and receptive fields of cells in an anatomically defined region of the superior temporal sulcus in the monkey. *Brain Research, 35*, 528–32.

Goldstein, K., & Gelb, A. (1918). Psychologische Analysen hirnpathologischer Fälle auf Grund von Untersuchungen Hirnverletzter. I. Abhandlung. Zur Psychologie des optischen Wahrnehmungs- und Erkennungsvorganges. *Zeitschrift für die gesamte Neurologie und Psychiatrie, 41*, 1–42.

Grüsser, O.-J., & Landis, T. (1991). *Visual agnosias and other disturbances of visual perception and cognition.* Boca Raton: CRC Press.

Hess, R.H., Baker, C.L., & Zihl, J. (1989). The "motion-blind" patient: low level spatial and temporal filters. *Journal of Neuroscience, 9*, 1628–40.

Jung, R. (1949). Über eine Nachuntersuchung des Falles Schn . . . von Goldstein und Gelb. *Psychiatrie, Neurologie und Medizinische Psychologie, 12*, 353–62.

Livingstone, M.S., & Hubel, D.H. (1987a). Segregation of form, color and stereopsis in primate area 18. *Journal of Neuroscience, 7*, 3378–415.

Livingstone, M.S., & Hubel, D.H. (1987b). Psychophysical evidence for separate channels for the perception of form, color, movement and depth. *Journal of Neuroscience, 7*, 3416–468.

Marcar, V.L., & Cowey, A. (1992). The effect of removing superior temporal cortical motion areas in the macaque monkey: II. Motion discrimination using random dot displays. *European Journal of Neuroscience, 4*, 1228–38.

Maunsell, J.H.R., & Van Essen, D.C. (1983a). Functional properties of neurons in middle temporal visual area of the macaque monkey. I. Selectivity for stimulus direction, speed and orientation. *Journal of Neurophysiology, 49*, 1127–47.

Maunsell, J.H.R., & Van Essen, D.C. (1983b). Functional properties of neurons in middle temporal visual area of the macaque monkey. II. Binocular interactions and sensitivity to binocular disparity. *Journal of Neurophysiology, 49*, 1148–67.

Morrow, M.J., & Sharpe, J.A. (1993). Retinotopic and directional deficits of smooth pursuit initiation after posterior cerebral hemisphere lesions. *Neurology, 43*, 595–693.

Movshon, J.A., Adelson, E.H., Gizzi, M., & Newsome, W.T. (1985). The analysis of moving visual patterns. In C. Chagas, R. Gattass & C.G. Gross (Eds), *Study group on pattern recognition mechanisms* (pp. 117–51). Vatican City: Pontifica Academia Scientiarum.

Nakayama, K. (1985). Biological image motion processing: A review. *Vision Research, 25*, 625–60.

Newsome, W.T., & Paré, E.B. (1988). A selective impairment of motion perception following lesions of the middle temporal visual area (MT). *Journal of Neuroscience, 8*, 2201–11.

Newsome, W.T., Wurtz, R.H., Dursteler, M.R., & Mikami, A. (1985). Deficits in visual motion processing following ibotenic acid lesions of the middle temporal visual area of the macaque monkey. *Journal of Neuroscience, 5*, 825–40.

Pasternak, T., & Merrigan, W.H. (1994). Motion perception following lesions of the superior temporal sulcus in the monkey. *Cerebral Cortex, 4*, 247–59.

Plant, G.T., & Nakayama, K. (1993). The characteristics of residual motion perception in the hemifield contralateral to lateral occipital lesions in humans. *Brain, 116*, 1337–53.

Plant, G.T., Laxer, K.D., Barbaro, N.M., Schiffman, J.S., & Nakayama, K. (1993). Impaired visual motion perception in the contralateral hemifield following unilateral posterior cerebral lesions in humans. *Brain, 116*, 1303–5.

Poppelreuter, W. (1923). Zur Psychologie und Pathologie der optischen Wahrnehmung. *Zeitschrift für die gesamte Neurologie und Psychiatrie, 83*, 86–152.

Rizzo, M., Nawrot, M., & Zihl, J. (1995). Motion and shape perception in cerebral akinetopsia. *Brain, 118*, 1105–27.

Salzman, C.D., & Newsome, W.T. (1994). Neural mechanisms for forming a perceptual decision. *Science, 264*, 231–7.

Schiller, P.H., Logothetis, N.K., & Charles, E.R. (1990). Functions of the colour-opponent and broad-band channels of the visual system. *Nature, 343*, 16–17.

Sereno, M.I., Dale, A.M., Reppas, J.B., Kwong, K.K.K., Belliveau, J.W., Brady, T.J., Rosen, B.R., & Tootell, R.B.H. (1995). Borders of multiple visual areas in humans revealed by functional magnetic resonance imaging. *Science, 268*, 889–93.

Shallice, T. (1977). Case study approach in neuropsychological research. *Journal of Clinical Neuropsychology*, *1*, 183–211.

Shipp, S., de Jong, B.M., Zihl, J., Frackowiak, R.S.J., & Zeki, S. (1994). The brain activity related to residual motion vision in a patient with bilateral lesions of V5. *Brain*, *117*, 1023–38.

Siegel, R.M., & Andersen, R.A. (1986). Motion perceptual deficits following ibonentic acid lesions of the middle temporal area (MT) in behaving rhesus monkeys. *Society for Neuroscience Abstracts*, *12*, 1183.

Tanaka, K., Hikosaka, K., Saito, H., Yukie, M., Fukuda, Y., & Iwai, E. (1986). Analysis of local and wide-field movements in the superior temporal visual areas of the macaque monkey. *Journal of Neuroscience*, *6*, 134–44.

Thurston, S.E., Leigh, R.J., Crawford, T, Thompson, A., & Kennard, C. (1988). Two distinct deficits of visual tracking caused by unilateral lesions of cerebral cortex in humans. *Annals of Neurology*, *23*, 266–73.

Tootell, R.B.H., Reppas, J.B., Kwong, K.K.K., Malach, R., Born, R.T., Brady, T.J., Rosen, B.R., & Belliveau, J.W. (1995). Functional analysis of human MT and related visual cortical areas using magnetic resonance imaging. *Journal of Neuroscience*, *15*, 3215–30.

Vaina, L.M. (1989). Selective impairment of visual motion interpretation following lesions of the right occipito-parietal area in humans. *Biological Cybernetics*, *61*, 347–9.

Vaina, L.M., Lemay, M., Bienfang, D.C., Choi, A.Y., & Nakayama, K. (1990). Intact "biological motion" and "structure from motion" perception in a patient with impaired motion mechanisms. A case study. *Visual Neuroscience*, *5*, 353–69.

Watson, J.D.G., Myers, R., Frackowiak, R.S.J., Hajnal, J.V., Woods, R.P., & Mazziotta, J.C. (1993). Area V5 of the human brain: evidence from a combined study using positron emission tomography and magnetic resonance imaging. *Cerebral Cortex*, *3*, 79–94.

Zeki, S.M. (1974). Functional organization of a visual area of the posterior bank of the superior temporal sulcus of the rhesus monkey. *Journal of Physiology (London)*, *277*, 73–90.

Zeki, S. (1978). Functional specialisation in the visual cortex of the rhesus monkey. *Nature*, *274*, 423–8.

Zeki, S. (1990a). A century of cerebral achromatopsia. *Brain*, *113*, 1721–77.

Zeki, S. (1990b). Colour vision and functional specialisation in the visual cortex. *Discussions in Neuroscience*, *IV(2)*, 64.

Zeki, S. (1991). Cerebral akinetopsia (visual motion blindness). A Review. *Brain*, *114*, 811–24.

Zeki, S. (1993). *A vision of the brain*. Oxford, UK: Blackwell Scientific Publications.

Zeki, S. and Shipp, S. (1988). The functional logic of cortical connections. *Nature*, *335*, 311–17.

Zihl, J., von Cramon, D., & Mai, N. (1983). Selective disturbance of movement vision after bilateral brain damage. *Brain*, *106*, 313–40.

Zihl, J., von Cramon, D., Mai, N., & Schmid, C. (1991). Disturbance of movement vision after bilateral posterior brain damage. Further evidence and follow up observations. *Brain*, *114*, 2235–52.

CHAPTER TWO

Cerebral achromatopsia

C.A. Heywood
Department of Psychology, Science Laboratories,
University of Durham, UK

A. Cowey
Department of Experimental Psychology, University of Oxford, UK

INTRODUCTION

The apparent effortlessness of our vision belies its complexity. The latter is reflected in the amount of cortical tissue devoted to vision, estimated at some 54% in the macaque monkey. Estimates of 25% in man are no less impressive. The last three decades have witnessed substantial progress in elucidating the organisation and function of visual cortex such that few would deny the general conclusion that in the monkey it is composed of some 25 areas that are exclusively or predominantly concerned with visual processing and an additional half dozen areas that are bimodal or multimodal and involved in other tasks as well (Felleman & Van Essen, 1991). At first glance, as is apparent in Fig. 2.1 (Young, 1992), the visual areas appear to be so interconnected as to defy any attempts at unravelling the role that any one of them plays in visual perception.

Distinct areas have been identified on the basis of one or more criteria, namely a specific pattern of connections, the presence of a topographic map of the contralateral half-field, receptive field characteristics (see below), a characteristic architecture revealed by histochemical or immunocytochemical techniques, and finally by the selectivity of the behavioural deficit following a circumscribed lesion. It is the rarity with which this last criterion has been successful in identifying a visual cortical area in the monkey that is of current concern because the rarity is inconsistent with neuropsychological reports of strikingly selective disorders following naturally occurring brain damage in man. Yet the characteristic

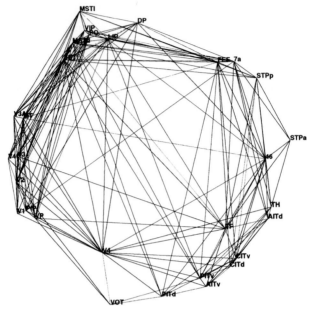

FIG. 2.1   The topological arrangement of the macaque cortical visual areas derived from multi-dimensional scaling. Adapted from Young (1992). Reprinted with permission from *Nature* © (1992) Macmillan Magazines Limited.

behavioural deficit is likely to be the best signpost to function when trying to find the elusive answer to the question of why there are so many visual areas. It has been natural to assume that a particularly promising clue to the function of each visual area of the patchwork might stem from the properties of the receptive fields of the cells that reside in each area. Early studies suggested that several areas contained a relatively high proportion of cells that responded optimally, and were narrowly tuned to, a particular psychophysical dimension such as colour, orientation, disparity and direction of motion. More recent results of recording the activity of single neurones (see Fig. 2.2) have not confirmed this sharp functional segregation (Felleman & Van Essen, 1987). This, along with the paucity of experimental evidence for a selective increase in threshold for the discrimination of a particular psychophysical dimension following the surgical ablation of a single area, has resulted in a decline in popularity of the view that a single area can be assigned a single function (Cowey, 1994).

However, there is a notable exception to this account, namely cortical area V4, a region located on the prelunate gyrus of the macaque monkey. Figure 2.3 shows the place occupied by V4 on the lateral surface of the macaque brain.

An early study of the properties of the cells contained in this region placed its function firmly in the realm of colour vision (Zeki, 1973). Bolstered by the clinical observation that brain damage in man can lead to the selective and total

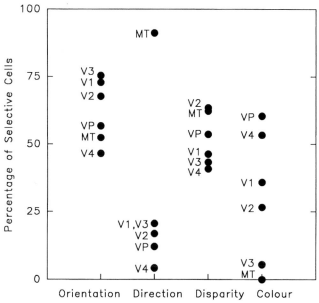

FIG. 2.2 The percentage of cells, in each of six visual cortical areas, that respond selectively to orientation, direction of motion, disparity and color. Each point is the mean of the results from several laboratories and the variation among them is thus concealed. Nevertheless, note that an area is not readily identified by the proportion of cells that respond to a single visual attribute. The figure is adapted from Cowey (1994) from data presented by Felleman and Van Essen (1987). Reprinted with permission Lawrence Erlbaum Associates, Inc.

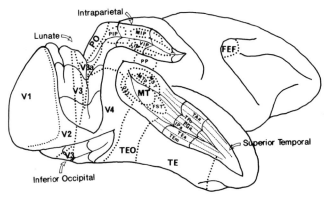

FIG. 2.3 The lateral view of the right hemisphere of a macaque monkey, showing the location of some of the visual areas. The lunate, superior temporal, intraparietal and inferior occipital sulci have been opened out to reveal their depths. Area V4 can be seen anterior to the lunate sulcus on the lateral surface. Area TE corresponds to the lateral extent of the tissue removed in an inferotemporal lesion. The figure is taken from Cowey (1994). Reprinted with permission Lawrence Erlbaum Associates, Inc.

abolition of colour vision, a condition known as cerebral achromatopsia, the view was proposed that achromatopsia is the result of damage to the human homologue of V4, a single cortical area (Zeki, 1990a). An impressive arsenal of techniques has been marshalled in the study of achromatopsia, a condition where neuropsychological examination of rare but informative single cases has guided research on human and nonhuman primates into the wider question of the organisation of cortical and subcortical visual pathways.

CEREBRAL ACHROMATOPSIA

Cerebral achromatopsia is a condition where brain damage in man results in a severe (but rarely, if ever, wholly selective) loss of colour vision. In its extreme form, patients may spontaneously complain that their visual world has become pale and washed out, devoid of colour and appears only in shades of grey. Patients are quite unable to perform the Farnsworth Munsell 100-hue test which requires the sequential ordering of a number of isoluminant coloured disks in terms of their chromaticity. The deficit may frequently be more substantial for blues and greens than for reds (Pearlman, Birch, & Meadows, 1979). In contrast, patients make few errors in arranging a series of achromatic, grey disks in terms of their lightness (Heywood, Wilson, & Cowey, 1987). They can neither match nor correctly name colours and the failure to discriminate isoluminant colour differences sharply distinguishes achromatopsia from other disorders of colour processing that can result from brain damage. For example, the failure either to name or point to a named colour, as in colour anomia, is not accompanied by a difficulty in telling those colours apart (Oxbury, Oxbury, & Humphrey, 1969). Similarly there is nothing awry about the perceptual colour-world of patients who fail to respond correctly when asked to provide the appropriate colour name when provided with the verbal label of a common object, e.g. when asked to state the colour of a banana (Kinsbourne & Warrington, 1964; Luzzatti & Davidoff, 1994). Finally, disorders of short-term colour memory may prevent patients from naming coloured samples but not interfere with the ability to indicate the correct colour when provided with the colour word (Davidoff & Ostergaard, 1984). In none of these disorders is colour vision itself disrupted. While poor performance on the Farnsworth Munsell 100-hue test is an invariable consequence of achromatopsia, another conventional test of colour vision, the Ishihara pseudoisochromatic plates, yields ambiguous results. Some patients are able to read some or all of the plates (Meadows, 1974; Victor et al., 1989), while others may only read them under certain test conditions (Green & Lessell 1977; Albert et al., 1975; Heywood et al., 1987). The extent of the colour deficit doubtless reflects the extent of brain damage but a cautionary note concerning terminology is in order. The term *dyschromatopsia* is frequently used to refer to cases of incomplete achromatopsia, yet the same term is correctly used elsewhere to refer to another condition where the visual world is uniformly tinged

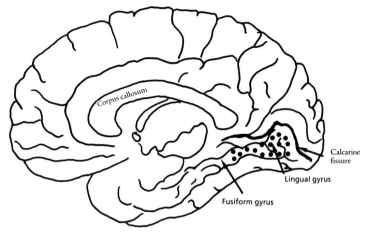

FIG. 2.4   Medial view of the human brain with the occipital lobe to the right. The stippled area represents the region which, when damaged, results in cerebral achromatopsia. The crucial region was established by determining which area of damage was common to all of a number of neuropathological cases of cerebral achromatopsia.

with hue (Plant, 1991). The severity of the disturbance is also related to the nature of the deficits that accompany achromatopsia, which are notably consistent. In a timely and early review of 14 achromatopsic patients, which rekindled interest in the disorder, Meadows (1974) drew attention to the co-occurrence (12 of the 14 cases) of achromatopsia and prosopagnosia, a severe impairment in the recognition and identification of faces. Moreover, in a collation of case studies reporting purely altitudinal field defects, Meadows demonstrated that inferior altitudinal defects (16 cases) were never accompanied by achromatopsia. However, upper field defects frequently went hand-in-hand with achromatopsia (7 of the 12 cases). Why should this be so?

It is now widely accepted that the brain areas that are compromised in achromatopsia are located in the ventromedial occipital cortex in the region of the lingual and fusiform gyri (see Fig. 2.4).

This has been determined by post-mortem neurohistology (Damasio, Yamada, Damasio, Corbett, & McKee, 1980) and magnetic resonance imaging of patients (Kölmel, 1988; Heywood, Cowey, & Newcombe, 1991). The ventromedial location neatly explains the prevalence of upper field defects among achromatopsic patients. Damage in this vicinity is liable to encroach on the lower lip and bank of the calcarine fissure and/or the fibres innervating it, particularly if the damage is extensive enough to result in substantial impairments of colour perception. Since this portion of calcarine cortex contains the topographic representation of the upper visual field in primary visual cortex (cortical area V1), its disturbance results in a scotoma, or field defect, confined to the upper quadrants. Similarly, since prosopagnosia is not an invariable companion of achromatopsia, the most parsimonious explanation is that regions crucial for the processing of faces reside in areas adjacent to those involved in colour processes and that extensive damage to the latter is likely to encroach on to the former. More recently, neuroimaging of normal observers has been carried out with positron emission tomography (PET) while subjects passively viewed chromatic Mondrian displays (Lueck, Zeki, Friston, Deiber, Cope et al., 1989; Zeki, Watson, Lueck, Friston, Kennard, & Frackowiak, 1991). The region of increased brain activation, indicated by increased cerebral blood flow, was located in just the region implicated in achromatopsia. This region has been dubbed the "colour centre", emphasising its important role in colour vision (Zeki, 1990a, 1993).

Cerebral achromatopsia has had a chequered history (Zeki, 1990a) but the results of careful neuropsychological assessment of single cases coupled with the substantial inroads that have been made into our understanding of the organisation of the primate visual pathways has resulted in its widespread acceptance. Inevitably, the nature of the disorder is best derived from case studies. Yet studies of monkeys have been the best source of information about the anatomy and physiology of the visual system. In consequence, the development of our recent understanding of achromatopsia can be charted by describing the study of a single, profoundly achromatopsic, patient alongside a description of parallel behavioural studies of monkeys, often using identical tasks. Such an approach attempts to reconcile the findings from the disciplines of anatomy, physiology and behaviour, some of them discrepant.

A SINGLE CASE STUDY

Case history

In 1970, a 22-year-old police cadet, M.S., contracted a febrile illness initially resulting in severe headaches and vomiting. Shortly thereafter he became drowsy, deluded and was dyspraxic and agnosic with a severe impairment of colour vision. Antibody studies were negative and the diagnosis was idiopathic herpes encaphalitis, resulting in bilateral brain damage which was more substantial in the right hemisphere and accounted for a left homonymous hemianopia with macula sparing. Within six months M.S. was able to return home, but while his behavioural problems had resolved, he was left with agnosia, amnesia, topographic disorientation and disturbed colour perception. His Snellen acuity, at 6/6, was normal. A psychological assessment some two years later revealed an unchanged pattern of deficits but by now he could read and write normally and his verbal IQ of 101 on the WAIS contrasted with poor performance scores.

The results of magnetic resonance imaging (Heywood et al., 1991) identified the extent of damage in M.S. The second, third and fourth and the anterior portion of the fifth temporal gyri are destroyed in the right hemisphere, along with the temporal pole. In the left temporal lobe the damage is less extensive and confined largely to the temporal pole, the fourth gyrus, the hippocampal gyrus and the area of the mesial occipito-temporal junction. The lateral and medial aspects of the parietal lobe are intact in the left hemisphere but there is substantial white matter involvement in the inferior half of the inferior parietal lobule and the posterior portion of the superior parietal lobule of the right hemisphere. The calcarine cortex is present in the left hemisphere but the mesial and lateral aspects of the occipital lobe of the right hemisphere are destroyed. All sectors of the frontal lobe of each hemisphere remain intact. In short, the location of the brain damage is consistent with what has been reported in earlier cases of achromatopsia.

M.S. has been repeatedly tested from 1972 until the present day and his condition is stable. His colour vision has remained unchanged or no change is readily detectable, and studies of this rare and informative patient have provided insights into the nature of his disorder.

Neuropsychological assessment

The earliest report on patient M.S. (Newcombe & Ratcliffe, 1975) was primarily concerned with visual object recognition. However, the authors drew attention to the inability of M.S. to name, match or sort coloured tokens and it is this initially subsidiary finding that eventually became the chief focus of clinical investigations of M.S. More formally, M.S. achieved an error score of 1245 on the Farnsworth Munsell 100-Hue test, which indicated no better than a random arrangement of the coloured disks. This was in marked contrast to his ability to discriminate fine shades of grey. The seven responses that could be elicited on presentation of the Ishihara plates were all incorrect. It was clear that the per-formance of M.S. on such tasks fulfilled the conditions of cerebral achromatopsia. Several years later Mollon, Newcombe, Polden, & Ratcliffe (1980) showed that the deficit is of central origin by demonstrating that M.S. retains three functional cone mechanisms. By using the increment threshold technique of Stiles (1978), whereby M.S. was asked to detect a monochromatic flash presented against a monochromatic background and thresholds were established, it was possible to show that M.S. has access to signals from more than one class of photoreceptor. His retinal trichromatic mechanisms appear to be intact, but in the absence of the processes that compare the output of the three cone types, he can say nothing about the colour of a visually presented sample. What is the nature of these processes and where are they located?

Visual pathways in primates

There is substantial functional segregation in the visual pathways of primates (for reviews see Livingstone and Hubel, 1987a,b; Zeki & Shipp, 1988; Schiller, Logothetis, & Charles, 1990; Zeki 1990a,b). Pathways that process different attributes of the visual scene, such as colour, form and motion, originate in retinal ganglion cells and remain segregated up to primary and secondary visual cortical areas. Retinal ganglion Pβ cells project to the parvocellular (P) cells of the lateral geniculate nucleus (dLGN), which then project to layer 4Cβ of V1 and then to the cytochrome oxidase (CO) rich blobs and interblobs in cortical area V1. The thin stripes and interstripes in area V2 receive their input from the blobs and interblobs, respectively, and in turn project to area V4. This constitutes the P-channel of visual processing which is relatively distinct from its partner, the M-channel, which arises from the Pα retinal ganglion cells and projects, via the magnocellular (M) cells in dLGN, chiefly to layer 4Cα of area V1 and then to Layer 4B. Layer 4B projects both directly, and via the CO rich thick stripes in V1, to cortical areas V2, V3 and V5. The receptive field properties of cells in the two pathways provide a strong clue as to their role in visual processing. The P-channel provides colour-opponent information and has low luminance contrast gain. The cells in the CO blobs are wavelength but not orientation selective while orientation selectivity is prevalent in the interblobs in cells that are not wavelength selective. There are thus two arms to the P-channel providing inputs to regions in the temporal lobes. These are chiefly concerned with the coding of colour and form, respectively. In contrast, the high luminance contrast gain together with the orientation and direction selectivity of cells in the M-channel, in the absence of wavelength selectivity, is consistent with its proposed role in conveying motion and form information to areas residing in the parietal lobes. In summary, while the the P- and M-channels are principally and respectively concerned with colour and motion processing, both pathways appear to be associated with the analysis of form. While the differences in the response properties of cells in the P- and M-channels are substantial, it is not the case that the two channels can readily and unambiguously be assigned to two distinct groupings of visual cortical areas. Thus area V4 receives input from both the broad-band M-channel in addition to the better-known contribution from the colour-opponent P-channel (Ferrera, Nealey, & Maunsell, 1994). Conversely, area V5 which is normally assigned to the M-channel, can be activated via the P-channel (Maunsell, Nealy, & DePriest, 1990).

Cortical area V4 and its role in colour processing

The fourth visual area, cortical area V4, is located on the prelunate gyrus of macaque monkeys and extends on to the ventral surface of the brain. An early study reported that every one of the 77 cells sampled in this region showed selectivity to wavelength and this became the chief reason to conclude that it plays a leading role in colour vision (Zeki, 1973). A later study reinforced this view by showing that the area contains cells that are sensitive to the perceived colour of a visual stimulus despite wide variation in the wavelength composition of the reflected light, i.e. the cells show properties akin to colour constancy (Zeki, 1983). Once area V4 had been dubbed the "colour area", it was natural to suggest that achromatopsia is the result of damage to its homologue in the

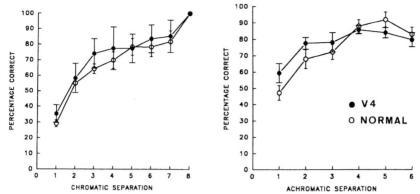

FIG. 2.5   Percentage correct performance for six monkeys required to select the odd-one-out from a display with a single target and eight distractors. On the left are the results for a task where the target was a target of one hue embedded in distractors of a different hue. Chromatic separation refers to the chromatic difference between targets and distractors, which were all in the red–green range. On the right are the results for a task where the target was a target of one luminance embedded in distractors of a different luminance. Achromatic separation refers to the luminance difference between targets and distractors. Vertical bars represent standard error bars. There were no differences in the performance of the three normal monkeys (open symbols) or the three with V4 ablation (solid symbols) in either condition.

human brain. This view has been adhered to despite more recent evidence that many cells in V4 are tightly tuned to orientation and even indifferent to wavelength (Schein, Marrocco, & De Monasterio, 1982; Desimone & Schein, 1987). The acid test of such a proposal is undoubtedly a comparison between the perceptual effects of surgically induced lesions to area V4 in the monkey and the performance of an achromatopsic patient when presented with identical tasks. The first such comparison provided no support for the involvement of area V4 in achromatopsia (Heywood, et al., 1991). When presented with three isoluminant chromatic Munsell plates, where two were identical and the third differed in hue, patient M.S. was quite unable to select the odd-one-out unless there was a substantial difference in their chromaticity. Even then he could not correctly name the hue. However, and this is the crux of the problem, it was unclear whether the plates were indeed isoluminant for M.S. Accurate performance may have been based on unintended brightness differences which are likely to be greater between plates of wider chromatic separation. After all, Munsell plates are isoluminant only for the hypothetical, average, young observer viewing the stimulus foveally. For many observers they are *not* isoluminant. When Munsell plates were used to test monkeys with V4 lesions, the results at best indicated a mild impairment in hue discrimination in an oddity task (Heywood & Cowey, 1987) or none at all (Dean, 1979). When such luminance cues were therefore made irrelevant or removed, by carefully controlling luminance and chromaticity on a display monitor, there was no evidence for any impairment (see Fig. 2.5) in either an oddity task for greys or colours following bilateral ablation of cortical area V4 (Heywood, Gadotti, & Cowey, 1992).

In striking contrast, M.S. responded randomly when asked to select a coloured target surrounded by distractors of a different, but isoluminant colour, or distractors composed of greys of differing luminance. However, he encountered no difficulties in selecting a grey target surrounded by greys of a different, but identical, luminance. In other words, monkeys with area V4 entirely removed can perform, without impairment, colour tasks that an achromatopsic patient can barely perform.

While these results should be sufficient to dispel the belief that achromatopsia is the consequence of destruction of the human homologue and analogue of area V4, they did little to suggest an alternative explanation. However, poor performance on the Farnsworth–Munsell 100-hue test, a test of colour ordering, is a reliable indicator of cerebral achromatopsia. When an analogous task was presented to both monkeys with V4 lesions and patient M.S., the results were consistent with another proposal that achromatopsia could be better accounted for as a selective destruction of all or part of the P-channel. The task required a discrimination between two spatially separated rows of isoluminant chromatic patches that abutted one another. In one row the colours were chromatically ordered, in the other they were jumbled. Neither the monkeys nor, more surprisingly, M.S. had the least difficulty in distinguishing between the two rows. The intact performance of monkeys lacking V4 came as no surprise. However, it posed the question as to how a patient who was unable to discriminate between any two of the colours presented in isolation could nevertheless indicate when their chromatic ordering was appropriate. In the absence of colour vision, M.S. could still detect the border between two adjacent isoluminant colours. Such borders are presumably more conspicuous in the jumbled row which lacked the fine gradation in chromaticity in an ordered series of hues where the borders are less prominent. One of the properties ascribed to the broad-band cells in the M-channel is that when a chromatic border falls in their receptive field, they cannot be rendered silent by any adjustment of the luminances of the colours of which the border is composed, i.e. they detect chromatic borders without signalling any information about the constituent colours (Saito, Tanaka, Isono, Yasuda, & Mikami, 1989). Perhaps, then, the P-channel is compromised in achromatopsia and residual vision is principally mediated by an intact M-channel. To confirm that it was the chromatic borders that signalled differences between the chromatically ordered and jumbled rows, a second task was devised. The display remained identical other than the introduction of a narrow grey strip between each of the patches of which the rows were composed, i.e. the patches were now discontiguous. Animals with V4 lesions continued to perform essentially flawlessly in the discrimination and were not, as in the previous condition, reliant on the salience of the chromatic borders to perform the task. In contrast, the discriminanda were indistinguishable to M.S., who was unable to tell the difference between the rows of colours when they were discontiguous.

The P-channel and Achromatopsia

If, as has been suggested, M.S.'s vision is best characterised by the nature of the information chiefly conveyed by the M-channel, then the proposal can readily be tested. At the very least, it is consistent with an intriguing observation reported by Mollon et al. (1980), who noted that reading the Ishihara pseudoisochromatic plates was greatly improved when M.S. viewed them at a distance of 2m. Optically blurring them has the same effect (Heywood et al., 1991). It was suggested that, under both conditions, the luminance contours defining each of the multiple small disks of which the figures are composed can no longer be resolved. What remains is the dominant and much larger hue boundary that defines figure and ground. It is this boundary which may be detected by cells in the M-channel, although all hue information is lost.

However, several related lines of evidence revealed that M.S. has access to signals other than those conveyed by the M-channel. First, thresholds were measured for the detection of light stimuli of different wavelengths to record a spectral sensitivity function (Heywood et al., 1991). If sensitivity were determined by the broad-band channel, a single broad peak would be expected at ~550nm (King-Smith & Carden, 1976). As shown in Fig. 2.6, the results indicated instead a reduced sensitivity with a clear contribution from colour-opponent mechanisms that are the preserve of the P-channel. Peaks of sensitivity occurred at 450, 525 and 600nm, and the last two peaks are characteristically displaced from the absorbance peaks of the medium- and long-wavelength cones, strongly suggesting opponent cone interactions (Sperling & Harweth, 1971).

Second, when a normal observer looks at a mixture of red and green light the resulting yellow appears conspicuously dimmer than would be expected on the basis of simple brightness additivity (Guth, 1965). This again is the result of opponent interactions between chromatic channels. Like normal trichromatic observers, M.S. showed a failure of such brightness additivity. Third, M.S. was presented with red/green, isoluminant horizontal sine wave gratings (Heywood, Cowey, & Newcombe, 1994). To a normal observer, if the grating is phase shifted by 180° at 1Hz (the red bars become green, and vice versa, each second), then the direction of apparent movement of the grating is ambiguous and frequently changes. By shifting the phase by only 90°, either upwards or downwards, the direction of motion is now unambiguous. However, in the absence of any information about which bar is red and which green, the ambiguity will remain. Remarkably, M.S. flawlessly indicated the "correct" direction of apparent movement although he was entirely unable to distinguish the colours of which the grating was composed when they were presented in an oddity task. Mysteriously, M.S. can detect the sign of colour contrast without experiencing the colours. Finally, measurements of chromatic contrast sensitivity, where thresholds were measured for the detection of sinusoidally modulated isoluminant chromatic gratings, show that M.S. has normal sensitivity to gratings up to 10

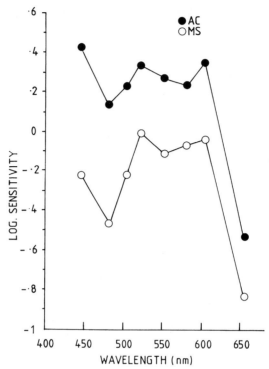

FIG. 2.6 Increment threshold spectral sensitivity for a 104min, 500ms circular target on a 30Cd m^{-2} white background, presented 2.5° to the right of fixation with binocular viewing. The open and closed symbols show the performance of M.S. and a normal observer, respectively.

cycles deg^{-1}, the highest spatial frequency tested. Moreover, such gratings elicit a visually evoked cortical potential (VECP) essentially indistinguishable from that of a normal observer (Heywood, Nicholas, & Cowey, 1996).

Residual visual processing in achromatopsia

The preceding account of M.S.'s residual ability, most notably the evidence of intact cortical chromatic opponent processes, including normal sensitivity to chromatic gratings, reinforces the notion that achromatopsia cannot be the result of total destruction of the P-channel. An early report of another patient did demonstrate normal VECPs to achromatic gratings but none to chromatic gratings (Damasio et al., 1980), supporting the view that in this patient the crucial lesion had destroyed all the cortical areas, or compartments within them, and pathways concerned with colour processing. However, consistent with the results from M.S., Victor and his colleagues (Victor, Maiese, Shapley, Sidtis, & Gazzaniga, 1989) described a case of incomplete achromatopsia where again normal VECPs to chromatic chequerboards accompanied normal acuity and colour contrast sensitivity. Their patient could identify 8 of the 9 Ishihara plates and select a coloured square surrounded by 39 irrelevant squares of the complementary opponent colour. They suggested that intact colour-opponent mechanisms in striate cortex could mediate such abilities. In contrast, deficits in the identification and sorting of colours were proposed as being the results of damage to extrastriate ventromedial regions. An alternative explanation is that the lesion in the "colour centre" may be incomplete and thus account for spared performance on the Ishihara plates and discrimination in an oddity task. Consistent with this proposal is the observation that profoundly achromatopsic patient M.S. is, unlike the patient of Victor et al. (1989), severely impaired at an oddity task and identification of the Ishihara plates at normal reading distance. This would not be expected if these tasks depended on the integrity of striate cortex, since M.S. also has normal sensitivity to sinusoidally modulated chromatic gratings which elicit a prominent visual evoked potential indicating no, or minimal, striate involvement. Thus, unimpaired oddity discrimination and correct performance of the Ishihara test are more likely to depend on the intact regions that survive a partial lesion to areas of ventromedial extrastriate cortex.

To summarise, it is not disputed that all cases of *complete* achromatopsia are unable to identify or sort colours. In cases of *incomplete* achromatopsia, residual colour vision cannot unambiguously be attributed to either intact striate cortex or remaining tissue in extrastriate regions. In the case of M.S., a profound achromatopsic, it has been argued that the nature of residual colour processes is inconsistent with their sole mediation by the M-channel. In addition, if the P-channel has been compromised, the location of the lesion in the ventromedial occipital cortex suggests that the loss occurs beyond striate cortex.

There are two distinct, but related interpretations of cerebral achromatopsia. The first (Zeki, 1990a, 1993) accounts for the impairment as the result of damage to cortical regions that are necessary for the "synthesis" or "construction" of colours, a role that is deemed inseparable from the phenomenon of colour constancy. An alternative interpretation, unlike the first, draws a distinction between the processes concerned with the generation of object colour and those concerned with colour constancy. The processes required for the rescaling required to achieve colour constancy in the face of changes in the composition of the illuminant are held to precede, and to be independent from, those that are involved in the reconstruction of colour that leads to the phenomenal experience of hue. Such constancy mechanisms may be peripheral, including classic von Kries adaptation (see Wandell, 1995, for review), or cortical.

Colour Constancy

Colour constancy refers to the phenomenon whereby an object's colour is perceived as unvarying or fairly stable despite considerable variation in the spectral composition of the illuminant. The perceived colour of an object is not simply determined by the wavelength composition of the illuminating light and reflected light from the object. To achieve this, the nervous system must compare intensities of different wavelengths reflected from the object with those reflected from the surround. The reflectance of a surface depends on the waveband of light incident on that surface. Hence when a multicoloured scene is illuminated with long-wavelength light, those regions with high reflectance for long-wavelength light will appear very light and those with low reflectance, dark. A description in this form of the entire scene constitutes the "lightness record" for long-wavelength light. Middle- or long-wavelength light will produce markedly different lightness records. The lightness of a region depends on a comparison of the intensity of the light reflected from that region compared with the intensity reflected from other regions, for a particular waveband of illuminant. One account of colour constancy suggests that colours are constructed by the brain on the basis of a comparison of "lightness records", derived from each of short, medium and long wavebands of light (Land, 1974). Many computational accounts of colour constancy require long-range colour interactions across large areas of the visual field. Cells in cortical area V4 have large receptive fields and widespread callosal connections. In addition, the response of the cells, unlike the response of cells in area V1, is not solely determined by the wavelength of light incident on the receptive field but depends on the wavelength composition of light from surrounding areas. Cortical area V4 has therefore been strongly implicated in colour constancy (Zeki, 1983). Not surprisingly, since area V4 of monkeys has been likened to the "colour centre" in man, destruction of which leads to achromatopsia, it has been entirely natural to interpret achromatopsia as a defect in colour constancy. Are there any characteristics of achromatopsia consistent with this view?

There is every indication, including spontaneous complaint, that patients with extreme achromatopsia perceive the world in shades of grey. This itself is puzzling if achromatopsia arises from destruction of the mechanism of colour constancy because simple primary colours should still look different. Yet M.S. cannot tell red and green apart. But one possibility, if the above account is correct, is that their vision now depends on a single lightness record. To assess this, Mr I., a patient reported by Sacks, Wasserman, Zeki, and Siegel (1988), was presented with chromatic "Mondrian" patterns under different illuminants. A Mondrian pattern is composed of a patchwork of coloured rectangles of different luminance. When viewed by normal observers under an illuminant of one waveband, each rectangle has a particular lightness. When the waveband is altered, the pattern of lightnesses changes in a predictable fashion. Mr I. was able to grade the lightnesses correctly when viewing the Mondrian in light of a single waveband. When the waveband was changed, Mr I. correctly regraded the lightnesses. Mr I. was asked to compare the Mondrian, simultaneously illuminated by three wavebands, with the same Mondrian individually illuminated by each of the three-component wavebands in turn (long-, medium- and short-wavelength).

The former condition produced a display that was deemed more similar to the Mondrian illuminated by middle-wavelength light than to either of the other two conditions. The conclusion was drawn that Mr I. operated on a single, middle-waveband lightness record. Moreover, it has been suggested that the lightness record is derived from the broad-band M-channel (Zeki, 1990a). Unfortunately, this view is untenable for patient M.S., as the evidence for P-channel, opponent processing is substantial.

It is, of course, evident that achromatopsics can process *wavelength* differences. This is to say no more than they possess a system which is differentially sensitive to light of different wavelengths. Thus Mr I. is indeed able to regrade correctly lightnesses of the coloured patches of which a Mondrian figure is constructed when the composition of the illuminant is changed (Zeki, 1990a). Such a system could, in addition, perform rudimentary discriminations, such as the selection of the odd-one-out from among three isoluminant stimuli where two are identical and the third differs widely in its chromaticity (Victor et al., 1989). Such discriminations should be an invariant feature of achromatopsia if patients are relying solely on a single middle-waveband lightness record. This latter point can be demonstrated in a normal observer by viewing such a display through a middle-wavelength (green) band-pass filter, where a red patch, presented alongside two green patches, appears darker. However, a problem arises that while rudimentary discriminations may well be performed by cases of *incomplete* achromatopsia (where vision is not mediated by a single lightness record), in cases of profound achromatopsia such as M.S. simple oddity discrimination is impossible between *any* suitably adjusted isoluminant hues. Thus reliance on a single lightness record can account for some of the properties of residual chromatic vision, for example the reported normal perception of a red/green isoluminant chromatic grating, and would additionally be consistent with severely impaired performance on tasks of colour sorting and the ordering of finely graduated hues. However, the spectral sensitivity function of M.S. suggests that the lightness record available to him is unlikely to be derived from the M-channel alone.

The notion that achromatopsia could be characterized as a failure of colour constancy arose primarily from the suggestion that area V4 of the monkey is homologous with the "colour centre" revealed by functional neuroimaging and that the former possesses properties consistent with a role in colour constancy. It is therefore informative, not only to test constancy in achromatopsic patients, but to examine the effects of bilateral ablation of area V4 in the monkey.

V4 and colour constancy

The capacity to assign a constant colour to a surface, regardless of changes in the wavelength composition of its illuminant, is said to depend on the comparison of different grey-level records. The sensation of colour is a product of our nervous system, i.e. colours are "constructed" from lightness records. This role has been attributed to the "colour centre" in the human brain. Partial destruction will lead to incomplete achromatopsia while more substantial involvement will result in the complete abolition of colour vision. There are two ways in which a failure of colour constancy may express itself, in a mild or more extreme form. In the mild form, perceived colour may be determined by the *wavelength* of light reflected from a visually presented object and an object would change its colour appearance with changes in the wavelength composition of the illuminant, i.e. there would be residual colour vision but no colour constancy. There is currently little evidence to suggest that this is the underlying deficit in achromatopsia since discrimination of isoluminant colours should be undisturbed even in severe achromatopsia and this is clearly not the case for M.S. In the extreme form of the hypothesis, it is proposed that colour vision is abolished in complete achromatopsia because of a failure to "construct" colours from a comparison of lightness records. Incomplete achromatopsia can then be accounted for by proposing that sufficient tissue remains in the "colour centre" to mediate rudimentary comparisons among lightness records. Under these circumstances, while testing colour constancy in the absence of colour vision would be fruitless (although the testing of lightness constancy could prove informative), examination of colour constancy in incomplete cases could prove informative. A recent study (Kennard, Lawden, Morland, & Ruddock, 1995) has described a patient with incomplete achromatopsia who made pronounced and predictable changes in the naming of surface colours with systematic changes in the illuminant, demonstrating a failure in colour constancy.

It has been argued above that the "colour centre" and area V4 in the monkey cannot be deemed homologous because bilateral ablation of the latter fails to render an animal colour blind, i.e. colours appear to be constructed in an essentially normal fashion. Given the chromatic response properties of neurones in V4, most notably their ability to discount the illuminant, it is sensible to ask whether V4 ablation results in a dissociation of hue discrimination and colour constancy, i.e. the ability to discount the illuminant, where the latter may be selectively compromised. Several authors have pursued this question (Wild, Butler, Carden, & Kulikowski, 1985; Walsh, Butler, Carden, & Kulikowski, 1993). Preliminary evidence is indeed consistent with a role for V4 in colour constancy mechanisms.

Random luminance masking

It is clear that residual vision in M.S. goes beyond processes mediated by the broad-band M-channel. This is evident from the shape of his spectral sensitivity function, the normal sub-additivity to mixtures of middle- and long-wavelength lights and his normal contrast sensitivity to isoluminant chromatic gratings. Thus chromatic processes remain which are quite dissociated from those that result in the conscious experience of colour. One way to investigate further the nature of these processes is to exploit the method of random luminance masking. This introduces fluctuations of luminance into the components of chromatic visual displays. Such fluctuations render the broad-band system ineffective in distinguishing between chromatic and luminance contrast. The detection of the chromatic properties of the display then relies on the integrity of the colour opponent pathway. Displays of this kind, composed of an achromatic chequerboard where the luminance differences among adjacent squares were randomly assigned from moment to moment, were presented to M.S. (Heywood et al., 1994). Three large squares, two red and one green, or vice versa, were embedded in a 28×38 chequerboard where each was composed of 5×5 smaller squares whose luminances were independently modulated. M.S. was unable to select the odd one out, confirming his inability to detect chromatic differences. Nevertheless, he had no difficulty in detecting the three squares themselves. Moreover, when a desaturated hue was introduced, while maintaining luminance modulation, into a single square in a 7×5 array, M.S. was unable to indicate its position. However, when nine of the smaller squares were replaced by a desaturated colour to form a cross (+), M.S. was unerring and rapid in detecting its presence and location on the screen. Chromatic and luminance boundaries can thus be perceptually segregated into figure and ground to reveal the cross. In short, M.S. can use wavelength to extract form but lacks any phenomenal experience of colour itself. Very similar results have been reported for cases of incomplete achromatopsia (Barbur, Harlow, & Plant, 1994). These authors first demonstrated that threshold detection of chromatic signals is unaffected by accompanying luminance contrast fluctuation. Furthermore, thresholds for the detection of a colour change and for the extraction of stimulus structure are indistinguishable in normal observers but are very different in cases of incomplete achromatopsia. This is consistent with there being different and independent processes underlying the generation of perceived object colour and the construction of spatially structured objects from chromatic signals. Can this readily be explained by what is known about the organisation of primate visual pathways? As indicated above, there are two arms to the P-channel arising from the cytochrome oxidase rich "blobs" and "interblobs", respectively, in cortical area V1. Cells in the "blobs" are largely selective for wavelength but not orientation, while the converse holds true for cells in the "interblob" regions. If cells in the "blobs" are implicated in the generation of perceived colour and those in the "interblobs" concerned with deriving spatial structure from chromatic signals, then cerebral achromatopsia could be the result of damage to the former with preferential sparing of the latter.

Another recent study using random luminance masking has reported colour *discrimination*, in the absence of a conscious percept of colour, in achromatopsic patients (Troscianco, Davidoff, Humphreys, Landis, Fahle, Greelee, Brugger, & Phillips, 1996). Subjects judged whether two spatially separated parts of an image were the same or different. The two parts differed in either colour or luminance or both. For a totally colour-blind observer, luminance judgements should not be affected by the introduction of colour into the display. However, performance was improved for two achromatopsic subjects and the authors argue that both patients had access to chromatic signals. Luminance noise was then added to the display which now appeared as chequerboards. The noise could either be static or of a high temporal frequency. For one achromatopsic, similarity judgements were not facilitated when colour differences accompanied luminance differences in the presence of static noise, which presumably abolished access to chromatic signals. However, performance was unaffected by rapid flicker. Since the P-channel is sensitive to static noise, but blind to rapid flicker, residual colour processes were presumed to be subserved by the P-channel. The second subject showed the opposite pattern of results. Performance was disrupted by rapid flicker but not static noise. In this case the M-channel is implicated in residual colour discrimination, with little or no P-channel contribution. The absence of sub-additive effects in the latter patient, along with the lack of evidence of colour opponency in measurements of spectral sensitivity, are consistent with this interpretation.

In summary, chromatic information can be used to signal form, but regions that are indispensable for the generation of object colour (ventromedial occipital cortex) have been lost or disconnected. This account differs from an interpretation of achromatopsia as a failure in colour constancy. The conventional use of the term "colour constancy" refers to the constant appearance of object colour despite changes in the wavelength composition of the illuminant, rather than the reconstruction of object colour. To establish whether these two processes are indeed inseparable it would be informative to assess *lightness* constancy in cases of complete achromatopsia to determine whether such mechanisms precede those responsible for the conscious representation of hue.

INFERIOR TEMPORAL CORTEX

Removal of area V4 fails to disrupt colour discrimination in macaque monkeys and is therefore an unlikely candidate for the homologue of the human "colour centre". This prompts the question as to whether there is any cortical lesion in the monkey that does cause the severe consequences for colour processing seen in achromatopsia? Cortical area V4 sends a prominent projection to the inferior temporal cortex, a region in the monkey brain known to be crucial for object identification. There have been sporadic reports that, when colours are carefully or fortuitously matched in luminance, inferotemporal lesions impair hue discriminations (Gross, Cowey, & Manning, 1971; Heywood, Shields, & Cowey, 1988). More recently, when monkeys with rostral inferotemporal ablation were tested on an oddity task for greys and colours, their performance was indistinguishable from that of M.S. who was tested on an identical display (Heywood,

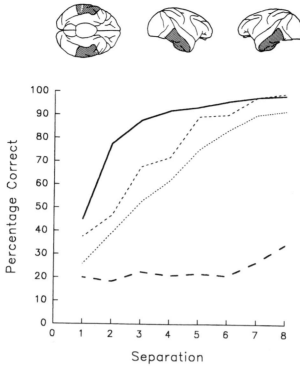

FIG. 2.7 Top: ventral and lateral views of the cerebral hemispheres of a macaque monkey with ablation of inferotemporal cortex, area TE. Bottom: The percentage correct performance of the monkey on an oddity task where the monkey was required to select the odd one out from a display with a single target and eight identical distractors. The target was either one coloured target among eight isoluminant distractors of another colour, or one grey that was brighter or dimmer than the other eight identical greys. Separation refers to the luminance or chromatic difference between targets and distractors. The solid line indicates preoperative performance for chromatic stimuli. The wide dashed line represents performance following bilateral inferotemporal (TE) lesions, where performance is little better than random responding. In contrast, the narrow and narrowest dashed lines represent performance on the greys. There was only a small post-operative decrement in performance. From Heywood, Gaffan, & Cowey (1995).

Gaffan, & Cowey, 1995). The ability to detect the chromatic target was no better than would be expected on the basis of random responding, contrasting with a small impairment in the discrimination of greys (see Fig. 2.7). Furthermore, in some monkeys there was retrograde degeneration in the lateral geniculate nucleus as a result of damage to the underlying optic radiations. Such damage resulted in a superior altitudinal field defect which commonly accompanies cerebral achromatopsia.

In one sense these results should come as no surprise. Cells sensitive to a particular region of colour space are more frequently encountered in medial portions of inferotemporal cortex than in area V4 (Komatsu, Ideura, Kaji, Yamane,

1992). However, the debilitating consequences of inferotemporal ablation on object identification in monkeys poses the question as to whether such a deficit is an invariable adjunct to cerebral achromatopsia in man.

FORM PROCESSING IN ACHROMATOPSIA

Although cerebral achromatopsia is frequently accompanied by deficits in form perception, perhaps because of the proximity of brain regions concerned with colour and form, respectively, there are isolated reports that the impairment is restricted to the perception of colour (Mackay and Dunlop, 1899; Kölmel, 1988; Damasio et al., 1980; Sacks et al., 1988). This raises some difficulties for the proponents of the view that human V4 is implicated in achromatopsia since bilateral ablation of V4 in the monkey invariably results in a disorder of form perception (e.g. Heywood & Cowey, 1987; Schiller & Lee, 1991; Schiller, 1995). Moreover, the same problem arises with the view that achromatopsia is the result of damage to regions homologous to rostral inferotemporal regions in the monkey. However, the evidence for a deficit restricted to colour is not, at present, compelling. For the handful of patients where the claim has been made, tests on form perception have been cursory and so the issue remains open.

CONCLUSIONS

Destroying the "colour centre" in humans leads to achromatopsia. Achromatopsia has been interpreted as a failure in colour constancy resulting in an inability to reconstruct colours. The response properties of cells in V4 and their widespread collosal connections make V4 a good candidate for the neural substrate of colour constancy. It has therefore been argued that monkey V4 is the homologue of the human "colour centre". However, if V4 is ablated, animals are not achromatopsic but preliminary evidence points to a failure in the ability to appropriately discount the illuminant when its spectral composition is varied during colour discriminations. The consequences of achromatopsia are greater than would be expected if it were the result of a failure of colour constancy (Rizzo, Smith, Pokorny, & Damasio, 1993). More rostral lesions, in inferotemporal cortex, do lead to achromatopsia in the monkey. It is then parsimonious to interpret achromatopsia as a failure to reconstruct colours, a mechanism that is carried out by regions beyond V4, while V4 itself, along with peripheral retinal mechanisms, may play a crucial role in colour constancy. It would be equally parsimonious to assume that colour and lightness constancy are subserved by the same mechanism. Given the difficulties of testing colour constancy in a patient bereft of colour vision, tests of lightness constancy would establish whether constancy mechanisms are indeed intact in achromatopsia. If so, then this would lend weight to the interpretation of achromatopsia as a failure of a process that generates object colour, a process that is distinct from those that underlie constancy.

The intriguing ability of achromatopsic patients to extract form from colour may be explained by the loss of only one arm of the P-channel. However, an alternative explanation is that it is the result of destroying or disconnecting rostral areas that are indispensable for the phenomenal awareness of hue, perhaps as a result of white-matter damage. The finding that inferotemporal lesions in monkeys lead to a dense achromatopsia naturally raises the question as to whether such lesions also spare the ability to segment figure from ground using colour cues. If similarities between the capacities of patients with achromatopsia and monkeys with inferotemporal lesions persist, then the view that V4 and the "colour centre" are homologous and analogous will be difficult to sustain. By pursuing such parallel studies in man and monkey, answers to these and other issues should be forthcoming.

REFERENCES

Albert, M.L., Reches, A., & Silverberg, R. (1975). Hemianopic color blindness. *Journal of Neurology, Neurosurgery and Neuroscience, 38,* 546–9.

Cowey, A. (1994). Cortical visual areas and the neurobiology of higher visual processes. In M.J. Farah, & G. Ratcliff (Eds), *The neuropsychology of high-level vision* (pp. 3–31). Hillsdale, New Jersey: Lawrence Erlbaum.

Damasio, A., Yamada, T., Damasio, H., Corbett, J., & McKee, J. (1980). Central achromatopsia: behavioral, anatomic, and physiologic aspects. *Neurology, 30,* 1064–71.

Davidoff, J.B., & Ostergaard, A.L. (1984). Colour anomia resulting from weakened short term memory. *Brain, 107,* 415–31.

Dean, P. (1979). Visual cortex ablation and thresholds for successively presented stimuli in rhesus monkeys. II Hue. *Experimental Brain Research, 35,* 69–83.

Desimone, R., & Schein, S.J. (1987). Visual properties of neurons in area V4 of the macaque: sensitivity to stimulus form. *Journal of Neurophysiology, 57,* 835–868.

Felleman, D.J., & Van Essen, D.C. (1987). Receptive-field properties of neurons in area V3 of macaque monkey extrastriate Cortex. *Journal of Neurophysiology, 57,* 889–920.

Felleman, D.J., & Van Essen, D.C. (1991). Distributed hierarchical processing in the primate cerebral cortex. [Review]. *Cerebral Cortex, 1,* 1–47.

Ferrera, V.P., Nealey, T.A., & Maunsell, J.H.R. (1994). Mixed parvocellular and magnocellular geniculate signals in visual area V4, *Nature, 358,* 756–58.

Green, G.J., & Lessell, S. (1977). Acquired cerebral dyschromatopsia. *Archives of Ophthalmology, 95,* 121–8.

Gross, C.G., Cowey, A., & Manning, F.J. (1971). Further analysis of visual discrimination deficits following foveal prestriate and inferotemporal lesions in rhesus monkeys. *Journal of Comparative and Physiological Psychology, 76,* 1–7.

Guth, S.L. (1965). Luminance addition: general considerations and some results at foveal threshold, *Journal of the Optical Society of America, 55,* 718–22.

Heywood, C.A., & Cowey, A. (1987). On the role of cortical area V4 in the discrimination of line and pattern in macaque monkeys. *Journal of Neuroscience, 7,* 2601–17.

Heywood, C.A., Cowey, A., & Newcombe, F. (1991). Chromatic discrimination in a cortically colour blind observer. *European Journal of Neuroscience, 3,* 802–12.

Heywood, C.A., Cowey, A., & Newcombe, F. (1994). On the role of parvocellular (P) and magnocellular (M) pathways in cerebral achromatopsia. *Brain, 117,* 245–54.

Heywood, C.A., Gadotti, A., & Cowey, A. (1992). Cortical area V4 and its role in the perception of colour. *Journal of Neuroscience, 12*(10), 4056–65.

Heywood, C.A., Gaffan, D., & Cowey, A. (1995). Cerebral achromatopsia in monkeys. *European Journal of Neuroscience, 7,* 1064–1073.

Heywood, C.A., Nicholas, J.J., & Cowey, A. (1996). Behavioural and electrophysiological chromatic and achromatic contrast sensitivity in an achromatopsic patient. *Journal of Neurology, Neurosurgery and Neuroscience, 61,* 638–43.

Heywood, C.A., Shields, C., & Cowey, A. (1988). The involvement of the temporal lobes in colour discrimination. *Experimental Brain Research, 71,* 437–41.

Heywood, C.A., Wilson, B., & Cowey, A. (1987). A case study of cortical colour "blindness" with relatively intact achromatic discrimination. *Journal of Neurology, Neurosurgery and Neuroscience, 50,* 22–9.

Kennard, C., Lawden, M., Morland, A.B., & Ruddock, K.H. (1995). Colour identification and colour constancy are impaired in a patient with incomplete achromatopsia associated with a prestriate cortical lesions. *Proceedings of the Royal Society (London), Series B, 260(1358),* 169–75.

King-Smith, P.E., & Carden, D. (1976). Luminance and opponent-color contributions to visual detection and adaptation and to temporal and spatial integration. *Journal of the Optical Society of America, 66,* 709–17.

Kinsbourne, M., & Warrington, E.K. (1964). Observations on colour agnosia. *Journal of Neurology, Neurosurgery and Neuroscience, 27,* 296–299.

Kölmel, H.W. (1988). Pure homonymous hemiachromatopsia: findings with neuro-ophthalmologic examination and imaging procedures. *European Archives of Psychiatry and Neurological Science, 237,* 237–42.

Komatsu, H., Ideura, Y., Kaji, S., & Yamane, S. (1992). Color selectivity of neurons in the inferior temporal cortex of the awake macaque monkey. *Journal of Neuroscience, 12,* 408–824.

Land, E.H. (1974). The retinex theory of colour vision. *Proceedings of the Royal Institution of Great Britain, 47,* 23–58.

Livingstone, M.S., & Hubel, D.H. (1987a). Segregation of form, color and stereopsis in primate area 18. *Journal of Neuroscience, 7,* 3378–415.

Livingstone, M.S., & Hubel, D.H. (1987b). Psychophysical evidence for separate channels for the perception of form, color, movement and depth. *Journal of Neuroscience, 7*(11), 3416–68.

Lueck, C.J., Zeki, S., Friston, K.J., Deiber, M.P., Cope, P., Cunningham, V.J., Lammertsma, A.A., Kennard, C., & Frackowiak, R.S.J. (1989). The colour centre in the cerebral cortex of man. *Nature, 340,* 386–9.

Luzzatti, C., & Davidoff, J. (1994). Impaired retrieval of object-colour knowledge with preserved colour naming. *Neuropsychologia, 32,* 933–50.

Mackay, G., & Dunlop, J.C. (1899). The cerebral lesions in a case of complete acquired colour-blindness. *Scottish Medical and Surgical Journal, 5,* 513–12.

Maunsell, J.H.R., Nealy, T.A., & DePriest, D.D. (1990). Magnocellular and parvocellular contributions to responses in the middle temporal visual area (MT) of the macaque monkey. *Journal of Neuroscience, 10*(10), 3323–34.

Meadows, J.C. (1974). Disturbed perception of colours associated with localized cerebral lesions. *Brain, 97,* 615–32.

Mollon, J.D., Newcombe, F., Polden, P.G., & Ratcliff, G. (1980). On the presence of three cone mechanisms in a case of total achromatopsia, In *Colour vision deficiencies,* Vol V, pp. 130–5. Bristol: Hilger.

Newcombe, F., & Ratcliff, G. (1975). Agnosia: a disorder of object recognition. In F. Michel and B. Schott (Eds) *Les Syndromes de disconnexion calleuse chez l'homme,* pp. 317–41. Lyon: Colloque International de Lyon.

Oxbury, J.M., Oxbury, S.M., & Humphrey, N.K. (1969). Varieties of colour anomia. *Brain, 92,* 847–60.

Pearlman, A.L., Birch, J., & Meadows, J.C. (1979). Cerebral color blindness: an acquired defect in hue discrimination. *Annals of Neurology, 5,* 253–61.

Plant, G.T. (1991). Disorders of colour vision in diseases of the nervous system. In D.H. Foster (Ed.) *Inherited and acquired colour vision deficiences: Fundamental aspects and clinical studies.* Vision and visual dysfunction, Vol. 7. Basingstoke: Macmillan Press.

Rizzo, M., Smith, V., Pokorny, J., & Damasio, A.R. (1993). Color perception profiles in central achromatopsia. *Neurology, 43*, 995–1001.

Sacks, O., Wasserman, R.L., Zeki, S., & Siegel, R.M. (1988). Sudden color-blindness of cerebral origin. *Society for Neuroscience Abstracts, 14*, 1251.

Saito, H., Tanaka, K., Isono, H., Yasuda, M., & Mikami, A. (1989). Directionally selective response of cells in the middle temporal area (MT) of the macaque monkey to the movement of equiluminous opponent color stimuli. *Experimental Brain Research, 75*, 1–14.

Schein, S.J., Marrocco, R.T., & De Monasterio, F.M. (1982). Is there a high concentration of colour-selective cells in area V4 of monkey visual cortex? *Journal of Neurophysiology, 47*, 193–213.

Schiller, P.H. (1995). Effects of lesions in visual cortical area V4 on the recognition of transformed objects. *Nature, 376*, 342–4.

Schiller, P.H., & Lee, K. (1991). The role of the primate extrastriate area V4 in vision. *Science, 251*, 1251–3.

Schiller, P.H., Logothetis, N.K., & Charles, E.R. (1990). Functions of the colour-opponent and broad-band channels of the visual system. *Nature, 343*, 16–17.

Sperling, H.G., & Harwerth, R.S. (1971). Red–green cone interactions in the increment-threshold spectral sensitivity of primates. *Science, 172*, 180–4.

Stiles, W.S. (1978). *Mechanisms of colour vision.* London: Academic Press.

Troscianko, T., Davidoff, J., Humphreys, G.W., Landis, T., Fahle, M., Greelee, M., Brugger, P., & Phillips, W. (1996). Human colour discrimination based on a non-parvocellular pathway. *Current Biology, 6*, 200–10.

Victor, J.D., Maiese, K., Shapley, R., Sidtis, J., & Gazzaniga, M.S. (1989). Acquired central dyschromatopsia: analysis of a case with preservation of color discrimination. *Clinical Vision Science, 4*, 183–96.

Walsh, V., Butler, S.R., Carden, D., & Kulikowski, J.J. (1993). The effects of V4 lesions on the visual behaviour of macaques: hue discrimination and colour constancy. *Behavioural Brain Research, 53*, 51–62.

Wandell, B.A. (1995). *Foundations of vision.* Sunderland, Massachusetts: Sinauer Press.

Wild, H.M., Butler, S.R., Carden, D., & Kulikowski, J.J. (1985). Primate cortical area V4 important for colour constancy but not wavelength discrimination. *Nature, 313*, 133–5.

Young, M.P. (1992). Objective analysis of the topological organization of the primate cerebral cortex. *Nature, 358*, 152–4.

Zeki, S.M. (1973). Colour coding in rhesus monkey prestriate cortex. *Brain Research, 53*, 422–7.

Zeki, S.M. (1983). Colour coding in the cerebral cortex: the reaction of cells in monkey visual cortex to wavelengths and colours. *Neuroscience, 9*(4), 741–65.

Zeki, S. (1990a). A century of cerebral achromatopsia. *Brain, 113*, 1721–77.

Zeki, S. (1990b). Colour vision and functional specialisation in the visual cortex. *Discussions in Neuroscience, IV*(2), Elsevier, Amsterdam, 64.

Zeki, S. (1993). *A vision of the brain.* Oxford: Blackwell Scientific Publications.

Zeki, S., & Shipp, S. (1988). The functional logic of cortical connections. *Nature, 335*, 311–17.

Zeki, S., Watson, J.D.G., Lueck, C.J., Friston, K.J., Kennard, C., & Frackowiak, R.S.J. (1991). A direct demonstration of functional specialization in human visual cortex. *Journal of Neuroscience, 11*, 641–9.

CHAPTER THREE

Integrative agnosia

Glyn W. Humphreys
Cognitive Science Research Centre, School of Psychology,
University of Birmingham, Edgbaston, Birmingham, UK

HISTORICAL BACKGROUND

Visual object recognition is undoubtedly a complex process. This is testified by the many attempts to build robust computer vision systems that are capable of recognising objects across a range of views, under different lighting conditions and in different contextual environments (see Brady, 1997; Lowe, 1987 for examples). It is also a commonplace assumption in the computer vision community that visual recognition comprises a number of distinct steps—these include: edge extraction, grouping of local image features, segmentation of objects from the background and from other objects that may be present, formation of a structural description of the object, and accessing stored structural and semantic information from the description assembled from the image (e.g. see Biederman, 1987; Marr, 1982). If the brain follows similar steps to achieve recognition, and if these steps are at least to some degree localised in different neural regions, we might expect visual recognition to break down in a variety of ways, according to the nature of the component processes involved.

In contrast to computational arguments for there being several necessary substages in object recognition, the neurological and neuropsychological literature on recognition disorders has traditionally adopted a dichotomous approach. This approach originates in the pioneering work of Lissauer (1890). Lissauer distinguished between two forms of recognition disorder or visual agnosia: apperceptive and associative. Apperceptive agnosia was diagnosed as an impairment that disrupts the formation of a normal percept for the visual stimulus,

41

although sensation of the basic properties of the image should be spared (e.g. brightness perception). Associative agnosia was diagnosed as being an impairment of the processes involved in retrieving stored memories from objects, despite perceptual processing being intact (see Chapters 4 and 9 for further discussion). Clinically, the distinction has often relied on the presence or absence of the ability of patients to copy objects that cannot be recognised. The label "associative agnosia" is applied to patients who can copy objects, and the term "apperceptive agnosia" is given to patients who fail to copy as well as recognise. This means of classifying patients is still in vogue today (e.g. see Behrmann, Moscovitch, & Winocur, 1994).

Despite the continuing popularity of the apperceptive–associative distinction, however, case studies over the past ten years have indicated that a finer-grained analysis of patients is possible. For example, several patients have now been documented who show impaired visual access to knowledge about the associative or functional properties of objects and yet can perform difficult object decision tasks at a high level (e.g. Hillis & Caramazza, 1995; Riddoch & Humphreys, 1987a; Sheridan & Humphreys, 1993; Stewart, Parkin, & Hunkin, 1992). Such object decision tasks require discrimination between real objects and non-objects formed by interchanging the parts of real objects to create unfamiliar, though perceptually "good" stimuli. Since non-objects may not be rejected from their general perceptual attributes, good performance is contingent on access to stored visual memories for familiar objects. In these patients, then, there can be access to stored visual memories without access to semantic information that defines the "meaning" of the stimulus. Such patients appear to represent "true" associative agnosics in the sense defined by Lissauer, since any deficit occurs after perceptual access to some forms of stored knowledge have taken place. Other patients perform relatively poorly at object decision but they are nevertheless able to carry out many apparently high-level perceptual tasks without difficulty—this can include matching objects presented in different views, where invariant perceptual properties must be extracted from objects (e.g. Forde, Francis, Riddoch, Rumiati, & Humphreys, 1997; Humphreys & Rumiati, 1998; Sartori & Job, 1988). Yet other patients are impaired at unusual view matching, though they are able to perform a variety of perceptual tasks at a reasonable level (e.g. finding a figure on a complex background, counting the number of three-dimensional figures present in two-dimensional line drawings with occluding parts etc.; Warrington & James, 1988; see Chapter 4). In some further cases, perceptual judgements about even rudimentary aspects of form can be severely impaired (judged by poor copying, impaired matching of line orientations, object sizes etc.), leading to the recognition problem. However, the same patients may be able to use the same properties of form for making actions (e.g. they show an appropriately scaled grasp aperture when reaching to objects of different size, despite being poor at perceptual judgements of size; see Milner, Perrett, Johnston, Benson, Jordan et al., 1991; Milner & Goodale, 1995, for example). Thus their impairment cannot be attributed to poor sensory discrimination, but rather perhaps some form of dissociation between visual information used for recognition and perceptual judgements, and visual information used for action. These dissociations indicate that within the broad distinction between apperceptive and associative agnosia, a number of different forms of recognition disorder can be found. Several attempts have been made to capture these different disorders within multi-stage models of vision (e.g. Humphreys & Riddoch, 1987a, 1993; Humphreys et al., 1994; Warrington, 1982, 1985).

One particular disorder, due to poor perceptual integration of form information, was identified in a single case study reported by Riddoch and Humphreys (1987b). In this chapter I review the initial evidence for "integrative agnosia" along with other data collected subsequently from the same patient. I relate the disorder found in the original patient to findings with other patients in the literature, and I discuss the implications of the results for understanding visual object recognition.

DEFINING INTEGRATIVE AGNOSIA

The patient studied by Riddoch and Humphreys (1987b), H.J.A., suffered an infarct of the posterior cerebral artery. This resulted in bilateral damage to the occipito-temporal regions of the cortex, involving the lingual and fusiform gyri (see Riddoch et al., 1999, for an MRI scan). There was a superior altitudinal defect for both visual fields, but brightness detection within his lower fields was preserved. Following the lesion, H.J.A. was profoundly impaired at a variety of vision-dependent tasks: object recognition, face recognition, word recognition and reading, colour perception and finding his way around his environment. These problems were modality-specific. H.J.A.'s tactile recognition of objects was good, and his ability to name objects from definition, and to give definitions of objects from their names, was entirely normal.

Like a number of other agnosic patients documented in the literature (e.g. Goldstein & Gelb, 1918; Grossman, Galetta, & D'Esposito, 1997; Sirigu, Duhamel, & Poncet, 1991; Wapner, Judd, & Gardner, 1978), H.J.A.'s attempts to identify objects were characterised by piecemeal descriptions of the forms. For example, when presented with a paintbrush H.J.A. remarked: "it appears to be two things close together but obviously it is one thing or else you would have told me." When presented with a line drawing of a pig he described each part of the object in turn and then deduced that it was a pig from the shape of its tail: "there is a round head joining what looks like a powerful body; there are four shortish legs; it doesn't say anything to me; ah but there is a small and curly tail so I think it must be a pig." When asked to describe how he went about identifying faces, H.J.A. said: "recently I've been going on the eyebrows but they don't help very much." These errors indicate that H.J.A. had little sense of familiarity for objects he failed to identify, and that he had some difficulty in perceiving objects as perceptual wholes. Indeed, one common tendency was for him to over-segment stimuli, so that parts of the same object became parsed as separate stimuli (as with the paintbrush example). Identification, when it occurred, was typically based either on the presence of some diagnostic local feature (the tail of the pig) or on a long process of deductive reasoning.

H.J.A.'s naming errors were always visually related to target objects and never related purely in terms of their semantic association (e.g. he named a line drawing of a nose as "a soup spoon" [due to the line representing the contour of the nose having an upturn at the bottom], a violin was named as "a mechanical tool with a turning bit" [the pegs], etc.). It is unlikely that such a pattern, of "pure" visual errors, reflects a deficit after access to forms of stored knowledge has been achieved (see Plaut & Shallice, 1993, for simulations of naming errors after lesioning different levels of a model of object naming). H.J.A. was also better able to identify real objects (at around a 60% level) than photographs (around 40%) and he was worst at identifying line drawings (around 30%, depending upon the items). Adding surface detail, and 3D depth information (via stereo, with real objects), benefitted performance. When surface detail was present, H.J.A. was less inclined to segment objects into separate parts. Surface information from objects thus seems to interact with the processes involved in integrating form elements together to form coherent perceptual wholes. When objects were mis-identified, H.J.A. was never able to indicate their use, by gesturing. He was also poor at matching tests requiring access to semantic information from objects (e.g. judging whether a hammer is used with a screw or a nail, when the stimuli were presented as pictures) and at object decision tasks. The problem was not one of naming but of recognition.

Yet, despite the indications of there being a visual locus for the deficit in H.J.A. (e.g. the visual errors and the effects of surface detail on recognition), he performed well on many standardised tests of perceptual processing. For example, he was able to reproduce highly accurate drawings of objects that he failed to identify. Figure 3.1 shows H.J.A.'s copy of an etching of St Paul's cathedral in London, which is highly accurate despite the picture being complex and containing many edge segments. Nevertheless, this particular picture took six hours to reproduce! So, although H.J.A.'s copies were accurate, they took an abnormally long time to complete. Also, H.J.A. often drew lines in an unusual order when copying, instead of following the parts of a single object in a coherent way (e.g. if one line fell across and occluded two parts of an object, he would move from one part of the object to follow the line instead of first reproducing the two parts of the same object together). Due the time taken and the unusual order of pencil strokes, Riddoch and Humphreys suggested that H.J.A.'s drawings were not necessarily reflecting a normal perceptual process, but rather a process of serially following each line without necessarily organising the lines into objects. It follows that, though the end product of copying may be good, we should be cautious in accepting accurate copies as evidence of intact perception.

FIG. 3.1   Copy by H.J.A. of an etching of St Paul's cathedral, London, during the blitz in World War II.

FIG. 3.2   Examples of stimuli from the Efron shape test (after Efron, 1968). The task requires squares to be discriminated from rectangles, matched for brightness.

In H.J.A.'s case, though, arguments about his perceptual processing did not rest solely on copying; he was in addition good at a test of shape perception, used to diagnose shape coding problems in other patients. This test, used originally by Efron (1968), requires that the patient judge whether shapes such as those shown in Fig. 3.2 are squares or rectangles. The squares and rectangles are equated for area and brightness, so the stimuli cannot be discriminated from these properties; differences between the shapes are then varied systematically to provide a sensitive measure of shape discrimination. H.J.A. performed normally on this task (Humphreys, Riddoch et al., 1992), whereas patients with impaired encoding of basic properties of form are impaired (Benson & Greenberg, 1969; Campion, 1987; Davidoff & Warrington, 1993; Milner et al., 1991). Furthermore, H.J.A. could make orientation and size-matching judgements at a normal level (Humphreys & Riddoch, 1984). And, in visual search tasks requiring detection of a target differing in the two-dimensional orientation of some of its lines relative to distractors, H.J.A. manifested (normal) flat search functions (where reaction times [RTs] are affected only minimally by the number of distractors present; Humphreys, Riddoch et al., 1992). Flat search functions are typically interpreted as evidence of parallel processing supporting the discrimination of targets from distractors. This last test is of some interest since it provides an on-line measure of processing efficiency. At least when the differences between targets and distractors were quite salient, H.J.A. demonstrated evidence of processing form information in a spatially parallel manner.

Thus the initial tests of visual processing were consistent with there being relatively good, parallel encoding of displays, and consequently they were consistent with the inference that the recognition deficit must be post-perceptual in nature: that is, H.J.A. had associative agnosia. The only contra-indication of this was with H.J.A.'s copying, though even here the finished drawings were satisfactory. Also it must be acknowledged that copying is a fickle behaviour to measure, and it is possible that H.J.A.'s slow, line-based strategy may occur too sometimes in normal subjects. To infer that there is some underlying perceptual deficit, more probing tests of visual processing are required.

Riddoch and Humphreys (1987b) reported data from a number of such additional tests.

1. Object decision performance was contrasted with line drawings and silhouettes. Silhouettes preserve the global outline shape of objects, but lose internal line details. Normal subjects find silhouettes more difficult than line drawings, presumably because they are able to use the extra details present in line drawings to identify the objects (or discriminate the objects from the non-objects, in object decision). In contrast to this, H.J.A. tended to perform better with silhouettes than with line drawings. This suggests that the internal details in line drawings disrupted rather than enhanced H.J.A.'s perception; for instance, internal lines may serve as segmentation cues which H.J.A. is abnormally sensitive to. Such cues, when present, lead to H.J.A. parsing the shapes incorrectly. More recently, Lawson and Humphreys (1999) have found similar effects in a picture-word verification task. Normal subjects are slow to verify silhouettes relative to line drawings, especially as objects are rotated away from a prototypical orientation. H.J.A. showed no sign of this disruption with silhouettes. Note that stored information about objects should be the same whether accessed by line drawings or silhouettes. The fact that performance can be somewhat better with silhouettes indicates an effect occurring at a pre-recognition stage.

2. H.J.A. was tested using sets of overlapping figures, with performance measured relative to baselines in which the same figures were presented alongside each other. H.J.A. was slowed disproportionately with overlapping figures relative to the non-overlapping baselines.

3. Object identification was compared across a range of presentation durations, using a set of line drawings that H.J.A. was often able to identify in free vision. H.J.A.'s identification performance decreased dramatically as the exposure duration shortened. With an unlimited exposure he named around 80% of the drawings correctly, with a 500ms exposure this decreased to around 30% and with a 100ms exposure only around 15% of the objects were named.

On all three tests in which the visual properties of the displays were made more difficult to assimilate, H.J.A. performed worse than controls. These results pointed to the presence of an underlying perceptual deficit, even though H.J.A. could copy objects and make basic shape discriminations. What characterises the tasks where H.J.A. did well and those where abnormalities were detected? The tasks where H.J.A. succeeded (copying, single shape discrimination) could all be done in a serial manner (e.g. with parts of objects being encoded one at a time), and they had unlimited presentation times (so there were no costs in accuracy due to the encoding of parts being serial). The tasks where he was impaired (1–3 above) (a) constrained the opportunity for serial encoding (e.g. by reducing the exposure time), and (b) used stimuli with multiple internal segmentation cues (with line drawings and overlapping figures, containing numerous T-junctions).

To account for the pattern of performance, Riddoch and Humphreys proposed that H.J.A. could process basic, local visual elements in a relatively normal way (e.g. as indicated by search for orientation-defined target lines), in parallel across the visual field. However, the processes involved in integrating those elements into perceptual wholes, by grouping, were impaired. Due to this poor grouping of visual elements, H.J.A. was abnormally sensitive to segmentation cues, and tended to parse stimuli inappropriately into separate parts. Human recognition is limited to just one object at a time (Baylis & Driver, 1993; Duncan, 1984). Segmentation processes in vision act to deliver a parsed visual field in which separate objects can be identified in turn. Thus segmentation may be viewed as the counterpart of grouping—the tendency to group elements together into a single object description competing against processes that act to segment displays into separate objects. Impairments to grouping will consequently lead to over-segmentation of the visual array, and poor recognition. Recognition processes may then operate in a piecemeal way, and be strongly affected by display time.

ANALYSES USING VISUAL SEARCH

Supportive evidence for H.J.A. having a problem in grouping local form elements was reported by Humphreys, Riddoch et al. (1992). They used visual search tasks which required the detection of a "form-conjunction" target from amongst distractors made up of similar local elements—an example would be to search for an inverted T amongst upright T distractors, all of which contain horizontal and vertical form elements, with targets distinguished from distractors by the way in which these elements conjoin. In studies of normal observers, Duncan and Humphreys (1989) and Humphreys, Quinlan, and Riddoch (1989) had demonstrated that search for form conjunctions was strongly affected by grouping relations between the stimuli. Search is relatively efficient (showing only weak effects of the numbers of distractors present) when distractors are homogeneous; search is inefficient and linearly related to the numbers of distractors present when distractors are heterogeneous (e.g. Ts rotated 90° left and right as well as upright). Heterogeneous distractors tend not to group with one another, and any grouping that does operate will be as strong between the distractors and the target as it is between distractors. Hence targets and distractors will not be segmented easily on the basis of parallel grouping operations. Search may then depend on serial selection of one stimulus at a time, leading to linear search functions. In contrast, homogeneous distractors (being identical) will tend to group together and be segmented from the target, making search more efficient. Indeed, RTs can be particularly fast to "target absent" trials with homogeneous displays, due to subjects responding to a homogeneous group of distractors.

H.J.A. was given similar tasks and manifested an unusual pattern of performance. He was as good as the control subjects on the tasks that controls find difficult—search for a target amongst heterogeneous distractors. He was poor at the normally easy task of searching for a target amongst homogeneous distractors. His RTs were affected by the number of distractors present, he made numerous errors, and there was no evidence of "fast absent" responses to homogeneous displays of distractors.

The fact that H.J.A. was no worse than the controls in the difficult search task indicates that he has no problems in serial search across visual displays. The selective deficit with homogeneous displays, however, is consistent with H.J.A. having impairments to a process used by control subjects to make search of these displays efficient—parallel grouping between the elements. Humphreys, Riddoch et al. (1992) replicated these findings with abstract forms as well as with letter stimuli, demonstrating that the effects were not confined to the use of letter-like forms (Ts at various orientations). One other point to note is that, when conducting serial search with heterogeneous displays, H.J.A. made few errors—his error rate was raised only with homogeneous displays. This suggests that H.J.A. attempted to process homogeneous displays in parallel (since with serial search his error rate would be low), but he was simply poor at doing this. It appeared that he could not prevent his visual system from attempting to group elements even when he would have benefitted by treating each element individually.

These results, showing a selective deficit in search with homogeneous (groupable) displays, have been simulated by Humphreys, Freeman, and Müller (1992). They used the SERR model of visual search, in which visual stimuli are selected by activating stored "templates" for targets and distractors used in search tasks (e.g. there might be templates for Ts at various orientations, to simulate the above studies). Elements in the visual field group together by virtue of their having identical local feature combinations, and different items compete with each other if they fall at the same location (e.g. two Ts at different locations would group and support one another, but a T would compete with an inverted

T to be represented at a given location). Templates are activated according to which items are represented most strongly in the visual field, and the strength of activation varies as a function of grouping. Normally, homogeneous items group and activate their template efficiently, enabling search to be efficient. Heterogeneous items compete, making search protracted. If an activated template belongs to a distractor rather than a target, then linked items are rejected and search continues until the target is detected. This leads to serial search functions being generated, matching the standard pattern of search found with normal subjects (Humphreys & Müller, 1993). Humphreys et al. (1992) modified the model by adding noise to the activation functions. This resulted in incorrect features in local elements sometimes being activated transiently. Once this occurred, however, grouping between homogeneous items could be disrupted and the model behaved as if heterogeneous items were present. Search with homogeneous items became slow and error-prone. Interestingly, there was relatively little effect with heterogeneous distractors since items tended to compete rather than group in any case. The results mimic the data from H.J.A. In the model, disruption to a specific process, distractor grouping, selectively affects search with homogeneous displays; this provides an existence proof that a similar impairment could underlie H.J.A.'s impairment.

ENCODING WHOLES AND PARTS

Much but not all of the data reported in Humphreys, Riddoch et al. (1992) and Riddoch and Humphreys (1987b) highlighted a problem for H.J.A. in grouping local features to form visual "gestalts". However an exception to this was his tendency to perform better with silhouettes than with line drawings (Riddoch & Humphreys, 1987b; see also Lawson & Humphreys, 1999). Earlier we attributed this to a tendency to over-segment visual objects into their parts, when internal line cues for segmentation were present (with line drawings but not with silhouettes). The result also suggests, though, that H.J.A. is sensitive to some more wholistic information in vision; for example, his object decisions with silhouettes were above chance, consistent with his using overall shape outline on at least some occasions. How might such wholistic representations be formed?

Humphreys, Riddoch and Quinlan (1985) investigated this issue using compound letters (i.e. large "global" letters formed from smaller "local" letters; see Navon (1977) for a first example). The task was to discriminate, on different blocks of trials, whether the global or the local stimuli were Ss or Hs. When responses were made to the global forms, the local forms could be consistent or inconsistent with the response (e.g. both Ss or 1S and 1H), or they could be neutral (e.g. an O). The same manipulation occurred when responses were made to the local forms (when the identity of the global forms could be consistent, inconsistent or neutral). Under appropriate conditions (e.g. when there is some uncertainly concerning the location of the target and the local elements are sufficiently dense), normal subjects respond faster to the global than to the local forms and the identity of the global forms affects local responses (e.g. there is interference when their identities are inconsistent) (see Navon, 1977). This provides one example of when the global "forest" seems to be identified before the local "trees".

Under equivalent conditions H.J.A., like control subjects, responded more quickly to the global than to the local letters (for H.J.A. RTs were as much as 300ms faster than global letters). Thus he was able to discriminate the global letters as perceptual wholes. In fact, H.J.A.'s responses to global letters were relatively normal and it was his responses to local letters that were slowed (when the letters appeared in the context of the global shape). However, unlike controls, H.J.A. showed no indication of any global interference on local responses. It might be argued that the lack of global interference arose precisely because H.J.A.'s local responses were slow; for example, any initial activation of a response by the global letter may have decayed by the time the local letter was identified. However, data with normal subjects show that interference effects occur across quite wide variations in local and global response times (Lamb & Robertson, 1988, 1989), making this account unlikely. Further, subsequent to this initial study Lamb, Robertson and Knight (1990) found somewhat similar results in a group study of patients with lesions to the superior temporal gyrus (STG) (of either hemisphere), though they showed a much smaller overall RT advantage for global letters (i.e. there was less disruption in responding to local forms; patients with right hemisphere lesions in fact showed a local advantage). This unusual pattern, of a global advantage without interference, suggests instead that the global and more local aspects of the forms may be processed independently, with interference arising only when the two forms of information are integrated perceptually. In H.J.A., and perhaps also patients with lesions of the STG, global aspects of shape can be derived, but these representations are not embellished efficiently with more detailed local form information. This may facilitate selective attention to the local and global aspects of form, minimising interference effects. In H.J.A.'s case the disruption in deriving local form information may mean that local and more global representations are never fully integrated, contributing to his recognition deficit. The STG communicates with the inferior occipito-temporal region via area MT (Kaas, 1988), and so STG lesions may disconnect this region from inferior temporal regions concerned with perceptual integration (which are damaged bilaterally in H.J.A.'s case).

What form might H.J.A.'s global representations take? At least two possibilities suggest themselves. One is that his global representations are based on low spatial frequency components in displays. The other is that they are based on coding the positions (but not the identities) of the local elements. If global forms are derived from position-based coding, then at least one form of grouping would seem to operate—grouping by proximity—even if other forms of grouping are impaired (e.g. grouping by similar identities). Whatever the case, information about the local identities of parts will not be specified (as they might be if grouping by similarity took place). To derive sufficient local information for object identification to operate, H.J.A. may then attempt to process parts serially, leading to piecemeal naming responses.

Other evidence supporting the proposal that H.J.A. can encode global shape information, but that this information is impoverished relative to the information derived by normal subjects, was reported by Boucart and Humphreys (1992). They had H.J.A. make perceptual matches to fragmented line drawings. The fragments in the line drawings could be aligned and collinear or they could be misaligned so that they were no longer collinear, but the overall shape had the same low spatial frequency components as before. Normal subjects are advantaged when they match forms with collinear segments. H.J.A. showed no evidence for this. He was sensitive to the orientation of the global form, however; he could better discriminate items whose global orientation differed than items with the same global orientation. Again it appears that there was impaired grouping by collinearity to support the global information that could be derived, either from low spatial frequency components or from a position-base analysis.

AGNOSIA AND SIMULTANAGNOSIA

The findings from H.J.A. indicate a deficit in integrating local elements into articulated representations of perceptual wholes, with perception breaking down into a parts-based analysis of objects on many occasions. One might ask, what is the relation between such a disorder and the syndrome of simultanagnosia, in which patients seem again to have limited ability to process visual information in parallel but this co-occurs with a relatively good ability to identify single objects (e.g. Balint, 1909; Coslett & Saffran, 1991; Humphreys & Price, 1994; Kinsbourne & Warrington, 1962)?

In behavioural terms, H.J.A. manifests few signs of simultanagnosia. He is able to report on the presence of several objects simultaneously (e.g. when asked to decide how many objects are present his RTs are relatively unaffected for up to four objects; Humphreys, 1998; Humphreys et al., 1985). He negotiates his environment successfully, picking up objects correctly and avoiding collisions (Humphreys & Riddoch, 1987b). In this respect, H.J.A. behaves quite differently from patients with simultanagnosia following bilateral lesions of the parietal lobes (Balint, 1909).

Humphreys (1998), as others before him, proposed that dorsal and ventral areas of the brain perform separate computational functions in vision (e.g. see also Milner & Goodale, 1995). According to Humphreys, ventral regions deal with the analysis of parts within objects; dorsal with the representation of at least a limited number of separate objects. It is this representation of a limited number of objects, within the dorsal visual stream, that provides us with some awareness of the spatial structure of the visual environment. Dorsal visual structures remain intact in H.J.A., and presumably enable him to move successfully in the environment (even if he does not recognise the objects present!). Within his ventral system, however, there is a limitation in the parallel grouping of visual forms, impairing object recognition. The opposite pattern of impairment may be found after bilateral lesions of dorsal visual areas. In this case, patients show poor awareness of the spatial structure of their environment. However, in tasks requiring the recognition of single objects such patients can show good performance and even evidence of processing visual parts in parallel (e.g. word identification can be unaffected by the number of letters present; Humphreys, 1998).

Farah (1990) distinguished between two forms of simultanagnosia, according to whether patients had lesions affecting ventral or dorsal visual areas. According to Farah, "ventral" simultanagnosia may be due to a limited visual short-term memory and "dorsal" to impaired disengagement of attention from objects. H.J.A., though, showed few deficits in visual short-term memory, at least as assessed in enumeration tasks. Whilst agreeing with the distinction between different functional deficits after ventral and dorsal lesions, it remains my contention that they are better characterised in terms of impairments in the construction of different forms of spatial representation (parts within objects and separate objects). Patients classed as ventral simultanagnosics following unilateral left ventral lesions (e.g. Kinsbourne & Warrington, 1962) may simply have a reduced version of the deficit suffered by H.J.A. after bilateral lesions. A unilateral left deficit may particularly impair the parallel grouping of parts within objects that are represented within the left hemisphere (words).

LONG-TERM VISUAL MEMORY

Although H.J.A. was severely impaired in visually recognising objects, he performed remarkably well at tasks designed to tap aspects of his visual memory for form. For example, his drawings from memory were as accurate as those produced by control subjects, and he produced detailed descriptions of objects from memory, including information about their visual properties (size, shape etc.)(Riddoch & Humphreys, 1987b). The only clear deficit on initial testing of long-term visual memory was with colour knowledge, which was quite poor. Such results suggested that, at least as far as form information is concerned, visual perceptual processes necessary to object recognition can be separated from long-term visual memory and the imagery processes that support performance in drawing and long-term recall (see Chapter 5 for further discussion of this argument). In this respect, colour knowledge may be somewhat different, and rely on the re-activation of perceptual representations of colour.

Subsequent studies, however, have indicated that H.J.A.'s long-term visual knowledge is not perfect, when probed using tasks similar to those where he shows a deficit in perception. Young, Humphreys, Riddoch, Hellalwell, and de Haan (1994) investigated H.J.A.'s long-term visual knowledge of faces. He showed good recall of individual features of faces but poor memory for more "configural" properties, which may require features to be integrated. This subtle deficit is consistent with perception and long-term memory recall tapping at least some common processes.

AGNOSIA 16 YEARS ON

H.J.A. suffered his brain lesions in 1981. In 1997, Riddoch et al. (1999) retested his performance on many of the original tasks used to diagnose his agnosia. H.J.A.'s ability to identify real objects showed some improvement. However, there was little change in his identification of line drawings, and he continued to be impaired on tests stressing the integration of form information, such as identifying overlapping figures and line drawings compared with silhouettes. This suggests that the basic underlying visual impairment had remained relatively constant, though he had become better able to use other forms of stimulation (e.g. stereo and texture cues, in real objects). A more pronounced improvement with real objects than with line drawings has been noted before in follow-ups of agnosic patients (e.g. Wilson & Davidoff, 1993). At a more detailed level, subsequent tests revealed that H.J.A. was still selectively impaired with overlapping figures, and he continued to perform relatively better with silhouettes than line drawings. The basic symptoms of integrative agnosia remained.

Interestingly, H.J.A.'s ability to recall the visual properties of objects did show some deterioration. For example, his line drawings of objects were less easy for control subjects to identify and his definitions specified fewer visual features. This was not due to some overall drop in performance, however; in fact his definitions contained more verbal detail than previously. These results suggest that long-term visual memory interacts with visual perception, at least in the sense that visual memories deteriorate unless updated by intact perceptual descriptions. Over the longer term, an integrative perceptual problem can also contribute to the loss of long-term visual knowledge about objects.

RELATIONS TO OTHER PATIENTS

As I noted above, the types of visual identification error made by H.J.A. resemble those described in several other case reports in the literature, in which patients attempt to name objects via the serial identification of their parts. The patient reported by Butter and Trobe (1994), when asked to describe how many objects were present when given single line drawings, even stated that there were several objects present, identifying parts as separate items. The patient reported by Shelton, Bowers, Duara and Heilman (1994) showed poor copying of objects when the parts had to be spatially related. Such responses are consistent with some form of problem in perceptual integration. Butter and Trobe also assessed their patient with overlapping figures and silhouettes. Similarly to Riddoch and Humphreys (1987b), there was a marked impairment with overlapping figures and relatively better performance with silhouettes than line drawings. Thus this pattern of performance is not unique to H.J.A.

DeRenzi and Lucchelli (1993) reported data on a patient who, like H.J.A., demonstrated relatively good shape perception on the Efron task (Fig. 3.2), along with poor performance on overlapping figures tests and on several tests requiring access to stored memory from line drawings (e.g. object decision). DeRenzi and Lucchelli's patient also found it very difficult to discriminate realistic from impossible figures, created by making local parts structurally inconsistent with one another. Such a task requires that the parts be integrated together. On similar tasks, H.J.A. too performed poorly. DeRenzi and Lucchelli's patient, however, was also impaired in recalling the perceptual details of objects from long-term memory. For example, she was poor at drawing objects from memory (though copying was relatively good) and she was often unable to describe the perceptual difference between two objects, when given their names. In such a case, the perceptual impairment seems to co-occur with a disorder of stored visual knowledge. Now, whilst it can be argued that, when probed, H.J.A. too had a deficit in recalling the kinds of visual attributes he had difficulty in perceiving (e.g. facial configurations; Young et al., 1994), the severity of any memorial deficit was less pronounced than his perceptual impairment. It seems likely that patients can have associated lesions, which generate substantial problems in long-term visual memory, in addition to any perceptual deficit (cf. DeRenzi & Lucchelli, 1993). A similar argument can be applied to the patient described by Grailet, Seron, Bruyer, Coyette, and Frederix (1990). Like H.J.A., the copies produced by this patient indicated some problems in parsing visual stimuli. For instance, surface reflectance properties were reproduced as if they were parts of objects. Drawing from memory, though, was impaired (this patient tended to reproduce general associative knowledge in his drawings; for example he introduced a container into the body of an animal when asked to draw a camel), and he was deficient in naming to visual definitions. The patient was in addition impaired in tactile object recognition. Grailet et al. proposed that their case had a central (cross-modal) problem in integrating parts into wholes, and suggested that H.J.A.'s deficit was at an earlier stage of binding visual features together. However the presence of a memory deficit in this patient could contribute to the cross-modal nature of his problem.

Riddoch and Humphreys (1987b) argued that, for H.J.A., there was relatively good encoding of basic properties of shape, along with poor integration of parts to wholes. They suggested that the processes of grouping parts into wholes is also necessary for accurate figure–ground coding to occur. For example, with overlapping figures the ability to link parts to one object may help in segmenting it from the background. The parts that enter into this integration process include correctly computed local contours. Subsequent to this, Davidoff and Warrington (1993) have posited that deficits in shape coding and deficits in figure–ground formation can doubly dissociate. They report a patient who was able to describe simple overlapping geometric forms, who could judge the number of three-dimensional line drawings present in a display, and who could make perceptual judgements about whether contours were aligned or not. However, the patient was poor at shape discrimination tasks, such as the Efron shape test. They argued that figure–ground coding was relatively intact in this patient, though shape coding was impaired. However, it is possible that figure–ground processes still rely on outputs from shape coding mechanisms, and for this pattern of deficit to occur. This would be the case if intact figure–ground coding processes can recover from poor shape input, at least when figure–ground is not taxed or measured under real-time conditions. Interestingly, in some of the tests used by Davidoff and Warrington to demonstrate intact figure–ground coding H.J.A. too performs at a high level. For example, he can discriminate letter fragments shown against a background of visual noise (the shape detection test from the VOSP battery; Warrington & James, 1991), and he can count the number of three-dimensional line drawings present (again using stimuli from VOSP). Deficits in grouping and segmentation are nevertheless apparent when time-based measures are used or time restrictions imposed.

CONCLUSIONS

H.J.A.'s case demonstrates that a form of visual agnosia can exist even though a patient shows relatively good basic coding of shape and even though stored knowledge of objects is largely preserved. The deficit appears to affect a stage of visual processing intermediate between basic shape coding and visual access to memory representations, concerned with parallel perceptual grouping and the integration of perceptual parts into wholes. It is revealed most strikingly under conditions that stress visual segmentation and grouping. It indicates that Lissauer's original distinction between apperceptive and associative agnosia needs to be fractionated further, to reflect the sub-processes involved at the different processing stages (see Humphreys & Riddoch, 1987a; Humphreys et al., 1994).

ACKNOWLEDGEMENTS

This work was supported by grants from the Medical Research Council (UK), the EU and the Human Science Frontier Programme.

REFERENCES

Balint, R. (1909). Seelenahmung des "Schauens": Optische ataxie, raumliche Storung der Aufmerkamsamkeit. *Monatschrift für Psychiatrie und Neurologie, 25*, 51–81.

Baylis, G., & Driver, J. (1993). Visual attention and objects: Evidence for hierarchical coding of location. *Journal of Experimental Psychology: Human Perception and Performance, 19*, 451–70.

Behrmann, M., Moscovitch, M., & Winocur, G. (1994). Intact visual imagery and impaired visual perception in a patient with visual agnosia. *Journal of Experimental Psychology: Human Perception and Performance, 20*, 1068–87.

Benson, D.F., & Greenberg, J.P. (1969). Visual form agnosia. *Archives of Neurology, 20*, 82–9.

Biederman, I. (1987). Recognition by components: A theory of human image understanding. *Psychological Review, 94*, 115–45.

Boucart, M., & Humphreys, G.W. (1992). The computation of perceptual structure from collinearity and closure: Normality and pathology. *Neuropsychologia, 30*, 527–546.

Brady, M. (1997). The forms of knowledge mobilized in some machine vision systems. *Philosophical Transactions of the Royal Society, B352*, 1241–8.

Butter, C.M., & Trobe, J.D. (1994). Integrative agnosia following progressive multifocal leukoencephalopathy. *Cortex, 30*, 145–58.

Campion, J. (1987). Apperceptive agnosia: The specification and description of constructs. In Humphreys, G.W., & Riddoch, M.J. (Eds), *Visual object processing: A cognitive neuropsychological approach*. Hove: Lawrence Erlbaum Associates.

Coslett, H.B., & Saffran, E. (1991). Simultanagnosia: To see but not two see. *Brain, 114*, 1523–45.

Davidoff, J., & Warrington, E.K. (1993). A dissociation of shape discrimination and figure–ground perception in a patient with normal acuity. *Neuropsychologia, 31*, 83–93.

DeRenzi, E., & Lucchelli, F. (1993). The fuzzy boundaries of apperceptive agnosia. *Cortex, 29*, 187–215.

Duncan, J. (1984). Selective attention and the organization of visual information. *Journal of Experimental Psychology: General, 113*, 501–17.

Duncan, J., & Humphreys, G.W. (1989). Visual search and stimulus similarity. *Psychological Review, 96*, 433–58.

Efron, R. (1968). What is perception? In R.S. Cohen, & M. Wartofsky (Eds), *Boston studies in the philosophy of science*. New York: Humanities Press.

Farah, M.J. (1990). *Visual agnosia*. Cambridge, Massachusetts: MIT Press.

Forde, E.M.E., Francis, D., Riddoch, M.J., Rumiati, R.I., & Humphreys, G.W. (1997). On the links between visual knowledge and naming: A single case study of a patient with a category-specific impairment for living things. *Cognitive Neuropsychology, 14*, 403–58.

Goldstein, K., & Gelb, A. (1918). Psychologische analysen hirnpathologischer Fall auf Grund von Unterschungen Hirnveletzter. *Zeitschrift für die gesemete Neurologie und Psychiatrie, 41*, 1–142.

Grailet, J.M., Seron, X., Bruyer, R., Coyette, F., & Frederix, M. (1990). Case report of a visual integrative agnosia. *Cognitive Neuropsychology, 7*, 275–310.

Grossman, M., Galetta, S., & D'Esposito, M. (1997). Object recognition difficulty in visual apperceptive agnosia. *Brain and Cognition, 33*, 306–42.

Hillis, A.E., & Caramazza, A. (1995). Cognitive and neural mechanisms underlying visual and semantic processing: implications from "optic aphasia". *Journal of Cognitive Neuroscience, 7*, 457–78.

Humphreys, G.W. (1998). The representation of objects in space: A dual coding account. *Philosophical Transactions of the Royal Society, B353*, 1341–51.

Humphreys, G.W., Freeman, T., & Müller, H.M. (1992). Lesioning a connectionist model of visual search: Selective effects on distractor grouping. *Canadian Journal of Psychology, 46*, 417–60.

Humphreys, G.W., & Müller, H.M. (1993). SEarch via Recursive Rejection (SERR): A connectionist model of visual search. *Cognitive Psychology, 25*, 43–110.

Humphreys, G.W., & Price, C.J. (1993). Visual feature discrimination in simultanagnosia: A study of two cases. *Cognitive Neuropsychology, 11*, 393–434.

Humphreys, G.W., Quinlan, P.T., & Riddoch, M.J. (1989). Grouping processes in visual search: Effects with single-and combined-feature targets. *Journal of Experimental Psychology: General, 118*, 258–79.

Humphreys, G.W., & Riddoch, M.J. (1984). Routes to object constancy: Implications from neurological impairments of object constancy. *Quarterly Journal of Experimental Psychology, 36A*, 385–415.

Humphreys, G.W., & Riddoch, M.J. (1987a). The fractionation of visual agnosia. In G.W. Humphreys, & M.J. Riddoch (Eds), *Visual object processing: A cognitive neuropsychological approach*. Hove: Lawrence Erlbaum Associates.

Humphreys, G.W., & Riddoch, M.J. (1987b). *To see but not to see: A case study of visual agnosia*. London: Lawrence Erlbaum.

Humphreys, G.W., & Riddoch, M.J. (1993). Object agnosias. In C. Kennard (Ed.), *Baillière's clinical neurology*. London: Baillière Tindall.

Humphreys, G.W., Riddoch, M.J., Donnelly, N., Freeman, T.A.C., Boucart, M., & Müller, H.M. (1994). Intermediate visual processing and visual agnosia. In M.J. Farah, & G. Ratcliff (Eds), *The neuropsychology of high-level vision*. Hillsdale, N.J.: Lawrence Erlbaum Associates.

Humphreys, G.W., Riddoch, M.J., & Quinlan, P.T. (1985). Interactive processes in perceptual organization: Evidence from visual agnosia. In M.I. Posner & O.S.M. Marin (Eds), *Attention, & Performance XI*. Hillsdale, N.J.: Lawrence Erlbaum Associates.

Humphreys, G.W., Riddoch, M.J., Quinlan, P.T., Price, C.J., & Donnelly, N. (1992). Parallel pattern processing in visual agnosia. *Canadian Journal of Psychology, 46*, 377–416.

Humphreys, G.W., & Rumiati, R.I. (1998). Stimulus specificity in visual recognition: Agnosia without prosopagnosia or alexia. *Cognitive Neuropsychology, 15*, 243–278.

Kaas, J.H. (1988). Changing concepts of visual cortex organisation in primates. In J.W. Brown (Ed.), *Neuropsychology of visual perception*. Hillsdale, N.J.: Lawrence Erlbaum Associates.

Kinsbourne, M., & Warrington, E.K. (1962). A disorder of simultaneous form perception. *Brain, 85*, 461–86.

Lamb, M.R., & Robertson, L.C. (1988). The processing of hierarchical stimuli: Effects of retinal locus, locational uncertainty and stimulus identity. *Perception & Psychophysics, 44*, 172–81.

Lamb, M.R., & Robertson, L.C. (1989). Do response time advantage and interference reflect the order of processing of global and local level information? *Perception & Psychophysics, 46*, 254–58.

Lamb, M.R., Robertson, L.C., & Knight, R.T. (1990). Component mechanisms underlying the processing of hierarchically organized patterns: Inferences from patients with unilateral cortical lesions. *Journal of Experimental Psychology: Learning, Memory and Cognition, 16*, 471–83.

Lawson, R., & Humphreys, G.W. (1999). The effects of view in depth on the identification of line drawings and silhouettes of familiar objects: Normality and pathology. *Visual Cognition, 6*, 165–196.

Lissauer, H. (1890). Ein Fall von Seelenblindheit nebst einem Beitrage zur Theorie derselben. *Archiv für Psychiatrie und Nervenkrankheiten, 21*, 222–70.

Lowe, D.G. (1987). Three-dimensional object recognition from single two-dimensional images. *Artificial Intelligence, 31*, 355–95.

Marr, D. (1982). *Vision*. San Francisco: W.H. Freeman.

Milner, A.D., & Goodale, M.A. (1995). *The visual brain in action*. Oxford: Oxford University Press.

Milner, A.D., Perrett, D.I., Johnston, R.S., Benson, P.J., Jordan, T.R., Heeley, D.W., Bettucci, D., Mortara, F., Mutani, R., Terazzi, E., & Davidson, D.L.W. (1991). Perception and action in "visual form agnosia". *Brain, 114*, 405–28.

Navon, D. (1977). Forest before trees: The precedence of global features in visual perception. *Cognitive Psychology, 9*, 955–65.

Plaut, D., & Shallice, T. (1993). Perseverative and semantic influences on visual object naming errors in optic aphasia: A connectionist account. *Journal of Cognitive Neuroscience, 5*, 89–117.

Riddoch, M.J., & Humphreys, G.W. (1987a). Visual object processing in optic aphasia: a case of semantic access agnosia. *Cognitive Neuropsychology, 4*, 131–85.

Riddoch, M.J., & Humphreys, G.W. (1987b). A case of integrative visual agnosia. *Brain, 110*, 1431–62.

Riddoch, M.J., Humphreys, G.W., Gannon, T., Blott, W., & Jones, V. (1999). Memories are made of this: The effects of time on stored visual knowledge in a case of visual agnosia. *Brain, 122*, 537–559.

Sartori, G., & Job, R. (1988). The oyster with four legs: a neuropsychological study on the inter-action of visual and semantic information. *Cognitive Neuropsychology*, *5*, 130–52.

Shelton, P.A., Bowers, D., Duara, R., & Heilman, K.M. (1994). Apperceptive visual agnosia: A case study. *Brain and Cognition*, *25*, 1–23.

Sheridan, J., & Humphreys, G.W. (1993). A verbal–semantic category-specific recognition impair-ment. *Cognitive Neuropsychology*, *10*, 143–84.

Sirigu, A., Duhamel, J.-R., & Poncet, M. (1991). The role of sensorimotor experience in object recognition: A case of multimodal agnosia. *Brain*, *114*, 2555–73.

Stewart, F., Parkin, A.J., & Hunkin, N.M. (1992). Naming impairments following recovery from herpes simplex encephalitis. *Quarterly Journal of Experimental Psychology*, *44A*, 261–84.

Wapner, W., Judd, T., & Gardner, H. (1978). Visual agnosia in an artist. *Cortex*, *14*, 343–64.

Warrington, E.K. (1982). Neuropsychological studies of object recognition. *Philosophical Trans-actions of the Royal Society, London, B298*, 15–33.

Warrington, E.K. (1985). Agnosia: The impairment of object recognition. In P.J. Vinken, G. Bruyn, & H. Klawans (Eds), *Handbook of clinical neurology*. Amsterdam: Elsevier Science.

Warrington, E.K., & James, M. (1988). Visual apperceptive agnosia. A clinico-anatomical study of three cases. *Cortex*, *24*, 13–32.

Warrington, E.K., & James, M. (1991). *VOSP: The visual object and space perception battery*. Bury St. Edmunds: Thames Valley Test Company.

Wilson, B.A., & Davidoff, J. (1993). Partial recovery from visual object agnosia: A 10 year follow-up study. *Cortex*, *29*, 529–42.

Young, A.W., Humphreys, G.W., Riddoch, M.J., Hellalwell, D.J., & de Haan, E.H.F. (1994). Recognition impairments and face imagery. *Neuropsychologia*, *32*, 693–705.

CHAPTER FOUR

Apperceptive agnosia: A deficit of perceptual categorisation of objects

Jules Davidoff
Goldsmiths' College, University of London, UK

Elizabeth K. Warrington
National Hospital, Queen Square, London, UK

HISTORICAL BACKGROUND

Models of human object recognition now quite standardly seek verification of their processing stages from neuropsychological research. These clarifications to the description in models of object recognition have all stemmed from the distinctions made in the classic paper of Lissauer (Lissauer, 1890; translation and commentary by Shallice & Jackson, 1988). It was Lissauer who initiated the current view that object recognition could be understood from its fractionation into component processes. In his paper, Lissauer made a simple division of recognition into two stages. These two stages were apperception and association. However, as these terms have been used somewhat differently by various authors, they will need some clarification. The essence of the distinction is simple. Apperception refers to some of the perceptual processes that take place prior to the access of meaning but subsequent to those required for intact elementary sensation; association refers to the meaning of the object, that is the links from all possible properly formed percepts of an object to its associated knowledge. Thus, apperception concerns the processing stage at which one has no difficulty seeing the world clearly and discriminating one object from another but nevertheless cannot grasp the visual equivalence of objects.

The two stages of Lissauer are commonly used to distinguish between two alternative types of an impairment in a patient's understanding of a visually presented object—an impairment that is known as visual agnosia. The term agnosia was introduced by Freud (1891) and literally means "without knowledge".

Thus, in the original sense, it is clear that only an impairment of the associative stage is a true agnosia. Nevertheless, patients may be functionally agnosic (unable to access associations and hence meaning of a visually presented object) because of difficulties that occur at an earlier or different stage in processing than that impaired in the true agnosia. The earlier stage in processing would correspond, in artificial intelligence terminology, to the structural descriptions that give the geometric and volumetric properties of an object. The agnosia that results from impairments to the corresponding structures in the human brain is often encompassed by the term apperceptive agnosia. The focus of the present chapter consists of some cases that have helped clarify the concept of apperception introduced by Lissauer.

Lissauer noted of his patient with associative agnosia and intact apperception that "It was clear from the way in which he was able to look at and handle objects that he was able to perceive visual stimuli . . . the patient could be made to draw simple familiar objects placed in front of him, a clear indication that he was able to perceive form." For a description of an impairment at the apperceptive stage, one could turn to Poetzl (1928). Poetzl wrote (see Levine, 1978) "Details that are normally irrelevant command attention, whereas the important details—those which form the nucleus for correct identification—often recede into the background or momentarily disappear . . . What Wertheimer called the centre of gravity of the Gestalt . . . is no longer stable . . . but at different moments, different complexes of parts emerge as the centre of gravity." Poetzl wrote, perhaps not surprisingly, as he denied Lissauer's division of apperception and association, as if the problem were at an intermediate stage in object identification.

The more recent work in clarifying the notion of an apperceptive impairment began with group studies conducted in the 50s and 60s. There emerged a growing body of evidence that the right hemisphere was critically involved with recognition of visual patterns (Milner, 1958; Kimura, 1963) and of meaningful objects that were presented in some non-optimal form. The non-optimal presentations have included those in the form of sketchy drawings (Milner, 1958) fragmented drawings of letters (Warrington & James, 1967; Faglioni, Scotti, & Spinnler, 1969) overlapping drawings (De Renzi & Spinnler, 1966; De Renzi, Scotti, & Spinnler, 1969) and rotated faces (Benton & Van Allen, 1968; De Renzi et al., 1969). The above impairments in object recognition arising from posterior right hemisphere lesions are those considered as apperceptive; they need to be distinguished from other (earlier) impairments that militate against the proper formation of a percept for a boundaried surface. For example, the normal ability to parse the visual field (i.e., the accurate segmentation into coloured or achromatic regions) can be compromised if the patient has impaired visual acuity, colour perception or shape perception. Damage to the occipital lobes, often from anoxia, may result in impairments of all three of these low-level visual abilities. However, each of these three abilities can be selectively lost or retained in the absence of the other two (Warrington, 1986). More recent research has shown that the processes required to form a coherent shape percept are more complicated than that given in the first systematic studies conducted by Efron (1968). Recent work by Warrington and her colleagues has shown that patients may have an inability to segment the visual input but retain some shape discrimination (Kartsounis & Warrington, 1991) or have virtually no usable shape discrimination in the presence of remarkably good segmentation (Davidoff & Warrington, 1993).

An advance in our understanding of apperceptive disorders came from the group study conducted by Warrington and Taylor (1973). The approach adopted in their study was to manipulate stimulus materials somewhat in the manner of classic constancy experiments and then to verify the extent to which the manipulation prevented correct identification. Acquired cortical lesions rarely affect the classical types of constancy; the neurological literature is sparse with respect to patients for whom colour or size constancy are lost—though each of these impairments has been recorded (Kennard, Lawden, Morland, & Ruddock, 1995; Wyke, 1960; Cohen, Gray, Meyrignac, Dehaene, et al., 1994). These constancies require the ability to detect the similarity between surfaces or objects as they are seen under different illuminations or at different distances. Shape constancy, however, is somewhat different as the object under test is rotated so that the retinal image is no longer similar (in the geometric sense) under the new condition of view. Though there appear to be no recorded cases of a cortical lesion causing such an impairment as tested in the manner of a constancy experiment, it is possible that patients with right parietal lesions and the consequent impairments on rotation tasks (Butters, Baron, & Brody, 1970) would show this impairment. The critical task used by Warrington and Taylor (1973) was, however, the rotation of meaningful objects rather than meaningless shapes. Warrington and Taylor found that the right posterior patients were not more impaired than left posterior patients when objects were transformed by size but they were impaired when objects were fragmented as in the Gollin figures (see Fig. 4.1 and Warrington & James, 1967) or rotated to present an unconventional view. In the unconventional views test, a series of 20 objects was photographed from two angles, i.e., from a conventional view and from an unconventional view (see Fig. 4.2). The unconventional view did not necessarily represent a view that was completely unfamiliar but was unlikely to be the choice of orientation if required to draw the object from memory. The 20 unconventional views were shown first to the patients and they were requested to identify each object either by naming or by description; these views were then followed by the objects shown from a conventional view. The patients with right posterior lesions, but not left lesions, were clearly impaired on the unconventional views without any similar impairment for conventional views. A similar impairment was subsequently found in right posterior patients by changing the angle of illumination rather than rotating the object (Warrington, 1982)—a manipulation also known to affect face matching

FIG. 4.1   Example of Gollin figure.

of two views of a face (Benton & Van Allen, 1968). Thus, the apperceptive impairment can be considered as one in which the patient has lost an ability to categorise different versions of the same object as equivalent.

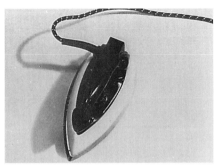

FIG. 4.2   Example of conventional and unconventional view object.

CASE STUDIES IN WARRINGTON & JAMES (1988)

The work with group studies has many virtues but the well-known arguments for the use of case studies in delineating models of cortical function demand that the apperceptive impairment be validated also from that methodology. The averaging techniques used in group studies may mask a valid dissociation and apparent dissociations could be artifactual due to differential task sensitivity. Three clear-cut cases have been studied (Warrington & James, 1988) with subsequent follow-up data and discussion (Rudge & Warrington, 1991; Warrington & Rudge, 1995); indeed, the cases of Warrington and James (1988) are so similar that they can be considered as replications.

Case 1 was a male right-handed 69 year old company director admitted to hospital after an acute episode of confusion and visual difficulties two weeks previously. There was a left homonymous hemianopia that spared the macula. A CT brain scan demonstrated a cystic cavity in the right parieto-occipital region. Case 2 was a 60 year-old male bricklayer who had been well up to one month previously when he became confused and bumped into things on the left. On examination, there was a left homonymous hemianopia and left-sided sensory inattention and some weakness in the left upper limb. A CT scan demonstrated a large cystic lesion in the right parietal lobe. Case 3 was a 60 year-old postman admitted for an investigation of increasingly severe headache and visual failure. There was a partial incongruent left homonymous hemianopia with a minor degree of motor weakness in the left arm; his gait was ataxic. A CT scan demonstrated a low-density lesion in the right posterior/parietal region with ring enhancement after contrast.

All three patients were assessed on the Wechsler Adult Intelligence Scale (WAIS). An estimate of their premorbid IQ level was obtained from their reading skills and the "Reading" IQ equivalents are given in Table 4.1. In each case

TABLE 4.1
Memory and Intelligence Test Scores (from Warrington & James, 1988)

	Case 1	Case 2	Case 3
Reading IQ equivalent	121	86	104
Verbal IQ	107	97	101
Performance IQ	89	89	96
Verbal memory	>50th %ile	>75th %ile	>75th %ile

their current level of functioning on the verbal scale of the WAIS was within the average range and in cases 2 and 3 very close to their estimated premorbid level. For cases 2 and 3, their current level of functioning on the Performance scale was also close to their optimum and only in case 1 was there a significant deterioration. A recognition memory test for words (Warrington, 1984) was also administered and the percentile score obtained by each case is given in Table 4.1. It is clear that, for these cases, verbal abilities had been left much intact. The next stage of the investigation was to ensure that the patients could adequately form a coherent percept of a boundaried surface. The following tests were given to each patient: shape detection, shape discrimination, and colour discrimination.

The most primitive segmentation task is to distinguish the presence of a figure from the background. The test stimuli used comprised a fragmented shape (X or O) superimposed on a random pattern background, the shape being present in half the stimuli and absent in the others (see Fig. 4.3). The patient is asked to state whether the shape is present or absent. All three cases scored 30/30 on this task and when one considers that normals may make errors on this task, is evidence of excellent performance. Good performance was also observed in a more demanding task of shape discrimination that was tested using an adaptation of the Efron squares test (1968). Each patient was required to judge whether a shape is a square or an oblong. The square was 50 × 50mm and the oblong matched for total flux was 46 × 55mm (see Fig. 4.4). Ten squares and ten oblongs are presented singly in pseudo-random order. Cases 2 and 3 made no errors and Case 1 made only one.

Testing the perception of coloured surface information was assessed by the Farnsworth–Munsell 100-Hue Test. The test asks the patient to arrange twenty or so small coloured chips to leave a series that systematically varies from one colour (e.g., red) to another (yellow). Given the small variation in colour between the chips and the known difficulties that patients with spatial difficulties have with this task (Zihl, Roth, Kerkhoff, & Heywood, 1988), the patients' normal performance shows clearly that these cases had no difficulty with colour perception.

So, even if the Warrington and James (1988) paper did not systematically assess the complexities of perceptual segmentation addressed in later papers (see Davidoff & Warrington, 1993 and Chapter 3 of this volume), the tests

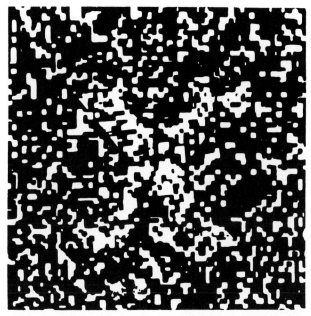

FIG. 4.3   Example of shape detection task—fragmented "X" against random pattern background.

FIG. 4.4   Example of square and oblong matched for total flux.

administered give good grounds to believe that the failure in perceptual categorisation (see below) did not arise from failure to form a coherent shape.

The apperceptive disorder was assessed in a series of six tests. Four of these have already been mentioned: these were the unconventional views test and two versions of the Gollin test (see Fig. 4.1 taken from Warrington & Taylor, 1973), a face matching task adapted from the work of De Renzi and colleagues (De Renzi et al., 1969) and the fragmented letters task (see Fig. 4.5) of Warrington and James (1967). Two further tests were added that considered more principled

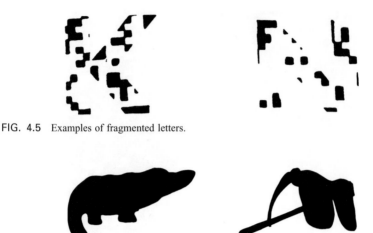

FIG. 4.5   Examples of fragmented letters.

FIG. 4.6   Examples of foreshortened silhouettes.

aspects of the finding in Warrington and Taylor (1973) concerning the difficulty
right posterior patients have with perceptual categorisation. These tests were
foreshortened silhouettes (see Fig. 4.6) and shadow image projection (see Fig. 4.7).
For the foreshortened silhouette task, the patient has to name or identify each
silhouette which is presented individually. The test has the advantage over the
unconventional views task of Warrington and Taylor (1973) in that the items are
manipulated to achieve a test of graded difficulty without a ceiling effect as
is the case with the conventional views. The gradation is effected by altering
the degree of foreshortening and hence the difficulty of recognition. The test is
known to be sensitive to right hemisphere damage (Warrington & James, 1991).
The shadow image projection test was taken from Warrington and James (1986).
Three-dimensioned (3D) shadow images of scale models of common objects
were produced by rotating the objects round either their horizontal (lateral rotation) or their vertical (base rotation) axes in an apparatus devised by Gregory
(1964). Five objects were viewed in each of the lateral and base rotation conditions. The object recognition threshold recorded was the angular rotation at
which the object was correctly identified. Table 4.2 shows that all three cases
were impaired, with only minor variation, at all these tasks measuring apperceptive (categorisation) abilities.

For consideration of the importance of these cases in Warrington and James
(1988) we need to discuss the other tasks at which these patients succeed. But
first one should say that the three cases were not devoid of problems in tasks that
required visual spatial analysis. One of the most primitive of spatial abilities is
location perception; this was tested by asking the patient to point to a spot of
light in 1 of 5 positions on the horizontal meridian in the visual field ipsilateral

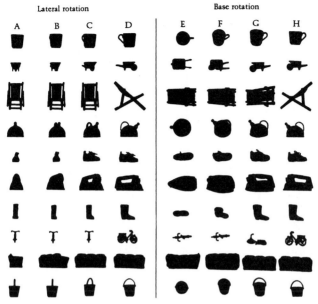

Lateral rotation   Base rotation

A   B   C   D   E   F   G   H

FIG. 4.7 Rotated three-dimensional shadow images: projected image of each object (drawn to scale). A & E, initial image; B & F, image of object recognised by 50% of control group; C & G, image of object correctly recognised by 100% of controls; D & H, image of object rotated through 90% (from Warrington & James, 1986).

TABLE 4.2
Scores on perceptual tests (from Warrington & James, 1988)

	Case 1	Case 2	Case 3	No. of controls	Controls, cut-off Scores	
					5%	25%
Unconventional views (no. correct)	7/20	8/20	6/20	62	13/20	16/20
Conventional views (no. correct)	17/20	18/20	20/20	62	18/20	19/20
Gollin pictures Version 1 (error score)	16	—	—	50	14	12
Gollin pictures Version 2 (error score)	—	58	28	41	31	26
Foreshortened silhouette objects (no. correct)	4/15	7/15	3/15	43	7/15	9/15
Shadow image projection (error score)	16	22	24	30	15	8
Face matching (no. correct)	13/20	17/20	13/20	62	15/20	17/20
Incomplete letters (no. correct)	10/20	2/20	18/20	62	16/20	18/20

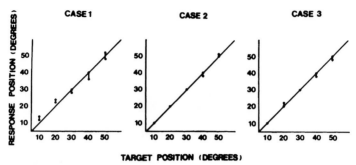

FIG. 4.8   Performance of three apperceptive cases on visual location task (from Warrington & James, 1988).

to the lesion. Figure 4.8 shows that all three cases showed a very high degree of accuracy in this simple task. Identity despite spatial rotation, a form of shape constancy, was assessed in an adaptation of Thurston and Jeffrey's (1956) flags test (see Fig. 4.9). Flags containing geometric patterns were presented in pairs half of which when rotated would be identical. Again the three cases showed no impairment. Nor was there any evidence of visual neglect. The cases, however, did not perform normally on other spatial tasks taken from the VOSP (Warrington and James, 1991). Position discrimination was assessed by asking which of two adjacent squares had a dot in the centre and which had the dot off-centre (see Fig. 4.9); all three cases were impaired. Cases 1 and 2 were also impaired on a test of spatial location; in this test, stimuli were two squares one containing many randomly placed numbers and the other containing a single dot (see Fig. 4.9). The task was to identify the number that in one square was occupying the location of the dot in the other. Only Case 2 was also impaired on a test of cube analysis; in this task, stimuli consisted of a series of 10 drawings of representations of bricks arranged in three dimensions (see Fig. 4.9) and the task was to indicate the number of bricks represented in each drawing, So, while the three cases were not completely free from problems other than those of perceptual categorisation, the other impairments were very few. Indeed, to our knowledge, there have been no "purer" cases reported in the neurological or neuropsychological literature.

The important tasks at which the three cases succeed concern semantic categorisation. De Renzi et al. (1969) noted that though the posterior right hemisphere damaged patients had problems in disentangling overlapping figures and matching two views of a face, they were not necessarily impaired on an object–figure matching test. The object–figure matching test required patients to match an object with a conventional view drawing of a non-identical object that would be given the same name. De Renzi et al. found that left hemisphere patients were those likely to be impaired on the object–figure matching task and without impairment on the tasks that were failed by the right posterior patients; these results suggest a different sort of categorisation system for the left hemisphere

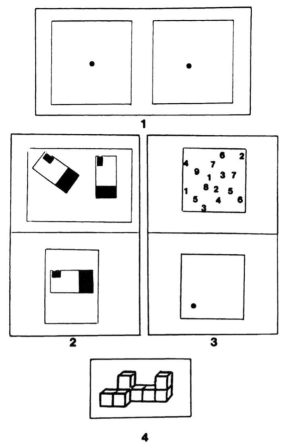

FIG. 4.9   Examples of tests of spatial skills: (1) position discrimination; (2) spatial rotation; (3) spatial location: (4) cube analysis (from Warrington & James, 1988).

(see also the distinction in Warrington and Taylor (1978) between a physical match and a functional match). A reason for a different type of object categorisation system would stem from the left hemisphere priority for language skills. A categorisation system sensitive to matches of non-identical versions of object that would be given the same name is essential for language production and other semantic tasks and has been incorporated into models of visual naming (Warren and Morton, 1982). The dissociation between a perceptual categorisation system and a semantic categorisation also finds support from a patient (Case 1 from Warrington, 1975). The patient was presented with both conventional and unconventional views of objects. On being presented with alternative views of the same object, the patient commented that he had been shown that object before and had already said that its identity was unknown to him. The

FIG. 4.10   Example of visual–visual matching test.

patient's observation, as Marr (1982) observed, shows that a stage of perceptual analysis could be fully complete before making contact with a representation used for identification. Thus, the situation with respect to intact semantics demanded investigation in the three patients reported in Warrington and James (1988).

Cases of visual agnosia have problems in attaching meaning to any view of an object and must be distinguished from the apperceptive disorder. Certainly, the apperceptive patients of Warrington and Taylor (1973) did not have problems with identifying objects when presented as conventional views; however, the only test administered was an identification task. The patients of Warrington and James (1988) were assessed in more detail. Using a multiple choice procedure taken from Warrington (1975), all three cases showed good evidence of associative and attribute knowledge of objects and animals depicted in drawings. They knew, for example, which of a choice of objects was found in a kitchen or which of a set of animals was most dangerous.

The three cases also showed good performance on two further tests administered to assess these types of semantics. In a variation of a test used by McCarthy and Warrington (1986), the patients were probed as to relative size of objects depicted in photographs without size cues. None of the cases had any difficulty with the task though an associative agnosic patient (McCarthy & Warrington, 1986) was significantly impaired on this task. A further test was devised to eliminate any verbal component in the assessment of associated knowledge. In a procedure adapted from McCarthy and Warrington (1986), stimuli were presented in two arrays. In each array there were five drawings (see Fig. 4.10). The patient's task was to match pairs of drawings that have a common function and name (e.g., two types of train or boat); the task was designed so that matches

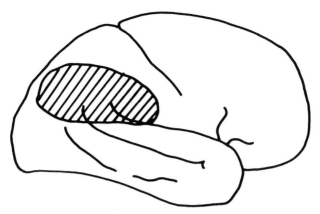

FIG. 4.11   Diagram of extent of the overlap of the lesions in the three patients with apperceptive agnosia (from Warrington and Rudge, 1995).

could not be made by physical similarity. All of the three patients in Warrington and James (1988) acquitted themselves very well on these tasks, showing that when given the conventional view of an object they had normal access to knowledge. It was only in the perceptual categorisation tasks that the patients found problems in dealing with their visual world.

The locus of impairment of perceptual categorisation (apperceptive agnosia) derived from these case studies is shown in Fig. 4.11 taken from Warrington and Rudge (1995). All the patients had unilateral right-sided lesions. In only one case was the temporal lobe involved, but in all, the inferior part of the parietal lobe and the adjacent occipital cortex on the right side was compromised. The lesion site of these three "pure" cases when superimposed on the sites found in the group study of Warrington and Taylor (1973) give the inferior part of the parietal lobe as the most likely site of the impairment.

ISSUES OF REPRESENTATION

The three cases in Warrington and James (1988) are clearly relevant to any neuropsychological model that considers object recognition. The paper gives the right hemisphere a critical role in what might be termed object constancy—the ability to recognise an object from different viewpoints after rotation. It further raises questions concerning the stored representations underpinning recognition. The two critical issues are (1) the principles by which representations for perceptual categorisation are laid down and (2) the number (or type) of different object representations required for the full range of visual abilities.

In considering the first issue, one might start from the influential view of object representation provided by Marr (1982). He made a distinction between descriptions that correspond to retinal input—i.e., those that are viewer-centred

—and those that define the relationships between parts of the object independently of the observer—i.e., object-centred views. In deriving the object-centred view, Marr argued that it would make sense if the representations for viewer-centred views were based on the principal axis of the object, because that is how he envisaged the representation for the object-centred view. The Warrington and Taylor (1973) findings would appear to fit with a hypothesis that right hemisphere viewer-centred descriptions were based on representations defined by the principal axis. In changing stimuli from a conventional to an unconventional view, most objects in the Warrington and Taylor (1973) study were presented with the principal axis foreshortened.

If representations are really based on the principal axis, then views that foreshorten the axis should impede recognition. So, the difficulty the patients had would derive from the inability to categorise a representation after these viewer-centred descriptions were no longer available. However, in foreshortening the principal axis by rotation, it also likely that some parts of the object are no longer visible. If representations were based on object parts (Biederman, 1985; Lowe, 1985, 1987), foreshortened views would also make for difficult recognition but for the reason that the critical parts (features) were out of sight or partially occluded. On the recognition by parts approach to object representation, recognition does not derive from representations based on the principal axis but rather on viewpoint consistency. The parts of objects in a "view" must be consistent with spatial relationship between parts. However, some parts may have more salience than others and it is the occlusion of these features that make for difficulty in recognition rather than occlusion of the principal axis.

Humphreys and Riddoch (1984) tested these two alternative approaches in five patients with right posterior lesions and found that for four of them it was the reduction in cues from foreshortening of the principal axis that made for impaired recognition of photographed objects. However, for the fifth patient it was reduction of features that compromised recognition. Yet it must be said that it is very difficult to present a foreshortened view without distorting some parts of the object and one must seriously consider whether all the impairments of the patients in Warrington and Taylor (1973) and Warrington and James (1988) could be explained from the principal axis approach. The Gollin figures (Fig. 4.1), for example, are incomplete drawings of objects that are progressively completed until there is a prototypical view. In none of the drawings is the principal axis modified, yet all the Warrington and James (1988) patients had difficulty with this task.

The shadow image projection test (see Fig. 4.7) as used in Warrington and James (1988) also gives some telling evidence against the principal axis view of representations in the right hemisphere. In an earlier use of the test (Warrington & James, 1986), data were obtained for the recognition of each object as it was rotated. No evidence of a "typical" function relating angle of view to identification emerged. In both the lateral-rotation and base-rotation conditions, there was considerable variation in the individual object recognition thresholds. Moreover, the shape of the recognition function for the lateral rotation was not necessarily the same in the base-rotation condition. Thus, there was little evidence of consistency across objects; both types of rotation yielded a distinctive pattern of performance without any systematic effect of the foreshortening of the principal axis. Warrington and James (1986) concluded—and hence for the three case studies of Warrington and James (1988)—that the principles by which right hemisphere object representations are organised is that of "minimal" views rather than views derived from the principal axes. Minimal views are those that contain sufficient features for the object to be reliably differentiated from other (physically) similar objects.

Another study that shows the importance of views that do not contain the principal axis is that of Perrett and Harries (1988); they asked subjects to inspect an object in order to commit it to memory. In their study, Perrett and Harries found that subjects chose to inspect side and end views; a finding rather against the principal axis view. Views chosen were those that minimised perspective distortion. So, the question arises as to how the prototypical or conventional view is derived from these end and side views. Perrett, Oram, Hietanen and Benson (1994) argue, in contrast to Warrington and James (1988), that the canonical view is not represented as such, but is the generalised output of other representations that are essentially viewer-centred.

When laying down representations for the objects we encounter, some "decision" has to be made about the number of different representations required. We clearly do not require a template for every possible view of an object even if we have the spare neural capacity to store them all. The Warrington and Taylor (1973) findings would seem to indicate that, because of their easier recognition, conventional views would be better than unconventional views if it came to a preference in allocating neural space, but nevertheless both types of representation are needed. However, the issue of the differences between left and right hemisphere representations with respect to the Warrington and James (1988) data is still an unresolved issue (see below).

The case studies of Warrington and James (1988) thus provide evidence for our first issue—the nature of the object representations impaired after right hemisphere damage. They also tell us important factors about the second issue—the interaction between these representations used for perceptual categorisation and other aspects of object recognition, including that of semantic representation. Warrington and Taylor (1978) had derived from the Warrington and Taylor (1973) group studies an essentially serial model. What they termed visual analysis, and is essentially segmentation of the visual input, was functionally sited in both hemispheres. After this visual analysis, information was passed to a perceptual categorisation stage in the right hemisphere sensitive to unconventional views for that object. Subsequently, in this stage model, information is transmitted to a left hemisphere semantic categorisation system (see Fig. 4.12a).

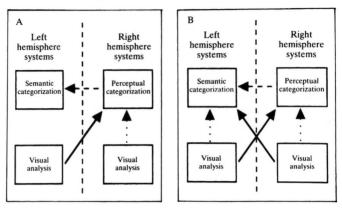

FIG. 4.12   Diagrams representing models of visual perception: (a) original model of Warrington and colleagues; (b) modified model proposed by Rudge & Warrington (from Rudge & Warrington, 1991).

There is a further flow forward in both hemispheres to memory and output systems. One of these feedforward systems operates directly from the perceptual categorisation system in the right hemisphere; this could be the system required to direct hand movements. Viewer-centred representations within the perceptual categorisation system would, by themselves, be sufficient for grasping an object. The identity of the object is unimportant and grasping could be achieved by a system without a memory for the object. Indeed, neurophysiological and neuropsychological studies suggest that the representations used for visually guided action differ from those used for identification (Milner, Perrett, Johnston, Benson, Jordan, et al., 1991; Perrett et al., 1994). However, despite all this evidence consistent with a serial stage model, the data from the case studies of Warrington and James (1988) requires some modification to the Warrington and Taylor (1978) model.

The paradox inherent in Warrington and James (1988) is that the patients with clear problems in perceptual categorisation have no impairments in everyday life and are able to perform adequately on a range of tests of visual semantic knowledge. If perceptual categorisation and semantic categorisation were in series as postulated in Warrington and Taylor (1978), then there ought to be at least some knock-on effect at semantic analysis. Warrington and James (1988) suggest an alternative model (see Fig. 4.12b). They argued that the right hemisphere perceptual categorisation system is an optional resource rather than an obligatory stage of visual analysis. The left hemisphere classification system must receive input directly from a precategorial visual analysis that could be as elementary as the $2\frac{1}{2}$D sketch proposed by Marr (1982); this would be the more direct route to meaning (rather than a route to object constancy). The right hemisphere system of perceptual categorisation would be put to use if the direct route to meaning fails.

Subsequent work has added neuroanatomical detail to the model proposed in Warrington and James (1988). In a study of impaired cognition after splenial tumours (Rudge and Warrington, 1991), the neuroanatomical locus of the connections between the right hemisphere perceptual categorisation system and the left hemisphere semantic system (see Fig. 4.12b) has been shown to be through the splenium. As with the patients of Warrington and James (1988), the patients of Rudge and Warrington (1991) had no difficulty in identifying photographs of objects presented in their conventional view but representations from unconventional views were not recognised. A curious fact about some of these patients was that despite relatively minor involvement of right parietal lobe tissue, these patients with callosal tumours exhibited the identical perceptual categorisation impairments of those cases in the Warrington and James (1988) study. So, it would appear that the use of the perceptual categorisation system requires intimate connection to a left hemisphere system and that connection must be callosal rather than subcortical. Conversely, the direct connection between the right hemisphere stage of visual analysis (see Fig. 4.12b), postulated in Warrington and James (1988) and the left hemisphere semantic system, must be subcortical. The evidence for the subcortical route comes from two of the patients in the Rudge and Warrington (1991) study who had right homonymous hemianopias. These patients prove the subcortical route because a right homonymous hemianopia ensures that early visual processing can be achieved only by striate and prestriate structures in the right hemisphere. The only available connections from the right hemisphere to the left hemisphere in these patients with callosal tumours is subcortical.

UNRESOLVED PROBLEMS

Major issues unresolved from the Warrington and James (1988) study are the properties of object representation used by the left hemisphere and its role in object recognition apart from semantic analysis. There is now a substantial body of evidence that suggests impairments in imagery from unilateral left hemisphere lesions (Basso, Bisiach, & Luzzatti, 1980; Farah, Gazzaniga, Holtzman, & Kosslyn, 1985; Grossi, Orsini, Modaferri, & Liotti, 1986; Riddoch, 1990; Bowers, Blonder, Feinberg, & Heilman, 1991; Goldenberg, 1992; Luzzatti & Davidoff, 1994). These impairments could be ascribed to deficits in generation of images stored in a prototypical representation (Kosslyn & Shin, 1994) and, therefore, these studies provide little difficulty for the model of apperception formulated in Rudge and Warrington (1991). However, there remains a further set of impairments, more to do with recognition, that can also result from unilateral left posterior lesions (Bisiach, 1966; De Renzi, Zambolin, & Crisi, 1987); these are more difficult for the model.

In particular, the study of De Renzi et al. (1987) poses problems. The patients in this group study of posterior left hemisphere lesions were asked to carry out a naming task. De Renzi et al. found consistent impairments on the naming of photographs compared to superior naming of real objects. The finding was confirmed in a subsequent case study with more systematic control of the stimuli (Davidoff and de Bleser, 1994); in that case study, a reduction in 3D cues in two conditions led to a systematic reduction in naming ability. The reductions used were viewing an object through a peephole and as a coloured photograph and were compared to tactile naming (see Table 4.3).

The difficulties found in identifying objects from photographs observed by De Renzi et al. (1987) and termed "photograph anomia" are not restricted to that study. In a review of optic aphasia (Davidoff and de Bleser, 1993), a type of patient was demonstrated whose errors in naming were usually visual and never semantic. All of these patients showed marked differences in identification between a picture condition and naming an object. While some of these patients had bilateral lesions and poor naming of both objects and photographs, a substantial number had unilateral left hemisphere lesions and excellent naming of objects (Damasio, McKee, & Damasio, 1979; Beauvois and Saillant, 1985 [case R.V.]; Larrabee, Leoin, Huft, Kay, & 1985 [case C.E.]). How do these patients with photograph anomia fit with the model derived from the Warrington and James (1988) cases?

The studies of photograph anomia have not usually presented stimuli in anything except a prototypical view; this could be a critical factor. One might suggest that the left hemisphere contains the representation of the prototypical form but not of other representations. Such a system for the left hemisphere would make sense if its use were as a link from a visual representation to a name. The representation would, however, have to cover a great variety of prototypical forms as many types of functional identity match are impaired by left hemisphere lesions (De Renzi et al., 1969; Warrington and Taylor, 1978). There are, however, still questions to answer. Why is access to this left hemisphere representation difficult from a photograph? And why is this form of degradation

TABLE 4.3

Correct naming responses (a) for each condition and significance levels (b) for paired comparisons between conditions using the McNemar test for the significance of changes (from Davidoff & De Bleser, 1994)

	Conditions			
(a)	*Objects visual*	*Photographs*	*Objects peephole*	*Objects tactile*
Number correct				
Max = 104	90	67	84	101

(b)				
Objects visual		$p = 0.0002$	ns	$p = 0.007$
Photographs			$p = 0.01$	$p = 0.0001$
Objects peephole				$p = 0.0005$

differently represented than others (e.g., fragmentation, rotation) that are important for right hemisphere function? The degradation from a real object to a photographic view reduces only 3D cues unless the observer gains additional views from head movements. It is not easy to see why the reduction of 3D cues is so important for access to these representations but, if it is, then some coherent proposal for photograph anomia can be given within the model produced in Warrington and James (1988). In situations where access to the left hemisphere representations is difficult, the patient will make use of the optional resource in the right hemisphere apperceptive system. If these patients have intact right hemispheres, by taking advantage of the information from different views, they could achieve excellent recognition and corresponding excellent naming.

An alternative explanation for the deficit of the left posterior patients could derive from the size differences in photographs compared to the those of real objects. McCarthy and Warrington (1986) showed that the comparison of identical objects of markedly different sizes could be affected by left hemisphere damage. Perhaps the unavailability of attribute information concerning size made it particularly difficult for the left hemisphere patients to access the correct object description from a photograph. Some element of hypothesis testing to establish identification occurs in normals, especially under degraded viewing conditions; in patients this could be exaggerated. The patient H.G. of Davidoff and de Bleser (1994), for example, made many gross visual errors but had no problem in fine within-category distinctions after the correct category was determined (she was, for example, not prosopagnosic) but had some difficulty in the prior stage of access to the correct structural description. Once the correct description was accessed, the patient behaved normally. It remains for future research to establish whether the difficulty in access to that description for left posterior patients was due to the incorrect size cues within photographs.

REFERENCES

Basso, A., Bisiach, E., & Luzzatti, C. (1980). Loss of mental imagery: A case study. *Neuropsychologia*, *18*, 435–42.

Beauvois, M.-F., & Saillant, B. (1985). Optic aphasia for colour and colour agnosia: A distinction between visual and visuo-verbal impairments in the processing of colours. *Cognitive Neuropsychology*, *2*, 1–48.

Benton, A.L., & Van Allen, M.W. (1968). Impairment in facial discrimination. *Journal of Neurological Science*, *15*, 167–72.

Biederman, I. (1985). Recognition by components: A theory of human image understanding. *Psychological Review*, *94*, 115–47.

Bisiach, E. (1966). Perceptual factors in the pathogenesis of anomia. *Cortex*, *2*, 90–5.

Bowers, D., Blonder, L.X., Feinberg, T., & Heilman, K.M. (1991). Differential impact of right and left hemisphere lesions on facial emotion and object imagery. *Brain*, *114*, 2593–609.

Butters, N., Barton, M., & Brody, B.A. (1970). Role of the right parietal lobe in the mediation of cross-modal associations and reversible operations in space. *Cortex*, *6*, 174–90.

Cohen, L., Gray, F., Meyrignac, C., Dehaene, S., et al. (1994). Selective deficit of visual size perception. *Journal of Neurological and Neurosurgical Psychiatry*, *57*, 73–8.

Damasio, A.R., McKee, J., & Damasio, H. (1979). Determinants of performance in colour anomia. *Brain and Language, 7*, 74–85.

Davidoff, J., & De Bleser, R. (1993). Optic aphasia: A review of past studies and reappraisal. *Aphasiology, 7*, 135–54.

Davidoff, J., & De Bleser, R. (1994). Impaired picture recognition with preserved object naming and reading. *Brain and Cognition, 24*, 1–23.

Davidoff, J., & Warrington, E.K. (1993). A dissociation of shape discrimination and figure-ground perception in a patient with normal acuity. *Neuropsychologia, 31*, 83–93.

De Renzi, E., Scotti, G., & Spinnler, H. (1969). Perceptual and associative disorders of visual recognition: Relationship to the site of lesion. *Neurology, 19*, 634–42.

De Renzi, E., & Spinnler, H. (1966). Visual recognition in patients with unilateral cerebral disease. *Journal of Nervous and Mental Disease, 142*, 513–25.

De Renzi, E., Zambolin, A., & Crisi, G. (1987). The pattern of neuro-psychological impairment associated with left posterior cerebral infarcts. *Brain, 110*, 1099–116.

Efron, R. (1968). What is perception? In: R.F. Cohen & M. Wartofsky (Eds), *Boston Studies in the Philosophy of Science*, pp. 137–73. New York: Humanities Press.

Faglioni, P., Scotti, G., & Spinnler, H. (1969). Impaired recognition of letters after hemisphere damage. *Cortex, 5*, 120–33.

Farah, M.J., Gazzaniga, M.S., Holtzman, J.D., & Kosslyn, S.M. (1985). A left hemisphere basis for visual mental imagery. *Neuropsychologia, 23*, 115–18.

Freud, S. (1891). *Zur Aufassung der Aphasien*. Wien: Deuticke.

Goldenberg, G. (1992). Loss of visual imagery and loss of visual knowledge: A case study. *Neuropsychologia, 30*, 1081–99.

Gregory, R.L. (1964). Stereoscopic shadow images. *Nature*, 1047–8.

Grossi, D., Orsini, A., Modaferri, A., & Liotti, M. (1986). Visuo-imaginal constructional apraxia: On a case of selective deficit of imagery. *Brain and Cognition, 5*, 255–67.

Humphreys, G.W., & Riddoch, M.J. (1984). Routes to object constancy: Implications from neurological impairments of object constancy. *Quarterly Journal of Expenmental Psychology, 26A*, 385–415.

Kartsounis, L.D., & Warrington, E.K. (1991). Failure of object recognition due to a breakdown of figure-ground discrimination in a patient with normal acuity. *Neuropsychologia, 29*, 969–80.

Kennard, C., Lawden, M., Morland, A.B., & Ruddock, K.H. (1995). Colour identification and colour constancy are impaired in a patient with incomplete achromatopsia associated with a prestriate cortical lesions. *Proceedings of the Royal Society of London, Series B, 260*, 169–75.

Kimura, D. (1963). Right temporal lobe damage: Perception of unfamiliar stimuli after damage. *Archives of Neurology* (Chicago), *8*, 264–71.

Kosslyn, S.M., & Shin, L.M. (1994). Visual mental images in the brain: Current issues. In: M.J. Farah & G. Ratcliff (Eds), *The Neuropsychology of High-Level Vision*. Hillsdale, N.J.: Lawrence Erlbaum Associates.

Larrabee, G.J., Levin, H.S., Huff, F.J., Kay, M.C., & Guinto, G.C. (1985). Visual agnosia contrasted with visual disconnection. *Neuropsychologia, 23*, 1–12.

Levine, D.N. (1978). Prosopagnosia and visual object agnosia: A behavioral study. *Brain and Language, 5*, 341–65.

Lissauer, H. (1890). Ein Fall von Seelenblindheit nebst einem Beitrag zur Theorie derselben. *Archiv für Psychiatrie, 21*, 222–70. Edited and reprinted in translation by M. Jackson (1988), *Lissauer on agnosia*. Cognitive Neuropsychology, *5*, 157–92.

Lowe, D. (1985). *Perceptual Organization and Visual Recognition*. Boston: Kluwer.

Lowe, D. (1987). Three-dimensional object recognition from single two-dimensional images. *Artificial Intelligence, 31*, 355–95.

Luzzatti, C., & Davidoff, J. (1994). Impaired retrieval of object-colour knowledge with preserved colour naming. Neuropsychologia, *32*, 933–50.

Marr, D. (1982). *Vision*. San Francisco: W.H. Freeman.

McCarthy, R.A., & Warrington, E.K. (1986). Visual associative agnosia: a clinico-anatomical study of a single case. *Journal of Neurological and Neurosurgurical Psychiatry*, *49*. 1233–40.

Milner, B. (1958). Psychological defects produced by temporal lobe excision. *Proceedings of the Association for Research in Nervous and Mental Disorders*, *36*, 244–57.

Milner, A.D., Perrett, D.I., Johnston, R.S., Benson, P.J., Jordan, T.R., Heeley, D.W., Bettucci, D., Mortara, F., Mutani, R., Terazzi, E., & Davidson, D.L.W. (1991). Perception and action in "visual form agnosia". *Brain*, *114*, 405–28.

Perrett, D.I., & Harries, M.H. (1988). Characteristic views and the visual inspection of simple faceted and smooth objects: "Tetrahedra and potatoes". *Perception*, *17*, 703–20.

Perrett, D.I., Oram, M.W., Hietanen, J.J., & Benson, P.J. (1994). Issues of representation in object vision. In: M.J. Farah & G. Ratcliff (Eds) *The Neuropsychology of High-level Vision*. Hillsdale, N.J.: Lawrence Erlbaum Associates.

Poetzl, O. (1928). *Die optisch-agnostischen Storungen*. Leipzig-Vienna: F. Deuticke.

Riddoch, M.J. (1990). Loss of visual imagery: A generation deficit. *Cognitive Neuropsychology*, *4*, 249–73.

Rudge, P., & Warrington, E.K. (1991). Selective impairment of memory and visual perception in splenial tumours. *Brain*, *114*, 349–60.

Shallice, T., & Jackson, M. (1988). Lissauer on agnosia. *Cognitive Neuropsychology*, *5*, 153–92.

Thurston, J.G., & Jeffrey, T.E. (1956). *Flags: A Test of Space Thinking*. Chicago: Industrial Relations Center.

Warren, C.E.J., & Morton, J. (1982). The effects of priming on picture recognition. *British Journal of Psychology*, *73*, 117–30.

Warrington, E.K. (1975). The selective impairment of semantic memory. *Quartely Journal of Expenmental Psychology*, *27*, 635–57.

Warrington, E.K. (1982). Neuropsychological studies of object recognition. *Philosophical Transactions Royal of the Society of London*, B., *298*, 15–33.

Warrington, E.K. (1984). *Recognition Memory Test*. Windsor: NFER-Nelson.

Warrington, E.K. (1986). Visual deficits associated with occipital lobe lesions in man. *Experimental Brain Research, Supplementum Series II*. Berlin: Springer-Verlag.

Warrington, E.K., & James, M. (1967). Disorders of visual perception in patients with localised cerebral lesions. *Neuropsychologia*, *5*, 253–66.

Warrington, E.K., & James, M. (1986). Visual object recognition in patients with right-hemisphere lesions: Axes or features? *Perception*, *15*, 355–66.

Warrington, E.K., & James, M. (1988). Visual apperceptive agnosia: A clinico-anatomical study of three cases. *Cortex*, *24*, 13–32.

Warrington, E.K., & James, M. (1991). *The Visual Object and Space Perception Battery*. Bury St Edmunds: Thames Valley Test Co.

Warrington, E.K., & Rudge, P. (1995). A comment on apperceptive agnosia. *Brain and Cognition*, *28*, 173–7.

Warrington, E.K., & Taylor, A.M. (1973). Contribution of the right parietal lobe to object recognition. *Cortex*, *9*, 152–64.

Warrington, E.K., & Taylor, A.M. (1978). Two categorical stages of object recognition. *Perception*, *7*, 695–705.

Wyke, M. (1960). Alterations of size constancy associated with brain lesions in man. *Journal of Neurological and Neurosurgurical Psychiatry*, *23*, 253–61.

Zihl, J., Roth, W., Kerkhoff, G., & Heywood, C. (1988). The influence of homonymous visual field disorders on colour sorting performance in the FM 100-hue test. *Neuropsychologia*, *26*, 869–76.

CHAPTER FIVE

Vision and visual mental imagery

Marlene Behrmann
Department of Psychology, Carnegie Mellon University, USA

Morris Moscovitch
*Department of Psychology, Erindale College, University of
Toronto, Canada; Rotman Research Institute, Baycrest Centre for
Geriatric Care, Toronto, Canada*

Gordon Winocur
*Department of Psychology, Erindale College, University of
Toronto, Canada; Rotman Research Institute, Baycrest Centre for
Geriatric Care, Toronto, Canada; Department of Psychology,
Trent University, Trent, Canada*

Visual mental imagery or "the ability to see with the mind's eye" refers to the recreation of a perceptual experience in the absence of visual input. This process in central to many cognitive processes and plays an important role in reasoning, memory, skill learning, language acquisition, and mental rotation (Farah, 1984, 1988, 1999; Kosslyn, 1994). Despite its centrality in cognition, the study of mental imagery has waxed and waned over time, at times occupying the mind of psychologists and philosophers, and, at other times, abandoned to the back-burner of science. In fact, interest in imagery dates back to Plato who emphasized its central role, believing that mental images are analogous to patterns carved onto wax tablets. In his view, individual differences in imaging ability such as clarity and vividness could be understood in terms of the properties of the wax (temperature, purity, and so on) (see Kosslyn, 1994; Kosslyn, Behrmann, & Jeannerod, 1995, for historical overview). This interest in imagery continued through the nineteenth century with both Wilhelm Wundt and William James expressing much interest in it and speculating about its function and basis. However, with the emergence of Watson's extreme form of behaviourism, the existence of mental imagery was denied and it ceased to be a legitimate topic for scientific study. In the late 1960s, released from the limitations and skepticism of behaviourism, and freed by the "cognitive revolution", a resurgence in the study of mental imagery occurred (Paivio, 1979). Since that time, questions about mental imagery, its operation and mechanisms have become increasingly more explicit and our understanding has grown accordingly. Sophisticated experimental techniques have provided crucial empirical data and these findings have been incorporated into increasingly more refined componential models of the processes involved in imagery (Farah, 1984, 1988; Kosslyn, 1980, 1987).

In the last decade or so, the study of imagery has advanced particularly rapidly, largely because of methodological developments that have allowed us to examine the neural mechanisms which give rise to imagery. These developments include single case neuropsychological investigations and, more recently, noninvasive methods for measuring electrophysiological change or regional cerebral blood flow during performance on imagery and corresponding perceptual tasks. While most of the emphasis of this work has been on visual mental imagery, a similar resurgence in auditory (Reisberg, 1992; Smith, Wilson, & Reisberg, 1995) and motor imagery (Annett, 1995a, 1995b; Decety Perani, Jeannerod, Bettinardi, Tadary et al., 1994; Jeannerod, 1994, 1995; Jeannerod & Decety, 1995; Parsons et al., 1995) has taken place. The focus of this chapter, however, is on visual mental imagery and specifically, the contribution of neuropsychology to our understanding of visual imagery, and it is to this topic that we now turn.

A number of central themes comprise the focus of current research on visual mental imagery and neuropsychology (Bruce, 1996; Cooper, 1995). These include, for example, whether there is a distinct component of the mental architecture dedicated to image generation and if so, what brain regions mediate this component (Farah, 1995, 1999; Stangalino, Semenza, & Mondini, 1995); what form the image representation takes, whether propositional or depictive (array-like) (see Kosslyn, 1994, for overview), and whether there are separate components selectively associated with spatial and with form imagery (Farah, Hammond, Mehta, & Ratcliff, 1989; Luzzatti et al., 1998). But the issue that has received the most attention and has generated the most vigorous debate is the extent to which mental imagery and visual perception share common processes and mechanisms (Miyashita, 1995).

During object recognition, the retinal image is processed and then mapped onto a stored long-term canonical representation that captures some of the invariant properties of the object (Pinker, 1984, 1985). During mental imagery, the visual appearance of an object is reconstructed from a canonical mental representation retrieved from long-term memory (Farah, 1984, 1985; Finke, 1985; Kosslyn, 1987). Recent research has suggested that these two processes—visual perception and visual imagery—draw strongly on the same set of stored representations or underlying codes (Farah, 1984, 1988; Kosslyn, 1980, 1987). Furthermore, many have proposed that both processes share a common neural substrate and that imagery utilises neural mechanisms which are ordinarily dedicated to visual perception. Following this view, in object recognition, an external image is projected onto the retina, passes through a visual buffer and various stages of early visual processing mediated by the parietal and temporal lobe until it is synthesized into a unique configuration which can be recognised through the activation of stored associative memories. During mental imagery, stored associative memories (from long-term visual memory) are activated and projected down the same visual pathways onto the same visual buffer which is used in object recognition. The generated image is then subject to inspection and further processing. This bidirectional flow of information is thought to be mediated by the direct cortico-cortico connections from higher-level visual areas to lower-level areas (Douglas & Rockland, 1992) and by the presence of afferent and efferent connections from each visual area to a second visual area (Van Essen, 1985).

In addition to having the appeal of parsimony, the view of common representations and neural substrate for visual imagery and perception has garnered much support from empirical research. Findings from a variety of studies on both normal and brain-damaged people have confirmed that perception and mental imagery are strongly associated. Despite this overwhelming evidence supporting such an association, there are now reports of patients with impaired imagery who have intact perception or object recognition (Farah, 1988; Riddoch, 1990). A critical question is how to accommodate this pattern of dissociation in the context of a model that proposes shared mechanisms for imagery and perception. One possible explanation for this single dissociation might be that imagery is just a more complex and demanding operation and, as such, is more vulnerable to the effects of brain damage than is perception (see Tippett, 1992 for review; also Kosslyn, Alpert, Thompson, Maljkovic, Weise, Chabris, Hamilton, & Buonanno, 1993). This would imply that there is a single common system but that imagery and perception are not equally complex and taxing processes. Following brain damage, the more complex and difficult task (i.e. imagery) would be impaired while the simpler perceptual task might remain unaffected. If this were the case, however, then one would not expect to find the converse pattern in which the supposedly more complex ability to form images is preserved while the supposedly simpler perception ability is impaired. There are, however, a growing number of reports of patients who conform to this pattern and have intact imagery despite a profound visual object recognition deficit (visual object agnosia). That the supposedly "more complex" function (imagery) is preserved while the "simpler" ability to perceive is impaired seriously undermines the view that imagery and perception are hierarchically arranged in terms of complexity. Instead, these cases support the existence of a double dissociation between imagery and perception. The separability or independence suggested by this double dissociation must be reconciled in the context of theories of shared mechanisms for imagery and perception.

In this chapter, we start by reviewing the evidence for the shared mechanisms, both at a functional and neural level, and then present the data for both sides of the double dissociation. We place special emphasis on the findings obtained from our studies of a patient with severe visual agnosia and intact imagery following a head injury but we also describe evidence from other, similar patients. Finally, we provide one interpretation of how the apparent association and dissociation between imagery and perception might both be accommodated within a single explanation and then raise some unresolved questions which will undoubtedly form the basis of continuing research in this area.

COMMON SYSTEMS FOR PERCEPTION AND IMAGERY

Results of numerous studies demonstrate the functional equivalence between perception and imagery (see Finke, 1985; Kosslyn, 1987, 1994; Kosslyn et al., 1993). For example, Finke and his colleagues (Finke, 1979; Finke, 1980; Finke & Schmidt, 1978) have found that visuomotor and orientation-specific adaptation (McCollough effect) are equivalent for images and percepts, as is the relation between eccentricity and resolution (Finke, 1989). The close relationship between images and percepts is further demonstrated by studies that have found facilitatory effects between these two processes. For example, in a recent study, Ishai and Sagi (1995) reported that equivalent facilitation was observed in the detection of a Gabor target when there were congruent flankers present in the display (perception condition) or when the subjects imagined the presence of congruent flankers (imagery condition). Interestingly, the imagery-induced facilitation shared many of the expected characteristics of the perception-induced facilitation, namely monocularity, specificity of orientation and retinal location. Similarly, Farah (1989) found that when subjects formed a mental image of a letter, the imaged prime facilitated detection of the subsequent target letter. In her experiment, subjects were instructed to detect the shape of a stimulus (H or T) which was preceded by an imaged prime stimulus (H or T) in the same or in a different location to the target. When the imaged prime and the target stimulus shared both shape and location, the subjects were better at detecting the subsequent target letter. These findings led to the conclusion that priming between imagery and visual perception is mediated through a common set of representations shared by the two processes (see also Stadler & McDaniel, 1990).

The representational commonality between imagery and perception is also noted in studies of patients with impaired perception (visual agnosia) who also have imagery deficits (Goldenberg, 1993; Ogden, 1993; Wilson & Davidoff, 1993). Perhaps even more compelling evidence for the common representations comes from patients who have both imagery and perception deficits but in whom these deficits are specific and selective for a particular domain. There are, for example, reports of agnosic patients who are unable both to perceive and image only faces and colours (Levine, Warach, & Farah, 1985), only facial emotions (Bowers, Blonder, Feinbery, & Heilman, 1991), only spatial relations (Levine et al., 1985; Farah, Hammond, Levine, & Calvanio, 1988), only object shapes and colours (Goldenberg, 1992), or only living things (Mehta, Newcombe, & De Haan, 1992). The same pattern is seen in patients with left visual hemineglect who fail to report perceptual information on the left side of space: these patients also image only the right side of a scene and report landmarks only on the right side of their internal image (Bisiach & Luzzatti, 1978).

Further evidence comes from studies that show that the imagery impairment is manifest only when mental imagery is tested on tasks which tap into the exact nature of the perceptual deficit. An interesting recent example is patient H.J.A., who is unable to recognise objects and has an impairment that affects his ability to integrate features and derive a coherent perceptual representation of the display (Humphreys & Riddoch, 1987a, b; Riddoch & Humphreys, 1987). H.J.A. is also impaired in face recognition and is at chance at judging the sex and facial expression of people. Somewhat surprising is the finding that H.J.A. was able to image single faces and to carry out feature-based comparisons between imaged faces; for example, he could answer questions about whether the people were balding or not, had dark or light hair or had facial hair. Interestingly, only when configuration-based imagery comparisons were required and he was required to integrate the features of his internal image, was a stable and severe imagery deficit uncovered (Young, Humphreys, Riddoch, Hellawell, & De Haan, 1994). For example, when H.J.A. was asked to image three people and to decide who looks most similar to the target ("who looks more like Elizabeth Taylor, Joan Collins, or Barbara Windsor?"), he performed poorly. The consistency between perception and imagery across particular domains endorses the claim that mental imagery activates the same stored representations that are engaged by an external stimulus during perception. When the common representations or perceptual procedures are affected, parallel deficits in imagery and perception are observed.

In addition to the evidence for shared representations, there is also considerable empirical support for the view of a shared neural substrate for imagery and perception. The claim is that circuitry in the early cortical visual pathways that mediate perception are also activated during mental imagery. When we engage in imagery, we make use of the explicit retinotopography of V1 and other low-level areas in visual cortex. This is achieved by activating these regions via the same back-projections from visual memory that are used in top-down hypothesis testing during normal visual perception (Kosslyn, 1994; Miyashita, 1995). Studies measuring regional cerebral blood flow using single photon emission computerised tomography (SPECT), for example, have found higher rates of blood flow in visual areas of the inferior occipital region (particularly in the left hemisphere) when the subjects were required to answer high-imagery questions (e.g. Is the green of pine trees darker than the green of grass?) than when they answered equally difficult low-imagery questions (e.g. Do leap years have 366 days?) (Goldenberg, Podreka, Steiner, & Willmes, 1987; Goldenberg, Steiner,

Podreka, & Deecke, 1992; see also Charlot, Tzourio, Zilbovicius, Mazoyer, & Denis, 1992). Similar results have been obtained on a study using positron emission tomography (PET) (Kosslyn et al., 1993; Kosslyn, Hamilton, Maljkovic, Horwitz, & Thompson, 1995; Kosslyn, Thompson, Kim, & Alpert, 1995) or functional magnetic resonance imaging (Le Bihan, Turner, Zeffiro, Cuenod, Jezzard, & Bonnerot, 1993) in which activation of primary visual cortex (areas 17 and 18) was noted during imagery tasks as well as during corresponding perception tasks. One very recent study has even found lateral geniculate activation as well as V1 activation during mental imagery in a high field 4 Tesla study (Chen et al., 1998). Finally, the selective involvement of the occipital regions in the generation of mental images is demonstrated by electrophysiological studies (Davidson & Schwartz, 1977; Farah & Peronnet, 1989) in which specific activation is shown at the occipital electrodes in imagery tasks. The observation that increased activation is seen during imagery in areas thought to be dedicated to visual perception lends further credibility to the view of a shared neural mechanism for these two processes.

A final source of evidence showing the close neural correspondence between imagery and perception comes from studies of patients with brain damage (see Levine et al., 1985, for overview). For example, patients with cortical blindness due to destruction of the occipital cortex (Brown 1966; Symonds & MacKenzie, 1957) are reported to have an associated loss of imagery, while patients with scotomas (blind spots) are reported to show equivalent blind spots in their mental imagery (Head & Holmes, 1911). In a similar vein, Farah, Soso and Dasheiff (1992) showed that, in a single subject who had undergone unilateral occipital lobectomy, the visual angle of the patient's "mind's eye" was reduced in the same way as was the visual angle of perception. The association between imagery and perceptual deficits which arose from removal of the same cortical substrate led the authors to conclude that images occur in a spatially mapped representational medium which is shared with visual perception (see also Kosslyn et al., 1993, Kosslyn, 1994; Kosslyn, Thompson et al., 1995). Taken together, the findings of these studies strongly favour the view that imagery and perception are associated and share a common neural substrate. The data are so compelling that some have claimed that output from early visual areas is "processed in the usual ways—regardless of whether the activity arose from immediate input from the eyes or from information stored in memory" (Kosslyn, 1994, p. 336).

EVIDENCE FOR DISSOCIATIONS BETWEEN PERCEPTION AND IMAGERY

Notwithstanding the strength of the evidence showing the relationship between imagery and perception, there are cases in whom imagery and perception are dissociable. That such dissociations exist potentially undermines the unitary account of perception and imagery. First, the studies reporting cases with imagery deficits with intact perception are reviewed and then the other, less common side of the dissociation is discussed: intact imagery and impaired perception.

Imagery deficits with intact visual perception/recognition

Evidence favouring a dissociation between imagery and perception comes predominantly from neuropsychological investigations of individual patients in whom imagery is impaired relative to recognition. The first case of sudden loss of mental imagery, reported by Charcot and Bernard in 1883, describes a patient who could not image even those objects he could identify in visual perception (Goldenberg, 1993; Trojano & Grossi, 1994). The same pattern has been reported in more recent cases. R.M., for example, was unable to draw from memory, had lost his dream imagery and was unable to describe objects from memory (Farah, Levine, & Calvanio, 1988; Farah, 1988). Furthermore, he was unable to answer yes/no questions that were verifiable only through the use of imagery (Eddy & Glass, 1981). In contrast, his performance in the recognition control conditions was perfect, as was his picture and object identification. These results led to the conclusion that R.M.'s deficit selectively affected image generation, the process by which stored representations from long-term memory are created in a short-term visual buffer.

Like R.M., patient D.W. (Riddoch, 1990) was unable to draw or to generate items from long-term memory. For example, he was unable to determine whether animals have long or short tails or whether letters have curved or straight sides when the names of the items are auditorily presented. In contrast, he was successful at recognising objects, at copying visually presented stimuli and at accessing the semantic system from vision. Two additional cases, A.P. (Grossi, Orsini, Modafferi, & Liotti, 1986) and the patient of Botez and his colleagues (Botez, Olivier, Vezina, Botez, & Kaufman, 1985) also displayed disproportionate failure to visualise objects and to draw from memory relative to their perceptual abilities. The deficit in all these cases is attributed to a deficit of the image generation procedure, thought to be mediated by posterior regions of the left hemisphere (Farah, 1984, 1995; Stangalino et al., 1995; Tippett, 1992; see also Behrmann, in press, for a recent review). This distinct generation component is thought to be unique to imagery and may be selectively affected without any adverse consequences for recognition.

Perception/recognition deficits with preserved imagery

While the pattern of an imagery deficit associated with good recognition seems to be clearly established, the existing evidence for the converse pattern is less definitive. The first report of such a case is that of Wilbrand's patient who could conjure up vivid images of buildings which she was unable to recognise in reality (Goldenberg, 1993). More recently, support for this dissociation comes from reports of patients with impaired object recognition or agnosia who are able to draw from long-term memory the very objects they typically misidentify (see Farah, 1984, for review of cases; Trojano & Grossi, 1994). Patient M.D. (Jankowiak, Kinsbourne, Shalev, & Bachman, 1992), for example, displayed reasonably good (but not perfect) drawing of objects and also performed remarkably well on a range of tests of mental imagery. Although the finding that M.D. showed relatively better imagery than perception is suggestive, the dissociation between these two processes is not very strong in this case and M.D.'s object recognition ability was reasonably well preserved under some conditions. For example, although he could only identify correctly 50% of black-and-white sketches of objects and symbols (e.g. $, %), his identification of real objects was good (91% accuracy) and he could interpret 5 out of 6 photographs of complex visual scenes. That M.D. could recognise visual stimuli well under some conditions undermines the claim of a clear dissociation between imagery and perception in his performance. Perhaps the strongest evidence for this dissociation comes from the study of our patient, C.K., who was profoundly impaired in object recognition but performed well on a range of visual mental imagery tests (Behrmann, Winocur, & Moscovitch, 1992; Behrmann, Moscovitch, & Winocur, 1994). Thus, C.K. provides the necessary evidence for the complement of the double dissociation between imagery and perception. First, we describe C.K.'s visual recognition deficit and then document his performance on a range of imagery tasks.

A CASE REPORT OF A PATIENT WITH INTACT IMAGERY AND VISUAL AGNOSIA

C.K., who was 35-years old at the time that this testing was started, is a right-handed man who emigrated from England to Canada in 1980. In January 1988, he sustained a closed head injury (acceleration–deceleration whiplash) in a motor vehicle accident. C.K. had no premorbid neurological problems but following the accident, he exhibited motoric weakness of the left side and a left homonymous hemianopsia. Neuropsychological testing conducted soon after the accident revealed major cognitive deficits including visuomotor slowing, limited learning ability, poor planning and organisation and distractibility. Memory was also poor initially but it improved markedly. Personality changes were noted including frequent mood swings and temper outbursts. Following the accident, C.K. received extensive rehabilitation training, focusing on planning and organisation as well as on improving his memory.

Neuropsychological testing conducted in September 1989 revealed a full-scale IQ score at the 20th percentile, a verbal score at the 40th percentile and a low average nonverbal score at the 10th percentile. In April 1991, a full

WAIS-R was administered and C.K. obtained a verbal IQ of 96 and a perform-ance score of 74. Prior to the accident, C.K. was an exemplary student enrolled in a Master's degree in history. He made a remarkable recovery from his injuries and, in 1991, completed his degree with the aid of multi-track tape recorders and a voice-activated computer. C.K. is now employed as a manager in a large organ-isation and after an initial period of adjustment, has adapted quite well despite his deficit (for further information, see Moscovitch, Winocur, & Behrmann, 1997).

The results of a CT scan (with transaxial scans performed in the temporal lobe and standard basal planes; December 1991) and of a magnetic resonance imaging scan (June 1992) revealed no focal mass nor abnormality. There was, however, a suggestion of thinning of the occipital lobes bilaterally on the MRI scan. An EEG (September 1991) showed some abnormality over the left fronto-temporal area (low voltage theta activity of 6 to 7 c.p.s.). Although this may seem unusual in a patient with object agnosia, because the abnormality from the head injury is non-specific, diffuse cortical changes are not surprising. At present, C.K. suffers from seizures of the partial complex form and takes anticonvulsant medication (Tegretol). On Goldmann perimetry testing (December 1990), the left field defect had resolved to a partial homonymous hemianopsia. Visual acuity was 6/7.5, O.U. with −1.00 lenses for distance vision and +1.00 for near visual tasks. Following the accident, C.K.'s ocular motility was normal, as were his pupils. Anterior segments and fundi were normal. There was some evidence of accommodative or convergence insufficiency but this has been corrected by lenses. The testing reported here was conducted between October 1991 and June 1993. C.K.'s language comprehension and spontaneous speech expression were normal, as revealed by his performance on those subtests of the standardised Western Aphasia Battery that do not require visual input (Kertesz, 1982).

Object recognition

C.K. was only able to recognise 16/23 (70%) three-dimensional common objects presented to him for an unlimited period of time (normal subjects score 23/23) and the size of the objects did not influence performance. His errors include calling a SMOKING PIPE → "a straw", a CARD OF MATCHES → "a card with writing", a PADLOCK → "an earring", a SAW → "a knife", PLIERS → "clothes peg" and he made no responses to PAPER CLIP and TOOTHBRUSH. He was, however, able to identify all 23 of the same objects with tactile presentation, suggesting that the object recognition deficit is restricted to the visual modality. He also defined all the objects correctly in detail when presented with the name auditorily. For example, he defined a DUCK as "an animal, marine life, with webbed feet and a bill", a CARD OF MATCHES as "a cardboard container, the container flipped open, the log sticks are struck against the cordite strip" and a PIPE as "a short, hollow object, larger on one end, 120° angle, for leisurely smoking using tobacco". The detailed and descriptive definitions which he was

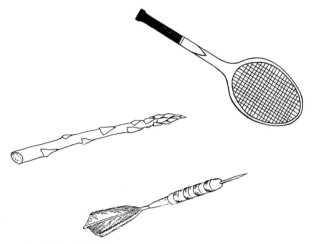

FIG. 5.1   Examples of stimuli which C.K. misnamed from the Boston Naming Test.

able to provide to an auditory label reflect the preservation of his knowledge of objects and confirm that his inability to recognise an object is restricted to the visual modality.

C.K.'s visual recognition deficit was perhaps even more marked for two-dimensional objects than for three-dimensional objects; he named correctly only 18 out of 60 line drawings from the Boston Naming Test, a significant impairment relative to the standardised norm of 56.6 obtained by age- and schooling-matched controls (Kaplan, Goodglass, & Weintraub, 1983). Errors included naming a picture of a DART → "a feather duster", a TENNIS RACQUET → "a fencer's mask" and an ASPARAGUS → "a rose twig with thorns" (see Fig. 5.1 for examples of these stimuli), all of which are predominantly visual confusions.

These visual errors indicate that although he is able to perceive parts of an object, C.K. is unable to integrate them into a meaningful whole. There is no evidence from his performance that his errors reflect simply the misnaming of visual objects that have been correctly recognised and for which semantics has been derived, a disorder known as optic aphasia (Iorio, Falanga, Fragassi, & Grossi, 1992; Plaut, & Shallice, 1993). Rather, it seems that C.K. is able to pick out some elements of the object and in some cases, the impoverished representation is sufficient to allow him to get reasonably close to the correct target—noting the presence of four legs on the object is sufficient to place it in the category of animal or perceiving the shape of the rhinoceros may be sufficient to generate the response "dinosaur" or "hippopotamus", both of which are semantically as well as visually related to the target. C.K.'s errors always shared some visual features with the target object and were never "purely semantic", suggesting that he did not gain access to semantic information for items on which visual misidentifications occurred.

Taken together, these findings are consistent with visual object agnosia as manifest in poor recognition of two- and three-dimensional objects only when presented in the visual modality. Both semantic knowledge and the ability to label objects are preserved, as noted through intact object recognition and good definitions of objects in modalities other than vision.

Recognition of other visual forms

C.K.'s visual recognition deficit extended beyond objects and his ability to recognise letters was also poor; for example, he was at chance when required to decide whether a letter was in its correct or reflected form. He was also poor at cross-case matching (17/28; 57%) when the upper and lower case letters were visually dissimilar (for example, R and r). Somewhat surprisingly, C.K. was able to name 36/52 (70%) single letters correctly when they were presented individually for an unlimited exposure duration. It is possible that because letters of the alphabet form a closed class of potential responses (and the stimuli were blocked on case), letter recognition is easier than object recognition. His letter recognition was well preserved when he was allowed to trace the stimuli, confirming the particular problem in the visual modality. C.K. was also unable to read any words aloud. He could identify some of the letters in a word individually; for example, for the stimulus "beard", he said "it is 'b' and there is a 'r' in it too". These findings provide clear evidence that C.K. is severely alexic and that his object recognition deficit includes a profound impairment in processing printed letters or words.

Despite the visual impairment in object and letter recognition, C.K. shows remarkably spared face recognition. For example, he scored 49/54 (normals 45.6/54) on the Benton et al. Face Recognition test (Benton, Hamsher, Varney, & Spreen, 1983), performing well even on those trials in which the target and the choices are photographed from a different angle or when the lighting conditions of the photographs are poor. He is able to identify photographs of famous people even those people who achieved fame after C.K. had sustained the head injury. C.K. is also able to learn new faces and his memory for these newly acquired faces is equivalent to that of the normal control subjects. C.K. also performs well on photographs with disguises and with caricatures (Moscovitch et al., 1997). His preserved face recognition is the subject of ongoing studies and can offer us an understanding of the operation of face recognition processes in the absence of processes involved in object recognition.

Nature of the perceptual deficit

Based on his errors in visual object naming, we have proposed that C.K. has a deficit in integrating features of a visual stimulus. Indeed, his performance appears to be similar to that of patients with deficits in intermediate stages of visual processing, known as "integrative agnosics" (Riddoch & Humphreys,

1987; see Chapter 3, this volume). C.K. was able to copy fairly complex geometric configurations but did so in a slavish and piecemeal fashion, suggesting that he failed to appreciate the overall shape of the depicted objects. This same segmental approach was seen in his copy of text, which he did accurately, although he produced each letter in a fashion (font and size) that directly replicates the input (see Behrmann et al., 1992).

C.K. was also unable to group together components of black-and-white line drawings of Poppelreuter-type objects where the objects overlap and the lines intersect. For example, given a display of four overlapping objects and asked to colour around the boundaries of each object in a different coloured crayon, C.K. was completely unable to demarcate the outline of the individual objects. He first marked in separate colours those components of the objects which jutted out from the central mass. When he reached an intersecting line, he was unable to decide how to continue and most often refused to carry on. He also performed poorly when required to point to a choice of six distractors and indicate which appeared in the superimposed display. These findings are consistent with a failure to segment or parse a complex display. Whereas he is able to match local information or components, he is unable to extract and integrate entire objects from the mass of intersecting lines (Behrmann et al., 1994).

C.K. also had difficulties when asked to decide whether an "x" was present in a modified version of the shape detection task from the Visual Object and Space Perception battery (Warrington & James, 1991). When the background was less noisy, he was somewhat successful but he was completely unable to pick out the target figure as the background became increasingly more fragmented and noisy. These data also implicate a problem in the integration and grouping of visual features.

C.K.'s deficit at intermediate levels of visual organisation, such as feature integration or figure-ground segregation, has been reported in other patients. For example, Riddoch and Humphreys (1987) report that their visual agnosic patient, H.J.A., had a specific deficit in integrating form information; whereas H.J.A. could identify letters, line drawings and geometrical shapes reasonably well, he was differentially impaired, relative to control subjects, when these same stimuli were superimposed on other stimuli and needed to be parsed. H.J.A. also failed on tasks in which grouping conjunctions of form features was required (Humphreys, Riddoch, Quinlan, Price, & Donnelly, 1992) and on tasks requiring grouping via collinearity and good configuration (Humphreys, Riddoch, Donnelly, Freeman, Boucart, & Muller, 1993). Similarly, the patient, Annalisa, described by De Renzi and Lucchelli (1993) was able to match complex objects but failed on tasks requiring the extraction of the form from a noisy background. Finally, Thaiss and de Bleser (1992) report a similar case, T.K., who failed to bind together local features into a perceptual whole. T.K. could copy the individual lines of a shape but was unable to relate these to the global form. She also failed to identify objects when they were overlapping and often recognised a part of an object without appreciating that it formed a part of a larger object. Thaiss and de Bleser (1992) postulated that T.K.'s impairment arose at intermediate stages of processing and that the disorder was attributable to a reduction of the attentional spotlight which facilitates global processing and shape integration (for other similar cases, see Grailet, Seron, Bruyer, Coyette, & Frederix, 1990; case G.K., Humphreys et al., 1993; Ricci, Vaishnavi, & Chatterjee, 1999; Sparr, Jay, Dreslane, & Venna, 1991; Williams & Behrmann, submitted).

Imagery for object size, colour and form

The critical question to be addressed in this chapter is to what extent imagery and perception share common mechanisms. Having shown that C.K. is profoundly impaired in perceiving visually presented stimuli, we administered a series of tests on which normal adults are known to rely on visual imagery (Farah, Hammond et al., 1988; Farah, Levine, & Calvanio, 1988) and on which patients have shown deficits in mental imagery (Farah, Levine, & Calvanio, 1988; Kosslyn, 1975, 1987; Kosslyn, Holtzman, Farah, & Gazzaniga, 1985; Riddoch, 1990). We focus specifically on those tasks that test knowledge of the physical appearance of objects such as their size, colour and form. We have, however, also tested C.K.'s spatial imagery abilities including his ability to determine the angle between hands on an imaged clock (Craik, & Dirkx, 1992; Paivio, 1979), to determine distance in imagery by choosing which of three cities is furthest from the other two (e.g. Manchester, Leeds, and Birmingham) and to decide on direction in an imaged navigation task (Brooks, 1968). C.K. performed normally on all these tasks, ruling out any deficit in spatial imagery (Behrmann et al., 1992).

When C.K. was asked to state the colour of an object in response to its verbal label (for example, a football, or the inside of a cantaloupe), he was able to report the correct colour for all 20 objects. In a test of animal body parts, generally considered to be a sensitive indicator of imagery ability, since facts about body parts and animals are usually only coded visually and are not represented in verbal memory (Farah et al., 1989; Kosslyn, 1975), C.K. was able to judge whether the animal had a long tail in proportion to its body size (for example, a kangaroo, a pig, 20/20) and also whether the ears of the animals were floppy or upright (for example, a doberman, a dachshund, 20/20). He was also able to make size comparisons in response to the auditory labels and to indicate which of a pair of similarly sized objects was larger (for example, a popsicle and a pack of cigarettes, a thimble and an eraser, 16/16).

In addition to tests that probe knowledge of the visual appearance of objects, we also had C.K. complete a sentence verification task in which half the sentences are rated as being high (e.g., The letter W is formed by three lines) and half as low on visual imagery (e.g., There are seven days in a week). This test has been shown to be a sensitive indicator of mental imagery in normal and brain-damaged subjects. Consistent with this is the finding that R.M., the patient with a selective imagery deficit (Farah, Levine, & Calvanio, 1988) performed significantly worse on the high than on the low imagery sentences. In contrast, C.K., like normal subjects, performed equally well on both high and low imagery sentences when given the sentence auditorily (total 59/68). Only one of C.K.'s errors was consistent across both the true and false versions of the sentence—he responded "true" to the sentence "the hot water handle on a sink is on the right" and "false" to the sentence "the hot water handle on a sink is on the left." This sentence probably unduly penalises C.K. as there is no obvious convention is the UK for the placement of the hot water tap on the sink.

These findings show that CK has retained detailed knowledge of the physical characteristics of many objects including their size, shape, and colour and that he can use this knowledge when sentences require imagery for verification. Because we do not have equivalent perceptual analogue tasks for the imagery tests, the data from these tasks provide compelling but not definitive evidence for the dissociation between imagery and perception. In fact, Kosslyn (1994) suggests that the data from C.K. do not constitute a serious challenge to the hypothesis of shared mechanisms because we did not demonstrate that C.K. fails on the perceptual versions of the imagery test. To make the argument even more convincing, therefore, we administered equivalent tests of perception and imagery to C.K. with the prediction that he should fail on the former and succeed on the latter.

Previous testing has revealed that C.K. has poor visual recognition of letters. To determine whether he knows the shape of letters and can image them, we asked C.K. to generate letters of the alphabet and judge their form. When asked to imagine an upper case letter and to judge whether it has any curved lines (for example, C versus L), or when asked to imagine a lower case letter and decide whether it has any lines ascending or descending from the body (for example, h versus p), C.K. did so perfectly (Kosslyn et al., 1985; Kosslyn, 1987; Riddoch, 1990, Sergent, 1989). In a size comparison task, similar to that described above, C.K. was required to compare the size of two objects. On the imagery version, the names of the objects were given to C.K. and, on the perceptual version, line drawings of the same objects were presented with the objects drawn in black and white and to equal scale. Thirty pairs of objects were used including "banana spider" and "scissors kite" (from Schwartz & Chawluk, 1990). Whereas C.K. was able to make the size judgements without error in imagery, performance was at chance on the perceptual version.

We also tested C.K.'s ability to draw objects that he failed to recognise perceptually. An initial observation made during preliminary testing showed that C.K. was able to draw objects from long-term memory in rich detail. C.K.'s drawing ability was noted to be particularly good and he had taken several art classes at school (see his rendition of a side view of a bicycle in Fig. 5.2). Because drawing is assumed to involve imagery and the generation of items

FIG. 5.2   Examples of C.K.'s spontaneous drawing of a bicycle from memory.

from stored knowledge (Trojano & Grossi, 1992; Servos, Goodale, & Humphrey, 1993; Van Sommers, 1989), if C.K. can draw the objects he fails to recognise, this provides further evidence for the dissociation between imagery and recognition. C.K. was presented with the names of 30 pictures from the Boston Naming Test that he failed to recognise. He drew easily recognizable pictures of 29 of the 30 objects (see Fig. 5.3), with the single error on the item "seahorse". He commented that he did not really know what a seahorse looked like and was not sure he had ever seen one.

The imagery tests together with the drawings suggest that C.K. is able to generate mental images that contain detailed knowledge of the visual appearance of the very objects that he failed to recognise when presented to him perceptually. The data thus far clearly demonstrate that in spite of the profound object recognition deficit, C.K.'s visual mental imagery remains intact.

Mechanisms for perceiving the internal visual image

The imagery experiments described above all required C.K. to make single judgements (size, shape, colour) on a static image that was generated from a long-term representation in response to a given label. For example, when asked to determine whether the ears of a doberman stick up or down, the identity of the internally generated object is already provided by the label and the image is generated "top-down" from a long-term store of representations. In contrast, consider the following task: "Take the letter H. Turn it on its side and drop off the bottom line" and report the identity of the image. In this task, the initial item is generated from the long term store but is then transformed and altered. The subject is then required to reinterpret the newly created image, to recognise it and assign it an identity. Are the mechanisms used for perceiving this new image internally the same as those used for perceiving the target letter "T" when

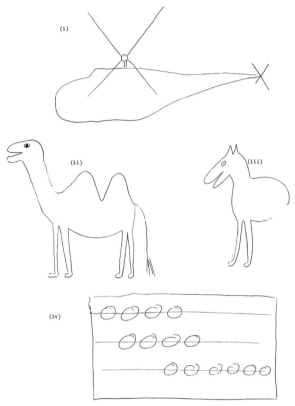

FIG. 5.3 Examples of C.K.'s drawings of items from the Boston Naming test from long-term memory. His error (the seahorse) is included (i) helicopter (ii) camel (iii) seahorse and (iv) abacus.

it is visually presented? If "internal perception" shares the same pathway as "external perception", then one might expect that C.K. would be impaired in both cases. If, however, the mechanisms used for seeing in the mind's eye are not equivalent to those used for perceiving a veridical object, then C.K. might succeed on the former and fail the latter, and this would provide further evidence for the separability of imagery and perception.

We used two tasks in which subjects are asked to generate a familiar pattern in imagery, alter it in some fixed way and then identify the transformed image. The one task was taken from Finke, Pinker and Farah (1989, Experiments 2 and 3) and the second was developed specifically for testing C.K. but, as in Finke et al. (1989), this task required the perception of an internally recreated image. For example, instructions for an item from Finke et al. (1989) are: "Imagine the letter B. Rotate it 90° to the left. Put a triangle directly below it having the same width and pointing down. Remove the horizontal line" (target response "heart"). When subjects fail to identify the item from imagery, they are generally asked to draw it. The subjects in Finke et al.'s experiment made an appropriate construal of the image on approximately 70% of the trials and an additional 10% of the trials (approximately) were correctly drawn and then identified. On the same task, C.K. was able to identify 11 out of the 12 objects from imagery. He was unable to identify the wine glass from imagery but drew it correctly. Our second, specially designed, task used a larger number of trials and items which, in their written form, refer to the full representation of the stimulus (i.e., alphabetic letters) rather than the schematic depictions as in the Finke et al. items. For example, a trial was as follows: "Take the letter H. Drop off the right vertical line. Add a horizontal line to the top and to the bottom" (target "E"). C.K. made only two errors on this test (normals: 21.6/24). On both the Finke et al. version and our version, when the targets were presented individually to C.K. on another occasion as black-and-white renditions, he failed to recognise many of them.

These data suggest that C.K. is able to "perceive" and recognise a newly created mental image. He is able to generate an item, transform it and recognise it from the internal image. On the few trials in which he failed to identify the image, he was able to draw it in a manner consistent with the instructions but still failed to identify it from the drawing. That C.K. can recognise the majority of items from "internal" input but not from "external" input suggests some separability between the mechanisms involved in these processes.

CONSISTENT EVIDENCE FROM OTHER PATIENTS

Consistent with evidence from other patients, the data from C.K. strongly suggest that perception and imagery are not absolutely equivalent and that there is some divergence between them. There is, however, one outstanding consideration that still might weaken the challenge to the shared mechanism hypothesis and that is that C.K. has some residual perception. Even though his object recognition is poor, C.K. is still able to perform some perceptual tasks (colour discrimination, line orientation) reasonably well. It is possible, then, that the processes underlying the residual perceptual abilities are also being used in the imagery tasks and thus there is no obvious dissociation between perception and imagery. This argument does not seem to hold, however, as there have now been reports of several cases who are profoundly impaired on even very simple perceptual tasks (apperceptive agnosia patients), and yet who still show well-preserved mental imagery.

For example, Servos and Goodale (1995) describe the impaired perception but spared imagery in patient D.F. who has profound visual agnosia resulting from an anoxia following carbon monoxide poisoning. The neural damage affected areas 18 and 19 primarily, leaving most of area 17 as well as most other areas of extrastriate cortex intact. D.F. had poor orientation discrimination, and could not recognise common objects (11% of 120 line drawings of common objects), familiar faces, letters nor even simple geometric forms. She could, however, draw common objects even though she could not identify them

(Humphrey, Goodale, Jakobson, & Servos, 1994; Servos et al., 1993), could use imagery for pantomime (how do you pick up a grapefruit), and had vivid and well-structured dreams (Goodale, Jakobson, & Keillor, 1994). Like C.K., she was able to perform size discriminations, make judgements on animals' body parts and alphabet tasks in imagery and could scan and generate new images using Finke et al. (1989) stimuli. Despite the inability to use bottom-up information about visual form to mediate even the simplest same–different judgements and matching tasks, D.F.'s imagery performance suggests that she has access to long-term representations of objects' forms. A very similar pattern has been described by Mapelli and Behrmann (personal communication) in which their patient, J.W., shows intact imagery on similar tasks despite an agnosic deficit so severe that his simple feature judgement on line orientation, symmetry judgments and size is poor.

Data from those patients with extensive destruction of visual cortex and preserved imagery present perhaps the most dramatic evidence favouring the separation between imagery and perception. These studies are reviewed in the discussion section. However, the presence of imagery despite almost total elimination of primary visual cortex is difficult to reconcile with the view of shared neural basis for imagery and perception.

DISCUSSION AND CONCLUSION

The findings from C.K., an "integrative agnosic" and other, lower-level "apperceptive agnosics" all suggest that it is indeed possible to see cases in whom mental imagery is preserved when visual perception is severely disturbed. These patients perform well on tasks of drawing from long-term memory, can make size and feature discriminations about objects, and, in some cases, can alter and manipulate images and then recognise them "internally" as new objects. Although the converse pattern of the dissociation (intact perception and impaired imagery) has been reported previously, compelling evidence for the preservation of imagery along with impaired perception has emerged only recently, as in the case of our patient C.K. That imagery and perception can each be selectively impaired while leaving the other process reasonably intact argues against a simple explanation of hierarchical ordering in which one of these processes is inherently more difficult than the other (Kosslyn et al., 1993; Tippett, 1992). Instead, this form of double dissociation is usually taken to mean that there is some independence or separation between the two processes (see Shallice, 1988, for a full discussion of the inferences from double dissociations). The first challenge, then, is how to reconcile the paradoxical findings of separation with the overwhelming evidence from normal subjects, neuropsychological cases and neuroimaging supporting the shared substrate for imagery and perception. The second question is, given that we will argue for some shared substrate, what exact neural structures mediate both imagery and perception.

Reconciling the associations and dissociations

The existing data supporting an association between imagery and perception are well established and accepted. The findings for a double dissociation are rather more novel and the problem is how to reconcile these opposing views, each of which has a strong empirical foundation. One possible reconciliation is that imagery and recognition are neither completely isolable nor completely integrated; instead imagery and recognition may overlap partially and yet still retain some unique components. It is obvious that there are some components of the visual system which are not equally shared by imagery and recognition. For example, the retina, while critical for recognition, is clearly not involved in imagery; damage to sensory stages of visual processing has little impact on imagery and congenitally blind people can generate images (Büchel, Price, Frackowiak, & Friston, 1998; Cornoldi, Cortesi, & Preti, 1991). Similarly, the impairment in imagery with intact perception is generally interpreted as a selective impairment in the generation component or the means whereby an image is created in the visual buffer from information stored in long-term visual memory (e.g. Farah, 1984, 1995; Kosslyn, 1980; Kosslyn, Flynn, Amsterdam, & Wang, 1990; Riddoch, 1990). Because generation is selectively involved in imagery and plays no role in perception, it may be damaged without any consequences for perception. Whereas this latter explanation may account for the selective impairment in imagery, it still does not shed light on the complementary pattern nor suggest what unique recognition processes or mechanisms may be selectively damaged, while leaving imagery intact.

A second way of reconciling the associations and dissociations and one that we favour, then, is to assume that imagery and perception do share some cortical areas but that parts of the system may be more involved or functionally special-ised for one or the other process. This approach does not parcel out some processes that are involved solely in imagery or solely in visual recognition but rather concedes that the same mechanisms are involved in both imagery and recognition but to differential extents. To understand this further, we turn to the second type of patient like case C.K. who has intact imagery and impaired percep-tion. As in many cognitive and computational models of visual object processing, we assume that there is a series of component stages through which object information passes prior to recognition (see Farah, 1990; Humphreys et al., 1993; Kosslyn et al., 1990; Marr, 1982; McCarthy and Warrington, 1986, 1990). At early stages, primitive features of the display are registered and edge detec-tion and orientation are carried out. At intermediate stages, processes involved in figure–ground segregation and feature grouping come into play, and at late stages, processes involved in activating stored knowledge are operational. We propose that these stages may be implicated in imagery and in perception to a greater or lesser degree. More specifically, we suggest that procedures such as grouping or segmentation are more involved in perception than in imagery.

When presented with a novel display, the observer must necessarily parse and organise the display. These processes do not play as central a role in visual imagery. Our findings have suggested that C.K.'s perceptual deficit affects the intermediate stages of processing which are required for grouping and segmentation of elements or features and that this "integrative agnosia" precludes the derivation of a coherent structural description of the display. The deficit, we would argue, disrupts access to higher-level processes which are, in themselves, fully functional. It is these intact, higher-level processes which operate in imagery and which access the stored representations. Thus, imagery of object size, shape and colour may be preserved even though access to this long-term knowledge may be impossible because of the visual deficit.

What remains to be explained is why intermediate procedures like segmentation and grouping are differentially involved in imagery and perception and why it is that C.K. can recognise objects "internally" (as in Finke et al. (1989) and our similar task) but not when the same objects are presented "externally" for recognition. Consider the processes involved in the "internal recognition" tasks. When asked to image the letter "H", for example, and to drop off some segments and re-recognise it, all the elementary features and their relations to each other are specified "top-down" from the long-term representation of the "H". Because all the elements are already assembled, the parts of the item and the spatial relations between them are known. Moreover, the instructions to the subject provide the parsing routine and specify what elements are to be segregated and manipulated. Thus, shifting the parts around to transform the image may be accomplished without the involvement of segmentation processes. This is especially so when the instructions to do the manipulations are explicit and unambiguous as is the case in the Finke et al. (1989) test and in our letter imagery task as well. When this recreated novel visual image must be reperceived, the reconstruction is straightforward and segmentation is known a priori. In this case, recognition circumvents the "bottom-up" disruption that produces the perceptual deficit. In contrast, consider the case of perceiving the letter "H". When this is shown to the observer, the components are not identified clearly and their location with respect to others is not explicitly tagged. Thus, segmentation and integration of the features of the display must be carried out from scratch and it is in this situation that C.K.'s deficit has its impact and prevents recognition. An analogous situation to the differences between imagery and perception might be the assembly of a jigsaw puzzle—when the puzzle is pre-assembled (as is the long-term representation) and the disassembly is under the control of the individual, reconstructing the puzzle is fairly trivial. The arrangement between the pieces was already given and, provided that one can keep track of this arrangement, putting the pieces back together is straightforward. On the other hand, if the puzzle pieces are presented randomly and the subject is instructed to produce a coherent picture, there is increased reliance on integration processes and the assembly is far more demanding and difficult.

There are various possible ways that this functional specialisation hypothesis might be tested. One way might be to construct an imagery task that will be more like perception—for example, devising a task in which the components are not quite identifiable or are broken down in unusual ways such that their tagging from the long-term representation does not help the reconstruction of the image. The second way, which is possibly easier, would be to construct a perception task that is more like imagery. In this task, the pieces would be pre-segmented and small components would be identified explicitly. The segmentation might be achieved through colouring the subparts in different colours, by applying different textures to demarcate the boundaries of the component parts or by explaining to C.K. how the pieces all fit together. Assembly of the subparts would then occur in a very obvious and straightforward way. The expectation is that, when the parsing is given to C.K., as is the case in imagery, his perception performance should improve. By modifying the perception task to be more akin to the demands required by imagery or vice versa, we might be able to tease apart the differential involvement of some processes in imagery and in perception.

By proposing a unifying framework and by showing how selective impairments can be observed in the context of a shared mechanism, we have been able to accommodate both the associations and dissociations between visual mental imagery and visual recognition. The thrust of this argument is that it is still possible to observe double dissociations in the context of a shared system even though the standard assumption has been that a double dissociation is diagnostic of separable and independent systems (see also Plaut, 1995). Although common representations and neural mechanisms may subserve both imagery and recognition, there may still be components of the shared system which are functionally specialized—in this case, higher stages of visual processing are involved in both imagery and in perception whereas earlier and more intermediate stages of information processing might be more involved in perception, and less involved in imagery. Following damage to these earlier and intermediate stages, imagery might be preserved but perception selectively disrupted.

The shared substrate

There is still one issue that remains to be addressed and that is the exact localisation of the shared neural substrate. We have argued that imagery and perception share (to a greater or lesser degree) functional processes and now the question becomes what structures mediate these shared processes. This issue remains controversial and is still a topic of much debate. A central claim of the view adopted by Kosslyn and his colleagues is that primary visual cortex is involved in both processes. While no one challenges the involvement of primary visual cortex in perception and recognition, the extent to which it is implicated in imagery is debated. As part of their model of visual imagery, Kosslyn and his colleagues and Farah and her colleagues have argued that primary visual cortex plays a crucial role in mental imagery. This claim is borne out by a host of neuroimaging studies not only showing activation in early cortical areas, including V1 and V2 (Kosslyn, Thompson, Kim, & Alpert, 1995; Le Bihan et at., 1993) but also showing that the size of the image is related to the location of maximum activity. This size–region relationship is what would be expected if the earliest visual areas which are spatially organised were mediating imagery.

This view of early visual area involvement is also supported by the findings from Ishai and Sagi (1995) who found equivalent facilitation between flankers present in a Gabor target detection task and an imagery condition in which subjects simply imagined that the flankers were present. As mentioned previously, of interest is the fact that the facilitation occurred only under specific conditions: the facilitation was monocular—when the perception task was performed with one eye closed and the following imagery task was performed with the other eye covered, there was no imagery-induced facilitation; the facilitation was also orientation specific—when the target and the masks were at different orientations, one vertical and one horizontal, no facilitation was obtained in either imagery or perception and finally, the facilitation was spatial-frequency specific. These characteristics are consistent with aspects of V1 functioning and suggest that the equivalence of imagery and perception are mediated by low-level visual areas.

In contrast to these findings, Roland and Gulyás (1994, 1995) have reported no activation in area V1 on PET studies using several experimental paradigms including route finding, recall of geometric patterns, letter and word visualization tasks. Area V1, however, is obviously crucial to perception, leading to the view that low-level visual areas are involved only in perception but not in imagery. Based on their data, Roland and Gulyás (1994, 1995) have argued that the sites of storage of long-term representations (parieto-occipital and temporo-occipital regions) are active during imagery but that primary visual cortex is not involved. Whereas there is general agreement that some higher-order visual areas in temporal and parietal lobes do play a role in imagery, the central question is whether lower-level visual areas are also involved, as would be expected on views that emphasise the sharing of topographic, retinotopically mapped areas of visual cortex. Interestingly, D'Esposito et al. (1997) also failed to obtain V1 activation in an imagery study in which subjects either passively listened to some words or mentally generated an image of the words' referent; whereas temporo-occipital activation was noted consistently across subjects and some subjects showed occipital activation, V1 was not activated. We return to the centrality of primary visual cortex activation during imagery in the final discussion.

In an exchange of papers, Kosslyn and Ochsner (1994) have challenged the conclusion reached by Roland and Gulyás (1994) on a number of fronts. They argue that the baseline subtraction conditions used by Roland and Gulyás (1994) may not have been appropriate; for example, Roland and Gulyás (1994) used a "rest" condition as the baseline and subjects were instructed to lie motionless with their eyes closed. If subjects had been visualizing during this "rest" condition, then it is not surprising that when this control condition is subtracted from the experimental imagery condition, no activation was observed in the crucial shared visual areas. Kosslyn and Ochsner (1994) also note that some of the tasks employed by Roland and Gulyás (1994) could be done without imagery. Finally, the absence of early visual area activation, according to Kosslyn and Ochsner (1994), may be attributable to individual differences because not every subject shows the expected activation of primary visual areas (17 and 18). It remains an open issue, then, as to whether primary visual cortex is actively involved in imagery or not.

How can we reconcile the discrepancy between studies that do find early visual area activation and those that do not? In a recent commentary on Roland and Gulyás' findings (1994), we have suggested that areas 17 and 18 may indeed be activated during imagery, and that the activation may be detected empirically, but that this does not mean that these regions are necessarily and mandatorily involved in imagery (Moscovitch, Behrmann, & Winocur, 1994). The activation may simply be epiphenomenal. If this is indeed the case, neuroimaging may not be the ideal method to definitively address this issue as there is no way of determining whether particular areas are obligatorily involved in imagery. Instead, we argued that evidence from two types of neuropsychological patients will carry more weight in adjudicating this issue: patients like C.K. who have intact imagery and impaired perception and patients with occipital lesions. We have already discussed C.K. and patients like him at length and so we turn to the occipital lesion patients before presenting our concluding remarks.

If imagery and perception necessarily share primary visual areas, then one prediction is that patients with complete cortical blindness following bilateral occipital lesions should not be capable of imagery. Thus, we argued, evidence from patients with complete loss or gross impairment of vision in both hemifields without retinal or ocular pathology might bear strongly on this issue. Indeed, since we wrote this commentary, a number of studies of patients with cortical blindness have been reported that address this very issue. The findings of one recent study of a patient with cortical blindness for over four years supports this prediction (Policardi et al., 1996). T.C., a 26-year-old university student, had only some residual visual competence in small regions of the visual fields following a traffic accident and a lengthy period in coma. Shape recognition was grossly defective although occasionally possible for fairly large targets and colour and brightness perception were severely impaired. T.C. failed a host of imagery tasks including those probing topographical imagery and structural imagery. For example, T.C. failed on tests of colour imagery, was unable to visualize well-known symbols (e.g. the Olympic symbol), and was impaired on tasks of animal (e.g. animals tails task, animals leg task) and object imagery (e.g. high/wide object tasks, sharp/round object task) tasks. The loss of cortical vision accompanied by the loss of imagery suggests that a common area (primary visual cortex in this case) mediates these two processes and is consistent with the view that early visual areas are involved in imagery.

As usual, however, the situation is not that clearcut and there are findings from cortically blind patients that support the alternative view. In one such study, Goldenberg, Müllbacher, & Nowak (1995) presented data from a patient with Anton's syndrome who denied her blindness despite extensive loss of cortical vision. Neuroimaging revealed almost complete destruction of primary visual cortex bilaterally with sparing of only small remainders of cortex at the occipital tip of the upper calcarine lip. Bilateral thalamic lesions were also noted. Notwithstanding the widespread and devastating occipital lesions, this patient was capable of generating such vivid imagery that she actually believed these were veridical perceptions (see also Kinsbourne, 1989; McGlynn, & Schacter, 1989). For example, when a set of keys were held up before her, she correctly identified the stimulus as a set of keys based on the auditory signal but then went on to present a fairly elaborate visual description of the keys (for example, there is a big ring on top and a dark bit on the key) even though she did not perceive the keys visually. That she was capable of imagery of this sort with such extensive damage to occipital cortex would suggest that the primary visual areas are not truly involved in imagery. There is, however, some room for doubt and for arguing that these data are still inconclusive: the patient had a small area of occipital cortex that was not completely destroyed and one might claim that this small, residual area of cortex might have been sufficient to mediate imagery. Further, even though the visual confabulations might have seemed very "perceptual" in quality, Goldenberg et al. (1995) did not examine their patient on tests which are specifically designed to assess imagery per se. There remains the possibility, remote though it is, that this patient did not have very well-preserved imagery.

More definitive evidence comes from a study of three cortically blind patients in which Chatterjee and Southwood (1995) conducted standard imagery tests as well as detailed evaluation of the lesion sites and visual abilities of the patients. The findings are most dramatic in one of the three cases who had exquisitely preserved visual imagery despite bilateral occipital lesions with an extension on the right into medial temporal lobe. This patient, who could not consistently differentiate light from dark and could not detect the movement of the examiner's hand in front of her, was not only able to perform well on the standard imagery tests but performed exceptionally well (in the upper range of normal performance) on imagery tasks designed to probe imagery for shape, colour, letters and faces. She also was able to complete spatial imagery tests (in what direction would you be travelling if going from Atlanta to Birmingham; is the angle of the hands of a clock showing the time at 10.30 greater or less than 90°?) and produced good depictions of objects in drawing. The finding that imagery is well preserved in the absence of functional occipital cortex remains a challenge to the notion that primary visual areas are equally involved in vision and in mental imagery.

CONCLUDING REMARKS

We have addressed a number of central issues concerning the relationship between visual mental imagery and visual perception or recognition. The primary focus of this paper was to examine the extent to which these two processes, visual perception and visual imagery, rely on common functional and neural mechanisms. While the evidence for a close coupling between these processes on both a functional and neural level has been obtained, there are also data from neuroimaging and neuropsychological studies which suggest that these processes may be dissociated. We have proposed one possible account for the existence of a dissociation in the context of a unitary mechanism and have argued that, even though the mechanisms may be shared, there may be differential reliance on the neural substrate and the functional processes for imagery and for vision. We have suggested that some visual processes, and in the case of C.K., segmentation and visual parsing, might play more of a central role in perception than in imagery. Because a visual scene needs to be parsed de novo, perceptual organisation and the intermediate stage of visual processing play an important role. These processes are, however, less implicated in imagery because the segmentation is often a by-product of the generation of the mental image top-down. We have suggested some ways in which this view might be tested more stringently. There are a number of outstanding issues in this domain which remain to be addressed (see Cooper, 1995), and the ongoing debate concerning the extent of the involvement of primary visual cortex in imagery awaits resolution.

ACKNOWLEDGEMENTS

This research was supported by a grant from the NIMH to M. Behrmann and by a grant from the Medical Research Council of Canada to M. Moscovitch and G. Winocur.

REFERENCES

Annett, J. (1995a). Motor imagery: Perception or action? *Neuropsychologia, 30*(11), 61–83.

Annett, J. (1995b). Imagery and motor processes: Editorial overview. *British Journal of Psychology, 86*, 161–7.

Behrmann, M. (in press). The mind's eye over the brain's matter. *Current Directions in Psychological Science*.

Behrmann, M., Moscovitch, M., & Winocur, G. (1994). Intact visual imagery and impaired visual perception in a patient with visual agnosia. *Journal of Experimental Psychology: Human Perception and Performance, 20*(5), 1068–87.

Behrmann, M., Winocur, G., & Moscovitch, M. (1992). Dissociation between mental imagery and object recognition in a brain-damaged patient. *Nature, 359*, 636–7.

Benton, A.L., Sivan, A.B., de Hamsher, N., Varney, N., & Spreen, O. (1983). *Contributions to neuropsychological assessment*. New York: Oxford University Press.

Bisiach, E., & Luzzatti, C. (1978). Unilateral neglect of representational space. *Cortex, 17*, 129–33.

Botez, M.I., Olivier, M., Vezina, J.L., Botez, T., & Kaufman, B. (1985). Defective revisualization: Dissociation between cognitive and imagistic thought. *Cortex, 21*, 375–89.

Bowers, D., Blonder, L.X., Feinberg, T., & Heilman, K.M. (1991). Differential impact of right and left hemisphere lesions on facial emotion and object imagery. *Brain, 114,* 2593–609.

Brooks, L. (1968). Spatial and verbal components of the act of recall. *Canadian Journal of Psychology, 22,* 349–50.

Brown, B.B. (1966). Specificity of EEG phoptic flicker responses to colors as related to visual imagery ability. *Psychophysiology, 2*(3), 197–207.

Bruce, V. (1996). Reality and imagination. In V. Bruce (Ed.), *Unsolved mysteries of the mind* (pp. 59–92). Hove, UK: Psychology Press.

Büchel, C., Price, C., Frackowiak, R.S.J., & Friston, K. (1998). Different activation patterns in the visual cortex of late and congenitally blind subjects. *Brain, 121,* 409–19.

Charlot, V., Tzourio, N., Zilbovicius, M., Mazoyer, B., & Denis, M. (1992). Different mental imagery abilities result in different regional cerebral blood flow activation patterns during cognitive tasks. *Neuropsychologia, 6,* 565–80.

Chatterjee, A., & Southwood, M.H. (1995). Cortical blindness and visual imagery. *Neurology, 45*(2), 2189–95.

Chen, W., Kato, T., Zhu, X.-H., Ogawa, S., Tank, D.W., & Ugurbil, K. (1998). Human primary visual cortex and lateral geniculate nucleus activation during visual imagery. *NeuroReport, 9,* 3669–674.

Cooper, L. (1995). Varieties of visual representation: How are we to analyze the concept of mental image? *Neuropsychologia, 33*(11), 241–8.

Cornoldi, C., Cortesi, A., & Preti, D. (1991). Individual differences in the capacity limitations of visuospatial short-term memory: Research on sighted and congenitally blind people. *Memory and Cognition, 19*(5), 459–68.

Craik, F.I.M., & Dirkx, E. (1992). Age-related differences in three tests of visual imagery. *Psychology and Aging, 7*(4), 661–5.

Davidson, R.J., & Schwartz, G.E. (1977). Brain mechanisms subserving self-generated imagery: electrophysiological specificity and patterning. *Psychophysiology, 14,* 598–601.

Decety, J., Perani, D., Jeannerod, M., Bettinardi, V., Tadary, B., Woods, R., Mazziotta, J.C., & Fazio, F. (1994). Mapping motor representations with positron emission tomography. *Nature, 371,* 600–2.

De Renzi, E., & Lucchelli, F. (1993). The fuzzy boundaries of apperceptive agnosia, *Cortex, 29,* 187–215.

D'Esposito, M., Detre, J.A., Aguirre, G.K., Stallcup, M., Alsop, D.C., Tippett, L.J., & Farah, M.J. (1997). Functional MRI study of mental image generation. *Neuropsychologia, 35,* 725–30.

Douglas, K.L., & Rockland, K.S. (1992). Extensive visual feedback connections from ventral inferotemporal cortex. *Society of Neuroscience Abstracts, 18*(1), 390.

Eddy, J.K., & Glass, A.L. (1981). Reading and listening to high and low imagery sentences. *Journal of Verbal Learning and Verbal Behavior, 20,* 333–45.

Farah, M.J. (1984). The neurological basis of mental imagery: A componential approach. *Cognition, 18,* 245–72.

Farah, M.J. (1985). Psychophysical evidence for a shared representational medium for visual images and percepts. *Journal of Experimental Psychology: General, 114,* 93–105.

Farah, M.J. (1988). Is visual imagery really visual? Overlooked evidence from neuropsychology. *Psychological Review, 95,* 307–17.

Farah, M.J. (1989). Mechanisms of imagery-perception interaction. *Journal of Experimental Psychology: Human Perception and Performance, 15*(2), 203–11.

Farah, M.J. (1990). *Visual agnosia.* Cambridge, MA: MIT press.

Farah, M.J. (1995). Current issues in the neuropsychology of image generation. *Neuropsychologia, 33*(11), 121–37.

Farah, M.J. (1999). Mental Imagery. In M. Gazzaniga (Ed.), *The cognitive neurosciences* (Second edition). Cambridge, MA: MIT Press.

Farah, M.J., Hammond, K.M., Levine, D.N., & Calvanio, R. (1988). Visual and spatial mental imagery: dissociable systems of representation. *Cognitive Psychology*, *20*, 439–62.

Farah, M.J., Hammond, K.M., Mehta, Z., & Ratcliff, G. (1989). Category-specificity and modality specificity in semantic memory. *Neuropsychologia*, *27*(2), 193–200.

Farah, M.J., Levine, D.N., & Calvanio, R. (1988). A case study of mental imagery deficit. *Brain and Cognition*, *8*, 147–64.

Farah, M.J., & Peronnet, F. (1989). Event-related potentials in the study of mental imagery. *Journal of Psychophysiology*, *3*, 99–109.

Farah, M.J., Soso, M.J., & Dasheiff, R.M. (1992). Visual angle of the mind's eye before and after unilateral occipital lobectomy. *Journal of Experimental Psychology: Human Perception and Performance*, *18*(1), 241–6.

Finke, R.A. (1979). The functional equivalence of mental images and errors of movement. *Cognitive Psychology*, *11*, 235–64.

Finke, R.A. (1980). Levels of equivalence in imagery and perception. *Psychological Review*, *87*(2), 113–32.

Finke, R.A. (1985). Theories relating mental imagery to perception. *Psychological Bulletin*, *98*, 236–59.

Finke, R.A. (1989). *Principles of mental imagery*. Cambridge, MA: A Bradford Book, MIT Press.

Finke, R.A., Pinker, S., & Farah, M.J. (1989). Reinterpreting visual patterns in mental imagery. *Cognitive Science*, *13*, 51–78.

Finke, R.A., & Schmidt, M.J. (1978). The quantitative measure of pattern representation in images using orientation-specific color aftereffects. *Perception and Psychophysics*, *23*, 515–20.

Goldenberg, G. (1992). Loss of visual imagery and loss of visual knowledge—a case study. *Neuropsychologia*, *30*(12), 1081–99.

Goldenberg, G. (1993). The neural basis of mental imagery. *Bailliere's Clinical Neurology*, *2*(2), 265–85.

Goldenberg, G., Müllbacher, W., & Nowak, A. (1995). Imagery without perception—a case study of anosognosia for cortical blindness. *Neuropsychologia*, *33*(11), 39–48.

Goldenberg, G., Podreka, I., Steiner, M., & Willmes, K. (1987). Patterns of regional cerebral blood flow related to memorizing high and low imagery words: An emission computer tomography study. *Neuropsychologia*, *25*, 473–86.

Goldenberg, G., Steiner, M., Podreka, I., & Deecke, L. (1992). Regional cerebral blood flow patterns related to the verification of low- and high-imagery sentences. *Neuropsychologia*, *30*(6), 581–6.

Goodale, M., Jakobson, L.S., & Keillor, J.M. (1994). Differences in the visual control of pantomimed and natural grasping movements. *Neuropsychologia*, *32*, 1159–78.

Grailet, J.M., Seron, X., Bruyer, R., Coyette, F., & Frederix, M. (1990). Case report of a visual integrative agnosia. *Cognitive Neuropsychology*, *7*, 275–310.

Grossi, D., Orsini, A., Modafferi, A., & Liotto, M. (1986). Visuo-imaginal constructive apraxia: On a case of a selective deficit in imagery. *Brain and Cognition*, *5*, 167–255.

Head, H., & Holmes, G. (1911). Sensory disturbances from cerebral lesions. *Brain*, *34*, 102.

Humphrey, G.K., Goodale, M., Jakobson, L.S., & Servos, P. (1994). The role of surface information in object recognition: Studies of a visual form agnosic and normal subjects. *Perception*, *23*, 1457–81.

Humphreys, G.W., & Riddoch, M.J. (1987a). *To see or not to see*. London: Lawrence Erlbaum.

Humphreys, G.W., & Riddoch, M.J. (1987b). The fractionation of visual agnosia. In G.W. Humphreys and M.J. Riddoch (Eds), *Visual object processing: A cognitive neuropsychological approach*. London: Lawrence Erlbaum.

Humphreys, G.W., Riddoch, M.J., Donnelly, N., Freeman, T., Boucart, M., & Muller, H.M. (1993). Intermediate visual processing and visual agnosia. In M. Farah and G. Ratcliff (Eds), *The neural basis of high-level vision*. Hillsdale, NJ: Lawrence Erlbaum.

Humphreys, G.W., Riddoch, M.J., Quinlan, P.T., Price, C.T., & Donnelly, N. (1992). Parallel pattern processing and visual agnosia. *Canadian Journal of Psychology*, *46*(3), 377–416.

Iorio, L., Falanga, A., Fragassi, N.A., & Grossi, D. (1992). Visual associative agnosia and optic aphasia: A single case study and review of the syndromes. *Cortex*, *28*(1), 23–37.

Ishai, A., & Sagi, D. (1995). Common mechanisms of visual imagery and perception. *Science*, *268*, 1772–4.

Jankowiak, J., Kinsbourne, M., Shalev, R.S., & Bachman, D.L. (1992). Preserved visual imagery and categorization in a case of associative visual agnosia. *Journal of Cognitive Neuroscience*, *4*(2), 119–31.

Jeannerod, M. (1994). The representing brain: Neural correlates of motor intention and imagery. *Brain and Behavioral Sciences*, *17*, 187–245.

Jeannerod, M. (1995). Mental imagery in the motor context. *Neuropsychologia*, *33*(11), 85–8.

Jeannerod, M., & Decety, J. (1995). Mental motor imagery: a window into the representational stages of action. *Current Opinion in Neurobiology*, *5*, 727–32.

Kaplan, E., Goodglass, H., & Weintraub, S. (1993). *Boston naming test*. Philadelphia: Lea and Febiger.

Kertesz, A. (1982). *Western aphasia battery*, New York: Grune and Stratton.

Kinsbourne, M. (1989). The boundaries of episodic remembering. In H.L. Roediger III, & F.I.M. Craik (Eds) *Varieties of memories and consciousness: Essays in honour of Endel Tulving*. pp. 179–91. Hillsdale, NJ: Lawrence Erlbaum.

Kosslyn, S.M. (1975). Information representation in visual images. *Cognitive Psychology*, *7*, 341–70.

Kosslyn, S.M. (1980). *Image and mind*. Cambridge, MA: Harvard University Press.

Kosslyn, S.M. (1987). Seeing and imagining in the cerebral hemispheres: A computational approach. *Psychological Bulletin*, *94*(2), 148–75.

Kosslyn, S.M. (1994). *Image and brain; The resolution of the imagery debate*. Cambridge, MA: MIT Press.

Kosslyn, S.M., Alpert, N.M., Thompson, W.L., Maljkovic, V., Weise, S.B., Chabris, S.F., Hamilton, S.E., & Buonanno, F.S. (1993). Visual mental imagery activates the primary visual cortex. *Journal of Cognitive Neuroscience*, *5*(3), 263–87.

Kosslyn, S.M., Behrmann, M., & Jeannerod, M. (1995). Perspectives on the cognitive neuroscience of mental imagery: Introduction to special issue on mental imagery. *Neuropsychologia*, *33*(11), 1335–44.

Kosslyn, S.M., Flynn, R.A., Amsterdam, J.B., & Wang, G. (1990). Components of high-level vision: A cognitive neuroscience analysis and accounts of neurological syndromes. *Cognition*, *34*(2), 203–77.

Kosslyn, S.M., Hamilton, S., Maljkovic, V., Horwitz, G., & Thompson, W.L. (1995). Two types of image generation: evidence for left- and right-hemisphere processes. *Neuropsychologia*, *33*(11), 151–76.

Kosslyn, S.M., Holtzman, J.D., Farah, M.J., & Gazzaniga, M. (1985). A computational analysis of mental image generation: Evidence from functional dissociations in split-brain patients. *Journal of Experimental Psychology: General*, *114*, 311–41.

Kosslyn, S.M., & Ochsner, K.N. (1994). In search of occipital activation during visual mental imagery. *Trends in Neuroscience*, *17*(7), 290–1.

Kosslyn, S.M., Thompson, W.L., Kim, I.J., & Alpert, N.M. (1995). Topographical representations of mental images in primary visual cortex. *Nature*, *378*, 496–8.

Le Bihan, D., Turner, R., Zeffiro, T.A., Cuenod, C.A., & Bonnerot, V. (1993). Activation of human primary visual cortex during visual recall: A magnetic resonance imaging study. *Proceedings of the National Academy of Sciences USA*, *90*, 11802–5.

Levine, D.N., Warach, J., & Farah, M.J. (1985). Two visual systems in mental imagery: Dissociation of "what" and "where" in imagery disorders due to bilateral posterior cerebral lesions. *Neurology*, *35*, 1010–18.

Luzzatti, C., Vecchi, T., Agazzi, D., Cesa-Bianchi, M., & Vergani, C. (1998). A neurological dissociation between preserved visual and impaired spatial processing in mental imagery. *Cortex, 34*, 461–9.

McCarthy, R., & Warrington, E.K. (1986). Visual associative agnosia: A clinicoanatomical study. *Journal of Neurology, Neurosurgery and Psychiatry, 49*, 1233–40.

McCarthy, R., & Warrington, E.K. (1990). *Cognitive neuropsychology*. London: Academic Press.

McGlynn, S., & Schacter, D. (1989). Unawareness of deficits in neuropsychological syndromes. *Journal of Clinical and Experimental Psychology, 11*, 143–205.

Mapelli, D., & Behrmann, M. (personal communication). Visual primitives in apperceptive agnosia.

Marr, D. (1982). *Vision: A computational investigation into the human representation and processing of visual information*. San Francisco: Freeman.

Mehta, Z., Newcombe, F., & De Haan, E. (1992). Selective loss of visual imagery in a case of visual agnosia. *Neuropsychologia, 30*(7), 645–55.

Miyashita, Y. (1995). How the brain creates imagery; Projection to primary visual cortex. *Science, 268*, 1719–20.

Moscovitch, M., Behrmann, M., & Winocur, G. (1994). Do PETS have long or short ears? Mental imagery and neuroimaging. *Trends in Neuroscience, 17*, 292–7.

Moscovitch, M., Winocur, G., & Behrmann, M. (1997). What is special about face recognition? Nineteen experiments on a person with visual object agnosia and dyslexia but normal face recognition. *Journal of Cognitive Neuroscience, 9*, 555–604.

Ogden, J. (1993). Visual object agnosia, prosopagnosia, achromatopsia, loss of visual imagery, and autobiographical amnesia following recovery from cortical blindness: Case M.H. *Neuropsychologia, 31*(6), 571–89.

Paivio, A. (1979). *Imagery and verbal processes*. Hillsdale, NJ: Lawrence Erlbaum.

Parsons, L.M., Fox, P.T., Downs, J.H., Glass, T., Hirsch, T.B., Martin, C.C., Jerabek, P.A., & Lancaster, J.L. (1995). Use of implicit motor imagery for visual shape discrimination as revealed by PET. *Nature, 375*, 54–8.

Pinker, S. (1984). Visual cognition: An introduction. *Cognition, 18*, 1–63.

Pinker, S. (1985). Visual cognition: An introduction. In S. Pinker (Ed.) *Visual cognition*. Cambridge, MA: MIT Press.

Plaut, D.C. (1995). Double dissociation without modularity: Evidence from connectionist neuropsychology. *Journal of Clinical and Experimental Neuropsychology, 17*, 291–321.

Plaut, D., & Shallice, T. (1993). Perseverative and semantic influences on visual object naming errors in optic aphasia: A connectionist account. *Journal of Cognitive Neuroscience, 5*(1), 89–117.

Policardi, E., Perani, D., Zago, S. Grassi, F., Fazio, F., & Làdavas, E. (1996). Failure to evoke visual images in a case of long-lasting cortical blindness. *Neurocase, 2*, 381–94.

Reisberg, D. (1992). *Auditory imagery*. Hillsdale, NJ: Lawrence Erlbaum Associates.

Ricci, R., Vaishnavi, S., & Chatterjee, A. (1999). A deficit of intermediate vision: Experimental observations and theoretical implications. *Neurocase, 5*, 1–12.

Riddoch, M.J. (1990). Loss of visual imagery: A generation deficit. *Cognitive Neuropsychology, 7*(4), 249–73.

Riddoch, M.J., & Humphreys, G.W. (1987). A case of integrative visual agnosia. *Brain, 110*, 1431–62.

Roland, P.E., & Gulyás, B. (1994). Visual imagery and visual representation. *Trends in Neuroscience, 17*(7), 281–7.

Roland, P.E., & Gulyás, B. (1995). Visual memory, visual imagery and visual recognition of large field patterns by the human brain: Functional anatomy by positron emission tomography. *Cerebral Cortex, 5*, 79–93.

Schwartz, M.S., & Chawluk, J.B. (1990). Deterioration of language in progressive aphasia: A case study. In M. Schwartz (Ed.) *Modular deficits in Alzheimer-type dementia*, pp. 245–96. Cambridge, MA: Bradford/MIT Press.

Sergent, J. (1989). Image generation and processing of generated images in the cerebral hemi-spheres. *Journal of Experimental Psychology: Human Perception and Performance, 15*(1), 170–8.

Servos, P., & Goodale, M. (1995). Preserved visual imagery in visual form agnosia. *Neuropsychologia, 33*(11), 49–60.

Servos, P., Goodale, M.A., & Humphrey, G.K. (1993). The drawing of objects by a visual form agnosic: Contribution of surface properties and memorial representations. *Neuropsychologia, 31*(3), 251–9.

Shallice, T. (1988). *From neuropsychology to mental structure.* New York: Cambridge University Press.

Smith, D., Wilson, M., & Reisberg, D. (1995). The role of subvocalization in auditory imagery. *Neuropsychologia, 33*(11), 99–120.

Sparr, S.A., Jay, M., Dreslane, F.W., & Venna, N. (1991). A historic case of visual agnosia revisited after 40 years. *Brain, 114,* 789–800.

Stadler, M.A., & McDaniel, M.A. (1990). On imaging and seeing: Repetition priming and interactive views of imagery. *Psychological Research, 52,* 366–70.

Stangalino, C., Semenza, C., & Mondini, S. (1995). Generating visual mental images: deficits after brain damage. *Neuropsychologia, 33*(11), 139–49.

Symonds, C., & Mackenzie, I. (1957). Bilateral loss of vision from cerebral infarction. *Brain, 80,* 28–48.

Thaiss, L., & De Bleser, R. (1992). Visual agnosia: A case of reduced attentional spotlight? *Cortex, 28,* 601–21.

Tippett, L.J. (1992). The generation of visual images: A review of neuropsychological research and theory. *Psychological Bulletin, 112*(3), 415–32.

Trojano, L., & Grossi, D. (1992). Impaired drawing from memory in a visual agnosic patient. *Brain and Cognition, 10,* 327–44.

Trojano, L., & Grossi, D. (1994). A critical review of mental imagery deficits. *Brain and Cognition, 24*(4), 213–43.

Van Essen, D.C. (1985). Functional organization of primate visual cortex. In A. Peters, & E.G. Jones (Eds) *Cerebral cortex.* New York: Plenum Press.

Van Sommers, P. (1989). A system for drawing and drawing-related neuropsychology. *Cognitive Neuropsychology, 6*(2), 117–64.

Warrington, E.K., & James, M. (1991). *The visual object and space perception battery.* London: Thames Valley Testing Company.

Williams, P., & Behrmann, M. (submitted). Object categorisation and agnosia.

Wilson, B.A., & Davidoff, M. (1993). Partial recovery from visual object agnosia: A 10 year follow-up study. *Cortex, 29,* 529–42.

Young, A.W., Humphreys, G.W., Riddoch, M.J., Hellawell, D.J., & De Haan, E.H.F. (1994). Recognition impairments and face imagery. *Neuropsychologia, 32*(6), 693–702.

CHAPTER SIX

Category-specific recognition impairments for living and nonliving things

Emer M.E. Forde
Institute of Psychology, Aston University, UK

Semantic memory refers to the store of knowledge that allows us to give meaning to the objects we see and to the words we hear and read. Over the past 25 years, cognitive neuropsychology has helped shed light on the structure, and on the principles that govern the organisation of semantic memory by detailed analysis of patients with semantic deficits. Amongst the most intriguing of these deficits are those affecting one particular category of objects, or a set of related categories (e.g. living things, Basso, Capitani & Laiacona, 1988; De Renzi & Lucchelli, 1994; Sartori & Job, 1988; Silveri & Gainotti, 1988; Sheriden & Humphreys, 1993; Warrington & Shallice, 1984).

More than fifty years ago, Nielsen (1946) suggested that visual recognition impairments for living and nonliving things might dissociate, and that our representations of different categories might be stored in anatomically distinct brain areas. He reported two case studies of patients with category-specific impairments. The first patient (C.H.C.) was documented as having "visual agnosia for inanimate objects while recognition and revisualisation of animate objects was retained". Nielsen (1946) reports as follows:

C.H.C., an unusually well developed and muscular self made man of 85 years who had during most of his life despised scientific medicine, was well until Dec. 21, 1937, when he woke at 3 in the morning unable to move his lower limbs. During the previous evening he had taken his usual walk of several miles about his estate for the exercise which he believed was the basis of his marvellous constitution . . . One morning in March 1938 the patient had a "dizzy spell" after which he said he could not understand what he saw printed. Examination disclosed visual verbal agnosia and agraphia except for retained ability to write his name . . . When a derby hat was held up before him he was unable to recognize it, even when he was allowed to hold it . . . He similarly failed to recognize a desk telephone by sight or by touch or by both. He did not recognize food until he had tasted it . . . Automobiles through the window were strange to him and he asked what "those things" were. Yet with all this visual disability relative to inanimate objects he recognized and revisualized all living things. He knew his most intimate friend, his doctor, and the six nurses in attendance. When it became so evident that he was drawing a sharp line between animate and inanimate objects, both for recognition and revisualization, a flower was presented to him and he was asked what it was. He immediately named it (a daffodil) correctly. He knew other flowers also, and not only identified them, but named them.

Nielsen (1946) reported a second case study of a patient, Flora D., with the reverse impairment to C.H.C.: she had "visual agnosia for animate objects with retained recognition of inanimate ones".

Flora D., a legal stenographer aged 46 years, was admitted Oct. 17, 1941 . . . She correctly identified a penknife, a watch dangling from a chain, a pen, and a pencil, though she failed to recognize a key and a coin . . . She could not recognize that any person's face was a face though she said that it was pink . . . Revisualization as well as recognition of inanimate objects was good. She described the local city hall, streets and directions. She also revisualized the colours of a canary bird, the ocean etc. We neglected to test for revisualization of animate objects until it was too late".

Flora D. had a left occipital lobe lesion and C.H.C. had a left temporal and right occipital lesion and on the basis of these two case studies, Nielsen (1946) suggested that recognition of animate and inanimate objects might be based on anatomically distinct brain regions.

. . . as the patient [Flora D.] failed to recognize animate objects while still able to recognize inanimate ones, it is tempting to postulate that the inanimate objects were recognized by means of the right occipital lobe. In a case previously reported [C.H.C.] the patient showed the reverse of this clinical picture through destruction of the right occipital lobe, i.e., he failed to recognize inanimate objects but he recognized animate ones . . . one occipital lobe may serve in recognition of animate objects while the other serves for inanimate ones".

Nielsen's reports of neuropsychological patients provide interesting reading and his basic hypothesis that our representations of living and nonliving things may dissociate is still an important idea in cognitive neuropsychology today. However, Flora D. and C.H.C. seem to provide a clearer dissociation between recognising faces and objects (see Chapter 8) rather than a more general dissociation between all living things (including animals and plants) and nonliving things. For example, Nielsen reported that C.H.C. could name his doctors, nurses and friends but not nonliving things such as a hat or a telephone. Flora D., on the other hand, could not recognise any faces but could name nonliving things such as a watch and a pencil. The only piece of evidence that Nielsen reported to suggest the dissociation was more general was that C.H.C. could name faces and also flowers, but not manmade objects.

MODERN CASE STUDIES OF CATEGORY-SPECIFIC RECOGNITION IMPAIRMENTS

Warrington and Shallice (1984) reported the first systematic study of patients with category-specific recognition impairments. One of their patients (J.B.R.) contracted herpes simplex encephalitis when he was a young man (23 years old) studying at university. Following his illness, a CT scan revealed bilateral damage to the temporal lobes. A cognitive neuropsychological assessment showed that he had a verbal IQ of 102 and a performance IQ of 78 (on the WAIS). His spontaneous speech was relatively fluent and articulation and syntax were reported to be intact. His low-level perceptual skills were also generally preserved (e.g. he could match two different views of the same object) but he had severe problems in recognising everyday objects and faces that should have been familiar to him. He also showed dense retrograde and anterograde amnesia.

Warrington and Shallice (1984) were particularly interested in J.B.R.'s object recognition impairment and, to examine his performance on different categories, they gave him 48 coloured pictures of animals and plants and 48 coloured pictures of nonliving objects. Across categories, the items were matched for the frequency of their names. J.B.R. was asked to name each picture (or identify it by giving specific semantic information about that item) and also to define the corresponding words. J.B.R. correctly identified 90% of the pictures of nonliving things but only 6% of the living things. He was also significantly better at defining the names of nonliving things (79% correct) compared to living things (8% correct). His definitions for nonliving things were relatively detailed. For example, he defined a tent as a "temporary outhouse, living home", a compass as a "tool for telling direction you are going" and a torch as a "hand held light". However, his definitions of living things were sparse and he only seemed able to access very general information about the items. For example, for a daffodil he said "a plant", for snail he said "an insect animal" and for a parrot he said "I don't know".

Warrington and Shallice (1984) also assessed J.B.R.'s ability to identify food items. He was asked to name 30 coloured pictures of food items and 30 pictures of nonliving things. He was then asked to describe each item when given its name. J.B.R. was better at naming the pictures of nonliving things (40%) compared to the food items (20%), and also better at providing definitions given the names of nonliving things (77%) compared to food items (30%). On a separate day, J.B.R. was asked to gesture how he would eat the food items (e.g. banana, spaghetti) or use the nonliving things (e.g. skipping rope, umbrella). Again, he showed preserved knowledge about nonliving things (65%) compared to food items (20%).

Warrington and Shallice (1984) argued that J.B.R.'s difficulty in recognising living things was a semantic memory impairment since his early visual processing abilities were relatively intact. The intriguing question is, of course, why the impairment was limited to living things. One might argue that the data lend support for the idea that biological category is a fundamental organising principle of semantic memory (Nielsen, 1946). However, Warrington and Shallice (1984) offered an alternative explanation. They suggested that living and nonliving things might be stored in separate systems, not by virtue of their biological category, but because they depend on different types of information for identification. In particular, Warrington and Shallice (1984) argued that to distinguish between living things requires access to fine-grained sensory information but to distinguish between nonliving things depends on accessing stored functional information. For example, they suggested that to identify a strawberry, and to distinguish it from a raspberry, one would need to access relatively fine-grained information about its perceptual features, such as its colour, shape, size and texture. However, to identify a pencil, and to distinguish it from chalk, which is also used for drawing, requires access to precise functional information, such as the writing surface on which the target item is characteristically used (i.e. drawing paper rather than a blackboard). Warrington and Shallice (1984) suggested that a semantic system based on functional information might have evolved for the identification of nonliving things, and a separate semantic system based on sensory information for the identification of living things.

In a previous paper, Warrington and Shallice (1979) distinguished between two forms of semantic memory impairment, degraded semantic representations and impaired access routes to those representations, and they also outlined a number of criteria to distinguish between these two types of disorder (though see Forde & Humphreys, 1995, 1997; Rapp & Caramazza, 1993, for counter arguments to these claims). Warrington and Shallice (1979) suggested that degradation to stored semantic representations would be characterised by item-specific consistency over time, relatively preserved knowledge about high-frequency items, preserved superordinate knowledge compared to basic or subordinate information and no facilitation from semantic priming. On the other hand, an access disorder would be characterised by no item-specific consistency over time, no difference between high and low frequency items and no advantage for accessing superordinate information. They also predicted that patients with an access disorder would benefit from semantic priming. Warrington and Shallice (1984) were interested to see if J.B.R. had degraded semantic knowledge about living things or impaired access to otherwise intact representations.

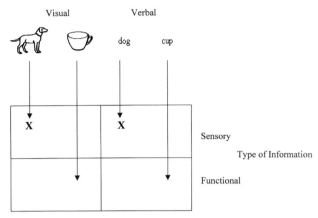

FIG. 6.1   Semantic memory is divided by modality and type of information stored. According to this account, J.B.R. has functionally independent impairments in the "visual/sensory" and "verbal/sensory" semantic systems (Warrington & Shallice, 1984).

J.B.R. was asked to name 40 pictures (mainly nonliving things) and to define the corresponding names. The picture-naming experiment was repeated later in the day to assess J.B.R.'s consistency on specific items within a modality. J.B.R. named 68% of the pictures on time 1 and on time 2 and gave correct definitions of 78% of the words. He showed item-specific consistency over time (for the picture-naming task), but not between picture naming and word definition. Warrington and Shallice (1984) suggested that the within-modality, item-specific consistency over time (between pictures on time 1 and time 2) reflected damage to stored semantic representations, rather than an impairment in accessing semantic memory from a particular modality. However, J.B.R. did not show item-specific consistency across modalities (words and pictures). To explain this inconsistency across modalities, Warrington and Shallice (1984) proposed that J.B.R. had impairments in two functionally independent semantic systems: a visual semantic system which would store information that could be accessed by pictures (or objects) and a separate verbal semantic system which would store information that could be accessed by words.

This visual/verbal distinction was orthogonal to the sensory/functional distinction so that semantic knowledge was divided up into a number of components, as shown in Fig. 6.1. According to this model of semantic memory, J.B.R. would have two functionally independent category-specific impairments: one to the sensory semantic representations accessed by pictures, and one to the sensory semantic representations accessed by words. More recently, Warrington and McCarthy (1994) have reiterated this idea: "in essence, our hypothesis is that processing domain (e.g. visual semantics vs verbal semantics) is orthogonal to category-specificity". McCarthy and Warrington (1994) also speculated on how these systems might develop. They suggested that children would acquire a visual semantic system first (as they started to recognise objects in the world) and then a verbal semantic system would develop by mirroring established representations within the visual semantic system. Consequently, the "ontologically primitive segregation of knowledge into 'biological' (sensory) and 'non-biological' (functional) protoconcepts might be carried over as a blueprint for organising verbal knowledge."

A somewhat different position was adopted by Warrington and McCarthy (1987), who modified the rather rigid distinction between sensory and functional semantics. They drew upon Lissauer's (1890) ideas on how we might learn and store information about objects. Lissauer (1890) suggested that

> the recognition of an object can only occur when at the time of its perception a number of ideas are evoked which relate to that object. These bring into consciousness those characteristics which the mind has learned to associate with it and those conditions in which it has been experienced previously . . . memories laid down through different sensory modalities contribute to these associations but it is only when they are brought into awareness and linked with the percept that the recognition of an object becomes complete.

He used the example of a violin to illustrate his ideas: "For anyone who has some knowledge of this instrument, there exist a number of recollections associated with its image, its name, its sound, the sensation and the tactile experiences which go along with handling it. In addition there will be the mental image of a violinist in his characteristic pose. It is only when the linkage between the percept of the instrument and such associated recollections occur promptly in consciousness that the individual will be able to interpret the object as a musical instrument, differentiate it from other instruments, and thus categorise it" (translations from Shallice & Jackson, 1988).

Warrington and McCarthy (1987) also proposed that semantic representations of objects would comprise information from a number of sensory (e.g. visual, tactile and olfactory) and motor channels, which would have different weightings (or importance) for different items. This system could be relatively complex because within each sensory channel (e.g. vision), there could be more fine-grained channels (e.g. colour, shape, size) which would have separate weightings. They suggested that "the information from each of the relevant channels would make a different quantitative contribution to the overall computational processes involved in the initial acquisition and comprehension of meaningful stimuli." Figure 6.2 illustrates the type of information that might be acquired through a particular sensory or motor channel. According to this model, living things (such as fruit and vegetables) would have relatively high weightings in the sensory channels and nonliving things in the motor channels, but they would not be

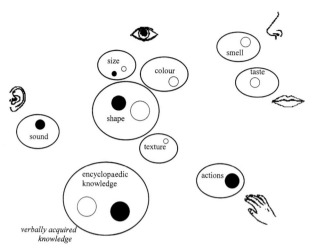

FIG. 6.2 Multimodal distributed semantic knowledge (Warrington & McCarthy, 1987). The distribution of stored knowledge across sensory and motor channels will differ for living things, such as fruit (grey circles), and nonliving things, such as tools (black circles).

stored in two functionally independent systems. This model is a more distributed, amodal account of semantic memory which resembles models outlined by Allport (1985), Damasio (1989), and Shallice (1988).

CATEGORY-SPECIFIC RECOGNITION IMPAIRMENTS: AN ARTIFACTUAL FINDING?

Warrington and Shallice (1984) proposed that living and nonliving things differ in the type of information that is necessary for recognition. However, living and nonliving things may also differ in a number of other respects. For example, we tend to see and use nonliving things everyday but have less direct experience with many living things (e.g. foreign animals). Living things (especially animals) also tend to be more visually complex than nonliving things. Funnell and Sheridan (1992) suggested that J.B.R.'s particular problem with living things may have been an artifactual finding resulting from differences between the categories in uncontrolled variables which can affect object recognition and naming (such as name frequency, concept familiarity and visual complexity).

Funnell and Sheridan (1992) reported a case study of a patient, S.L., who had been injured in a car accident when he was 20 (in 1987). Following the accident a CT scan showed contusions and oedema in the right cerebral hemisphere and a craniotomy was carried out which resulted in right temporal lobe damage. One year after the operation, she had a verbal IQ of 50 and a performance IQ of 78 (on the WAIS). In the first experiment S.L. named a set of pictures and defined the corresponding written and spoken words. The picture naming test and defining written words test were repeated on a separate occasion to assess within-modality, item-specific consistency over time. Funnell and Sheridan (1992) found that S.L. was highly consistent both within and across tasks, and argued that this pointed to a single locus of impairment within a unitary semantic system accessed by all modalities (rather than the multiple semantics model outlined by Warrington and Shallice (1984)).

Funnell and Sheridan (1992) also found that, combining across tasks, S.L. was significantly better with nonliving things compared to living things. For example, she defined a duck as, "one that walks, not sure" and for grapes said, "I don't know". In contrast, her definitions of nonliving things were relatively good. She defined an umbrella as something "to hold up if it's raining to protect you" and a glove as something "to wear on a very cold day, one on each hand".

However, S.L.'s performance was also affected by the familiarity of the item and in a second experiment, Funnell and Sheridan assessed the relative importance of semantic category (living/nonliving) and concept familiarity. S.L. was presented with a set of 48 pictures which were matched for familiarity, frequency and visual complexity. Half the pictures were highly familiar and half were less familiar. Within each familiarity band, half the pictures depicted living things and half nonliving things. With this set of carefully matched pictures, S.L.'s naming performance was still significantly affected by familiarity but no longer by semantic category. Funnell and Sheridan concluded that

> apparent category-specific deficits for the processing of living things arise from the fact that most items that can be classified as living things are relatively poorly represented by those properties responsible for success in tasks of object naming and identification (i.e. familiarity; name frequency; and in the case of some patients, the simplicity of the visual form). When such factors are not properly controlled, category-specific disorders will emerge.

Stewart, Parkin, and Hunkin (1992) reported a similar case study to Funnell and Sheridan and also drew very similar conclusions. They argued that studies of category-specific naming impairments had failed to control for variables such as frequency, familiarity and visual complexity, and concluded that, "at present, there is no convincing evidence to support the theory that semantic memory is organised into dissociable categories of living and nonliving things."

Interestingly, Funnell and Sheridan (1992) re-analysed J.B.R.'s naming performance on different categories, using the data reported in Warrington and Shallice (1984), and found that there was a significant correlation between the mean familiarity rating for the items in a particular category and J.B.R.'s ability to name items from that category. Funnell and Sheridan (1992) highlighted familiarity as a particularly important factor in determining naming performance and suggested that this was because familiarity reflects how much direct experience we have had with an object. Although animals, birds and insects may be relatively common, we do not have as much direct sensory experience of them compared to familiar manmade objects, which we can manipulate and examine more closely. This additional sensory experience facilitates object naming for nonliving things.

In a recent follow-up study on J.B.R., Funnell and De Mornay Davies (1996) specifically examined the effects of category, familiarity and frequency on his naming performance. They presented J.B.R. with a set of pictures of 54 living things and 54 nonliving things which were matched for concept familiarity and word frequency. There were 36 highly familiar items and 72 less familiar items, with equal numbers of living and nonliving things in each set. Funnell and De Mornay Davies (1996) found that there was no difference between living (67%) and nonliving things (72%) for the highly familiar items, but the advantage for nonliving things (reported by Warrington and Shallice, 1984) remained for the less familiar items (11% and 44% for living and nonliving things, respectively). This study highlights the importance of controlling for factors known to affect object naming, such as familiarity, but it appears that J.B.R.'s category-specific effect was still robust, at least for low-frequency items.

In a second test, J.B.R. was asked to provide definitions of the same items when given a spoken name. Again, there was no significant difference in his definitions for living and nonliving things for the highly familiar items (83% correct on both categories), but he was significantly better with nonliving things (58%) compared to living things (11%) for the less familiar items. Interestingly, there was no significant difference between J.B.R.'s performance on naming pictures and in defining spoken names and there was a significant degree of item-specific consistency across the two tasks. This contrasts with the earlier study on J.B.R. (Warrington & Shallice, 1984), which used the lack of consistency across modalities to argue for the existence of modality-specific semantic systems: visual and verbal semantics. Indeed, for J.B.R. there appear to be at least three pieces of evidence that point to a rather different conclusion, namely that there is a single impairment within a unitary semantic system that is accessed both by words and pictures (Caramazza, Hillis, Rapp, & Romani, 1990; Riddoch, Humphreys, Coltheart, & Funnell, 1988): (1) the item-specific consistency between modalities when a larger set of items was used, (2) the fact that J.B.R. shows a category-specific impairment for living things on picture naming and word definition, and (3) the similar overall levels of performance with words and pictures.

CATEGORY-SPECIFIC RECOGNITION IMPAIRMENTS: A RETURN TO THE IDEA THAT THESE MIGHT REFLECT DAMAGE TO A CATEGORICALLY ORGANISED KNOWLEDGE SYSTEM

In another important study on category-specificity, Sartori and Job (1988) suggested that recognition impairments for one particular semantic category may not necessarily reflect an impairment at the semantic level. Recognition of visually

FIG. 6.3   Example of a real and an unreal animal from an object decision task.

presented objects requires access to stored perceptual knowledge (structural descriptions) prior to semantic knowledge and Sartori and Job (1988) suggested that these presemantic structural descriptions may be categorically organised and selectively damaged in some patients. They reported a case study of a patient (Michelangelo) who, like J.B.R., sustained bilateral damage to the anterior temporal lobes following herpes simplex encephalitis. Following his illness, he had a verbal IQ of 82 and a performance IQ of 76 (on the WAIS). Michelangelo was presented with all 260 Snodgrass and Vanderwart (1980) pictures to name. He was significantly impaired at naming the line drawings compared to controls, and was particularly poor at naming animals (32%) and fruit and vegetables (36%) compared to nonliving things (75%). This was particularly striking since Michelangelo was an employee and active member of the World Wildlife Fund and before his illness would have known large numbers of different animals, fish, and birds.

Michelangelo did not have any general early visual processing impairments. For example, he was able to match two views of a target object regardless of its category. He was also able to name overlapping figures, name objects in unusual orientations, decide whether a line drawing depicted a real object or not and draw from memory, provided the stimuli were nonliving things. However, his drawings of living things were very impoverished and he was at chance on deciding whether a drawing depicted a real animal or not (e.g. see Fig. 6.3).

Sartori and Job (1988) assessed Warrington and Shallice's (1984) claim that category-specific impairments emerge from damage to a perceptual/sensory semantic system. Sartori and Job argued that if the impairment was fundamentally attribute specific (i.e. for perceptual properties rather than living things), Michelangelo should be impaired on all categories when tasks demanded the retrieval of relatively fine-grained perceptual information. However, Michelangelo was at ceiling when asked to provide the important features that distinguished between two nonliving things (e.g. a cup and a bowl), but he was impaired when the stimuli were living things (e.g. a tiger and a leopard, a strawberry and a gooseberry); consequently, Sartori and Job (1988) rejected Warrington and Shallice's (1984) hypothesis. Instead they argued that Michelangelo's fundamental problem was with living things. In addition, Sartori and Job (1988) suggested that since Michelangelo was poor at deciding whether a drawing depicted a real animal or not, a test that could be performed by accessing presemantic structural descriptions (see Riddoch & Humphreys, 1987), the locus of his impairment may be to a presemantic, categorically organised structural description system. Note, however, that there are case reports of patients with category-specific impairments who perform well on object decision for all categories, suggesting that category-specific impairments may emerge at different levels within the object recognition system (Humphreys, Riddoch, & Quinlan, 1988; Sheridan & Humphreys, 1993).

CATEGORY-SPECIFIC RECOGNITION IMPAIRMENTS: THE IMPORTANCE OF CATEGORY STRUCTURE

Humphreys et al. (1988) offered a further possible explanation for category-specific impairments in naming living things. Like Sartori and Job (1988), they suggested that these impairments may result from damage to presemantic representations, but suggested that the effects were related to the structural similarity between items within a category and not to a biological distinction between living and nonliving things. Within their model of object recognition there are three levels of representation: the structural description, semantic representations and phonological representations (see Fig. 6.4). The visual properties of objects necessary for identification would be stored in the structural description system, the functional and associative properties of objects in the semantic system, and the phonological representation in a phonological output lexicon. Humphreys et al. (1988) suggested that, when objects are viewed, a number of exemplars could be activated in parallel within each level of representation. For example, when a picture of an apple is presented, the structural descriptions of all items which share visual features with an apple (e.g. orange, pear) will be activated simultaneously. In order to allow the target item to be selected, there is competition between the activated representations, with strongly activated representations inhibiting those less strongly activated. This model operates in "cascade" so that the semantic and phonological representations of an item can be activated before processing is complete at the structural description level. Consequently, the semantic and phonological representations of items structurally similar to the target will also be activated before the target is selected. For example, as shown in Fig. 6.4, when an apple is presented, the semantic and phonological representations of structurally similar items such as an orange and a pear will also be activated.

Humphreys et al. (1988) showed that normal subjects took longer to name living things compared to nonliving things. They argued that the identification of living things relative to nonliving things required more fine-grained visual information to distinguish a target from its perceptual neighbours. For example,

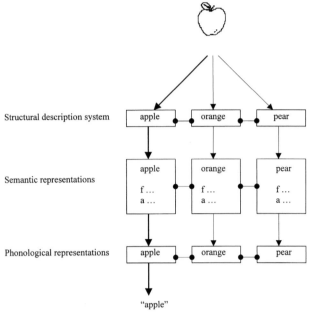

FIG. 6.4   The Cascade model of object naming (Humphreys et al., 1988).
Note: ⟶ represents activation and ●—● represents inhibition. f . . . and a . . . represent functional and associative attributes, respectively.

many animals share the same basic features and overall global shape so, for instance, when a dog is presented, the representations of a number of other animals will also be activated (see Fig. 6.5a). In contrast, nonliving things tend to be more structurally distinct within their category. Consequently, when a target item belongs to a category of structurally dissimilar things, fewer items will be activated at each level of representation. Within the category of kitchen items, a cup may activate the representation of a bowl, but in general, there will be less competition between the target and other activated items compared to a structurally similar category like animals (see Fig. 6.5b).

Gaffan and Heywood (1993) also suggested that living things were more difficult to identify because they belonged to "visually crowded" categories. In an interesting study, they showed that monkeys found it more difficult to learn to distinguish between line drawings of living things compared to nonliving things. Gaffan and Heywood (1993) also reported that there was a relatively steep increase in the difficulty of learning as the number of items increased in the set of living things, but not as items increased in the set of nonliving things. Since the monkeys would not organise their knowledge according to super-ordinate verbal labels (e.g. vegetables, tools, animals, body parts), and since they are not influenced by linguistic variables (e.g. name frequency), Gaffan

(a)

(b)

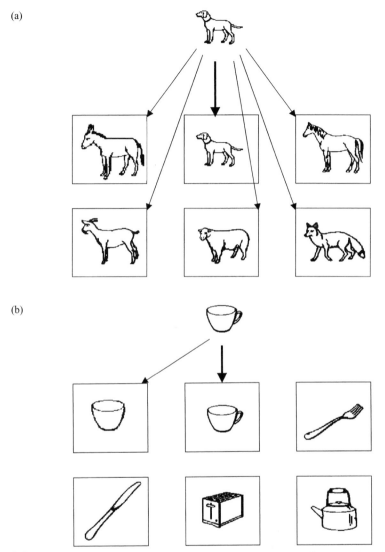

FIG. 6.5   (a) Living things (e.g. animals) belong to structurally similar categories; (b) nonliving things (e.g. kitchen items) belong to structurally disimilar categories.

and Heywood (1993) argued that the particular difficulty the monkeys had with living things must reflect differences in the visual discriminability of the stimuli. They proposed that living things belong to visually crowded categories in which individual exemplars are less visually discriminable. They concluded that category-specific impairments for living things in human patients arise because it is inherently more difficult to differentiate between living things compared to nonliving things. Consequently, patients who have difficulty in forming precise visual representations of objects will present with a relatively more severe impairment in identifying living things.

SUMMARY TO DATE

Despite the large number of reports of patients with category-specific impairments for living things, the case studies of J.B.R., S.L. and Michelangelo have illustrated that there is still considerable debate over the locus (loci) of the impairment in information-processing terms. Nielsen (1946) suggested that living and nonliving things may be represented in anatomically distinct brain areas. This view is reflected in functional models which hold that category-specific impairments for living things are due to selective damage within knowledge systems representing either: (1) pre-semantic structural knowledge (Sartori & Job, 1988); (2) multimodal semantic knowledge (Sheridan & Humphreys, 1993); or (3) semantic knowledge specific to each input modality (Warrington & McCarthy, 1994). Others have suggested that the problems do not reflect the biological category of the stimulus per se, but rather: (1) whether perceptual or functional information is required for identification (Warrington & Shallice, 1984; see also Farah & McClelland, 1991); (2) differences in name frequency, concept familiarity or visual complexity between the stimuli (Funnell & Sheridan, 1992; Stewart et al., 1992); or (3) the degree of differentiation required between category members for identification to proceed (Gaffan & Heywood, 1993; Humphreys et al., 1988).

In a recent paper, Forde, Francis, Riddoch, Rumiati, and Humphreys (1997) attempted to assess a number of questions arising from these different theoretical perspectives: (1) are category-specific impairments theoretically interesting or do they simply reflect differences in variables already known to affect naming performance (such as familiarity, frequency, and visual complexity)? (2) how important is perceptual overlap within a category? (3) if category-specific impairments are theoretically interesting, do they necessarily reflect damage at a semantic level? and (4) can category-specific impairments be restricted to one type of stimulus (e.g. visually presented objects but not written words or spoken names)?

S.R.B.

Forde et al. (1997) reported a case study of a patient (S.R.B.) who sustained damage to the left inferior medial temporal lobe extending posteriorly into the occipital lobe, following what appeared to be an arteriovenous malfunction. S.R.B.'s verbal IQ was 81 and his performance IQ was 99 on the WAIS. He had 12 years of school education and was working as a plumber prior to his brain injury. He showed no signs of low-level perceptual impairments (e.g. he could

TABLE 6.1
Mean reaction times and number correct for
different categories

Category	RT	Number correct	
Living things			
Animals	3,743	31/35	(89%)
Birds	4,051	7/8	(88%)
Insects	4,520	8/9	(89%)
Fruit	3,707	10/13	(77%)
Vegetables	13,966	4/10	(40%)
Mean	4,572	60/75	(80%)
Nonliving things			
Tools	1,112	10/10	(100%)
Vehicles	1,909	9/9	(100%)
Household items	1,654	24/25	(96%)
Furniture	1,612	6/6	(100%)
Clothes	1,625	20/20	(100%)
Mean	1,710	69/70	(99%)

Note: RTs are given in milliseconds

match two views of the same object) or unilateral visual neglect (e.g. he made no errors on star cancellation). However, S.R.B. reported problems in naming objects and faces. In particular, S.R.B. had problems in naming fruit and vegetables when he went shopping and consequently, we were interested to see if he showed a category-specific impairment for all living things compared to nonliving things. He was presented with all 260 Snodgrass and Vanderwart (1980) pictures and asked to name them as quickly and accurately as possible. We found that S.R.B. was significantly worse at naming living compared to nonliving things in terms of both accuracy and reaction time (see Table 6.1). To ensure that this category-specific impairment was not an artefact reflecting differences in the frequency, familiarity or visual complexity between categories, we submitted his reaction times to a multiple regression with the factors category (living/nonliving), name frequency, concept familiarity and visual complexity. We found that the only variable to significantly affect his performance was category, and concluded that S.R.B.'s impairment with fruit, vegetables and animals was not because they were less familiar, less frequent or more visually complex than nonliving things. However, in this experiment category was confounded with structural similarity and in a second regression analysis on a subset of the pictures we included a measure of structural similarity (the percentage of contour overlap between exemplars). In this second analysis we found that S.R.B.'s naming performance was significantly affected by contour overlap, but not by category, familiarity, name frequency or visual complexity. This analysis suggests that structural similarity, and not category, may be the most important factor accounting for S.R.B.'s inability to name living things.

Humphreys et al. (1988) suggested that naming of an exemplar from a category of structurally similar things required access to relatively fine-grained perceptual information. From this we may predict that S.R.B. should be impaired at naming all items which require differentiation from a relatively large set of structurally similar items, regardless of category. To assess the relative importance of category and structural similarity, we presented S.R.B. with two sets of colour photographs of structurally similar items, one of nonliving things (cars) and one of living things (dogs). S.R.B. was interested in both categories premorbidly and his wife reported that, prior to his brain injury, he would have been able to name all the stimuli presented. S.R.B. scored 4/23 (17%) with the set of dogs and 8/14 (57%) with the cars. He was significantly impaired on both categories compared to his wife (who scored 20/23 (87%) and 13/14 (93%) on dogs and cars, respectively). These results indicate that S.R.B. was relatively poor at retrieving subordinate names for nonliving as well as living things (cars as well as dogs): that is, his difficulties were not completely restricted to living things when more detailed visual differentiation was required to name nonliving things. We concluded that recognition impairments that are predominantly for living things are theoretically interesting, but can reflect differences in the structural similarity between exemplars within a category rather than any biological distinction.

To assess S.R.B.'s ability to access relatively detailed information about the visual properties of objects, he was asked to name definitions that stressed different types of knowledge. For each item (e.g. squirrel) there was a definition that stressed visual/perceptual properties (e.g. a small animal with a long fluffy tail. It may be rusty red or grey in colour) and another based on functional/encyclopaedic properties (e.g. this animal stores nuts in winter). Overall, S.R.B. was significantly impaired at naming the visual/perceptual definitions (39/76, 51%) compared to the functional/encyclopaedic definitions (73/76, 96%) (see also Gainotti & Silveri, 1996; Silveri & Gainotti, 1988).

In addition, S.R.B. was impaired at drawing living things relative to nonliving things from memory and also in describing the perceptual differences between two items when they were two animals (e.g. a donkey and a zebra) or two fruits (e.g. apricot and plum), but not when they were two nonliving things (e.g. a match and a toothpick). He was also significantly worse at providing the correct colour for living (22/44, 50%) compared to nonliving things (30/33, 91%). These tests suggest that there is a correlation between S.R.B.'s ability to name objects and to remember their visual/perceptual features. This lends support for Humphreys et al.'s (1988) hypothesis that there may be a causative link between loss of visual knowledge and category-specific impairments for "living things": these categories are particularly vulnerable because differentiating between the exemplars requires access to fine-grained visual information.

This visual information may be stored separately from other types of semantic information (Warrington & Shallice, 1984), represented in specialised areas within a distributed unitary semantic system (Allport, 1985; Shallice, 1988; Warrington & McCarthy, 1987) or in presemantic structural descriptions (Humphreys et al., 1988; Sartori & Job, 1988). S.R.B. was impaired on object decision tasks with living things compared to nonliving things, suggesting that the locus of his impairment may be within the structural description system. This suggests that representations within the structural description system are not only involved in on-line visual recognition but in all tasks that require access to the visual properties about objects, such as drawing from memory or describing the perceptual differences between objects (Riddoch et al., 1988).

We were also interested in assessing Warrington and Shallice's (1984) claim that different types of stimuli (in particular, objects and words) would access functionally independent semantic stores (visual and verbal semantics, respectively) (see also McCarthy & Warrington, 1994; Warrington & McCarthy, 1994). Warrington and Shallice (1984) formulated this hypothesis to explain why J.B.R. did not show item-specific consistency across pictures and words, despite having a category-specific impairment when presented with stimuli in these two modalities. Their model predicts that patients could show a category-specific impairment when tested in one modality (say, with objects or pictures), but not with another (e.g. with words or perhaps from taste or touch). However, on more detailed testing, with a larger number of items, Funnell and De Mornay Davies (1996) found that J.B.R. did in fact show significant item-specific consistency and argued that this pointed to a unitary semantic representation which could be accessed by all modalities. We presented S.R.B. with a set of 41 real objects to name from vision: 20 nonliving objects and 21 fruit and vegetables. On a separate occasion he was blindfolded and asked to name a subset of these objects from touch. Following this, he was asked to name a subset of the items from taste. S.R.B. was significantly better at naming the nonliving objects from vision and touch (20/20 (100%) for both modalities) compared to the fruit and vegetables (12/21 (57%) and 9/18 (50%), respectively). In addition, he was relatively poor at naming the fruit and vegetables from taste (3/9 (33%) correct). Interestingly, S.R.B. showed a relatively high degree of item-specific consistency across naming from vision, taste and touch: he was consistent for 8/13 (62%) of the items that were presented in all three modalities. In a separate experiment, we found that there was significant item-specific consistency between S.R.B.'s ability to name photographs (of fruit, vegetables and faces) and to provide definitions from the spoken names. To accommodate S.R.B.'s data within the model of semantic memory outlined by Warrington and Shallice (1984) one would have to argue that S.R.B. had very similar, but functionally independent impairments to visual semantics, verbal semantics and presumably to "tactile semantics" and "taste semantics", if these also have modality-specific semantic representations. A more parsimonious explanation would be that S.R.B. had sustained damage to representations of "living things" which could be accessed from all modalities (visual objects, taste, touch, words). Interestingly, the results suggest that if this problem lies in the structural description system or in regions of a distributed semantic store specialised for visual information, then these knowledge systems are recruited when objects are named from all modalities (including touch and taste). For instance when naming a strawberry from taste, we might need to re-activate knowledge of what a strawberry looks like.

CATEGORY-SPECIFIC IMPAIRMENTS FOR NONLIVING THINGS

Given the relatively large number of reports of category-specific impairments for living things and the interest in understanding why this deficit may arise, it is striking that there have been only a handful of reports of patients with a recognition disorder restricted to nonliving things. This point in itself merits some thought. According to Humphreys et al. (1988) and Gaffan and Heywood (1993) this may be because living things belong to structurally similar, or visually crowded, categories and are consequently intrinsically more difficult to distinguish from one another. However, according to the models outlined by Warrington and Shallice (1984) or Sartori and Job (1988) there are no a priori reasons why category-specific impairments for living things should be more prevalent.

The first case study of a patient with a category-specific impairment for nonliving things was documented by Nielsen (1946) and has already been described. To summarise briefly, C.H.C. was unable to recognise a car, a hat, or a telephone, despite good recognition of living things, such as faces and flowers. More recently, Warrington and McCarthy (1983, 1987, 1994) have outlined three case studies of patients with global aphasia who had particular problems with nonliving things on matching to sample tasks. For example, in spoken word/picture matching V.E.R. was better with flowers (93%) and animals (86%) compared to nonliving objects (63%) (Warrington & McCarthy, 1983); Y.O.T. was better with animals (86%) and flowers (86%) compared to nonliving objects (67%) (Warrington & McCarthy, 1987); D.R.S. was better with animals (95%) compared to nonliving objects (74%) (Warrington & McCarthy, 1994).

Hillis and Caramazza (1991) reported two case studies of patients with category-specific naming impairments. One patient (P.S.) had a particular impairment with living things (animals and vegetables) and the other (J.J.) with all categories except animals (vegetables, fruit, food, body parts, clothing, transport, and furniture were relatively impaired). Thus Hillis and Caramazza (1991) showed a double dissociation in naming living and nonliving things, using the same items and experimental procedures across patients. They argued that this supported the idea that semantic information was organised along categorical boundaries in the brain. They suggested that semantic information was represented in a distributed network in which exemplars from the same category (e.g. animals) shared features (e.g. four legs, tail, head). Consequently, if some of these semantic features were degraded, all the items (e.g. cat, dog, horse) defined in terms of those features would be impaired (see Damasio, 1990, for a related view). Note also that Hillis and Caramazza (1991) have provided evidence for more fine-grained category-specific impairments than are usually reported, since J.J.'s performance was good with animals but not fruit and vegetables (see also Hart & Gordon, 1992).

Sacchett and Humphreys (1992) also reported a case study of a patient (C.W.) with a category-specific impairment for inanimate objects. C.W. was significantly better at naming line drawings and at performing picture–word matching tasks for living things (despite the fact that they were less familiar, more visually complex and matched on frequency to the nonliving things). Sacchett and Humphreys (1992) suggested that C.W.'s impairment might reflect degraded semantic representations or impaired access routes to the name from semantic memory. They argued that C.W.'s performance provided evidence for the idea that semantic representations are categorically organised, and they outlined a number of possible reasons to explain why the semantic system should be organised in such a way. Firstly, they proposed that our associations would differ for particular object categories; for example, nonliving things would be strongly associated with their corresponding actions, and living things with their sensory properties. Secondly, Sacchett and Humphreys (1992) suggested that not only do the semantic associations differ, but the type of information needed for identification may also differ for the two classes of object. For example, differences in function would be important for distinguishing between nonliving things, but differences in perceptual properties (e.g. colour, size and texture) for living things (Warrington & Shallice, 1984). Thirdly, they proposed that the representation of parts may differ for the two categories: nonliving things might have the same parts but with different spatial arrangements between the parts (e.g. a cup and a bucket); living things (e.g. animals) might have the same parts in the same spatial arrangements, and the scaling of the parts would be the critical factor for identification. They suggested that category-specific impairments for nonliving things might, therefore, arise for a number of reasons: because important semantic associations (e.g. between visual properties and functional properties) had been lost, because functional information critical for object recognition had been lost or because the patient had a deficit in representing the correct position of individual parts. The corollary would be that category-specific impairments for living things may also arise for a number of reasons: because important semantic associations for living things (e.g. between visual properties and smell or taste) had been lost, because visual information critical for recognition had been impaired or because the patient had a deficit in scaling the relative size and shape of the parts. As already discussed, there does seem to be some consistent empirical support for the importance of intact visual knowledge in recognising living things, but the importance of functional information for identifying nonliving things, and the role of the representation of parts in each type of disorder, remain interesting avenues for future research.

REFERENCES

Allport, D.A. (1985). Distributed memory, modular systems and dysphasia. In S.K. Newman & R. Epstein (Eds), *Current perspectives in dysphasia*. Edinburgh: Churchill Livingstone.

Basso, A., Capitani, E., & Laiacona, M. (1988). Progressive language impairment without dementia: A case study with isolated category-specific semantic defect. *Journal of Neurology, Neurosurgery and Psychiatry, 51*, 1201–7.

Caramazza, A., Hillis, A.E., Rapp, B.C., & Romani, C. (1990). The multiple semantics hypothesis: Multiple confusions? *Cognitive Neuropsychology, 7*, 161–89.

Damasio, A.R. (1989). Time-locked multiregional retroactivation: A systems-level proposal for the neural substrates of recall and recognition. *Cognition, 33*, 25–62.

Damasio, A.R. (1990). Category-related recognition defects as a clue to the neural substrates of knowledge. *Trends in Neuroscience, 13*(3), 95–8.

De Renzi, E., & Lucchelli, F. (1994). Are semantic systems separately represented in the brain? The case of living category impairment. *Cortex, 30*, 3–25.

Farah, M.J., & McClelland, J.L. (1991). A computational model of semantic memory impairment: Modality specificity and emergent category specificity. *Psychological Review, 120*, 339–57.

Forde, E.M.E., Francis, D., Riddoch, M.J., Rumiati R., & Humphreys, G.W. (1997). On the links between visual knowledge and naming: A single case study of a patient with a category-specific impairment for living things. *Cognitive Neuropsychology, 14*, 403–58.

Forde, E.M.E., & Humphreys, G.W. (1995). Refractory semantics in global aphasia: On semantic organization and the access-storage distinction in neuropsychology. *Memory, 3*(3/4), 265–307.

Forde, E.M.E., & Humphreys, G.W. (1997). A semantic locus for refractory behaviour: Implications for access-storage distinctions and the nature of semantic memory. *Cognitive Neuropsychology, 14*, 367–402.

Funnell, E., & De Mornay Davies, P.D. (1996). J.B.R.: A re-assessment of concept familiarity and a category specific disorder for living things. *Neurocase, 2*, 461–74.

Funnell, E., & Sheridan, J. (1992). Categories of knowledge? Unfamiliar aspects of living and nonliving things. *Cognitive Neuropsychology, 9*(2), 135–53.

Gaffan, D., & Heywood, C.A. (1993). A spurious category-specific visual agnosia for living things in normal human and nonhuman primates. *Journal of Cognitive Neuroscience, 5*(1), 118–28.

Gainotti, G., & Silveri, M.C. (1996). Cognitive and anatomical locus of lesion in a patient with a category-specific semantic impairment for living beings. *Cognitive Neuropsychology, 13*(3), 357–89.

Hart, J., & Gordon, B. (1992). Neural subsystems for object knowledge. *Nature, 359*, 60–4.

Hillis, A.E., & Caramazza, A. (1991). Category-specific naming and comprehension impairment: A double dissociation. *Brain, 114*, 2081–94.

Humphreys, G.W., Riddoch, M.J., & Quinlan, P.T. (1988). Cascade processes in picture identification. *Cognitive Neuropsychology, 5*, 67–103.

Lissauer, H. (1890). Ein Fall von Seelenblindheit nebst einem Beitrag zur Theorie derselben. *Archiv für Psychiatrie, 21*, 222–70. Edited and reprinted in translation by Shallice, T. & Jackson, M. (1988). Lissauer on agnosia. *Cognitive Neuropsychology, 5*, 157–92.

McCarthy, R., & Warrington, E.K. (1994). Disorders of semantic memory. *Philosophical Transactions of the Royal Society of London, 346*, 89–96.

Nielsen, J.M. (1946). *Agnosia, apraxia, aphasia: Their value in cerebral localization* (2nd edition). New York: Hoeber.

Rapp, B.A., & Caramazza, A. (1993). On the distinction between deficits of access and deficits of storage. *Cognitive Neuropsychology, 10*, 113–142.

Riddoch, M.J., & Humphreys, G.W. (1987). Visual object processing in optic aphasia: A case of semantic access agnosia. *Cognitive Neuropsychology*, *4*(2), 131–85.

Riddoch, M.J., Humphreys, G.W., Coltheart, & Funnell, E. (1988). Semantic system or systems? Neuropsychological evidence re-examined. *Cognitive Neuropsychology*, *5*, 3–25.

Sacchett, C., & Humphreys, G.W. (1992). Calling a squirrel a squirrel but a canoe a wigwam: A category-specific deficit for artefactual objects and body parts. *Cognitive Neuropsychology*, *9*, 73–86.

Sartori, G., & Job, R. (1988). The oyster with four legs: A neuropsychological study on the interaction of visual and semantic information. *Cognitive Neuropsychology*, *5*(1), 105–32.

Shallice, T. (1988). *From neuropsychology to mental structure*. Cambridge: Cambridge University Press.

Shallice, T., & Jackson, M. (1988). Lissauer on agnosia. *Cognitive Neuropsychology*, *5*, 153–92.

Sheridan, J., & Humphreys, G.W. (1993). A verbal-semantic category-specific recognition impairment. *Cognitive Neuropsychology*, *10*(2), 143–84.

Silveri, M.C., & Gainotti, G. (1988). Interaction between vision and language in category-specific semantic impairment. *Cognitive Neuropsychology*, *5*(6), 677–709.

Snodgrass, J.G., & Vanderwart, M. (1980). A standardised set of 260 pictures: Norms for name agreement, familiarity, and visual complexity. *Journal of Experimental Psychology: General*, *6*, 174–215.

Stewart, F., Parkin, A.J., & Hunkin, N.M. (1992). Naming impairments following recovery from herpes simplex encephalitis. *Quarterly Journal of Experimental Psychology*, *44A*, 261–84.

Warrington, E.K. (1981). Concrete word dyslexia. *British Journal of Psychology*, *72*, 175–96.

Warrington, E.K., & McCarthy, R. (1983). Category-specific access dysphasia. *Brain*, *106*, 859–78.

Warrington, E.K., & McCarthy, R. (1987). Categories of knowledge: Further fractionations and an attempted integration. *Brain*, *110*, 1273–96.

Warrington, E.K., & McCarthy, R. (1994). Multiple meaning systems in the brain: A case for visual semantics. *Neuropsychologia*, *32*(12), 1465–73.

Warrington, E.K., & Shallice, T. (1979). Semantic access dysphasia. *Brain*, *102*, 43–63.

Warrington, E.K., & Shallice, T. (1984). Category-specific semantic impairment. *Brain*, *107*, 829–54.

CHAPTER SEVEN

Optic aphasia:
A review of some classic cases

M. Jane Riddoch
School of Psychology, University of Birmingham, UK

INTRODUCTION

Optic aphasia was the term used by Freund (1889) to describe a patient who was unable to name visually presented objects, but who was able to name the same items when they were presented tactilely. However, Freund did not clearly distinguish between a disorder of *visual recognition* and a disorder of *visual naming*. In a later paper he attempted to separate visual agnosia (a modality-specific disorder in which visual recognition is compromised), optic aphasia (a modality-specific disorder in which visual recognition is not compromised), and anomia (a cross modality naming disorder) (see Lhermitte & Beauvois, 1973). In this account the critical defining feature was "intact visual recognition" in addition to the modality specificity of the naming disorder. A paper by Lhermitte and Beauvois in the 1970s described a patient who was always able to gesture the use of objects that he was unable to name (Lhermitte & Beauvois, 1973). Gesturing ability was taken to indicate that visual recognition was intact. More recently, definitions of optic aphasia have been provided by Farah (1990) and Hodges (1994). In both instances, the ability to pantomime the use of a visually presented object (while being unable to name it) is taken as indicating that the object has been recognised. Thus Farah (1990) defines optic aphasia as "A condition in which patients can (1) name an object if it is presented nonvisually (e.g. by hearing a definition of the object), (2) demonstrate their recognition of the object if it is presented visually (e.g. make an appropriate pantomime showing the use of the object), but (3) cannot name the object when presented visually"

133

(Farah, 1990, p. 161). A similar definition is given by Hodges (1994): ". . . patients with optic aphasia can recognise items visually, as demonstrated by their accurate pantomiming of their use, even though they cannot access their names" (Hodges, 1994, p. 84).

According to Freund (1889), the disorder represented a disconnection of the language areas of the left hemisphere from visual information coded via the occipital lobes. The critical lesion was thought to implicate the posterior left hemisphere and include involvement of the corpus callosum (in so far as the association tract between the right occipital visual structures and the left tem- poral region would be impaired). Thus visual processing in the right hemisphere would remain intact and allow access to semantic information in that hemi- sphere (so that recognition occurs), but naming would be impaired as a result of the left hemisphere lesion. Lhermitte and Beauvois (1973) accepted that Freund's (1889) anatomical account of the critical lesion site was consistent with what was known at that time. In the light of the then more recent knowledge, how- ever, they amended the account and proposed that the crucial lesion for optic aphasia would be an interruption of the pathways between the left occipital association areas and the left occipito-temporal region (either the inferior longi- tudinal tract, or the occipital part of the fasciculus arcuatus), and there may also be disruption of the links between the left and right occipital lobes due to damage to the splenium or the white matter of the left occipital lobe (Lhermitte & Beauvois, 1973). In a recent review of the literature, Iorio, Falanga, Fragassi, and Grossi (1992) have proposed that optic aphasia tends to be associated with left unilateral lesions in the infero-temporo-occipital region (100% of the cases they report); while visual associative agnosia is associated with bilateral lesions in the infero-temporo-occipital region (59% of the cases they report) or with left unilateral lesions (41% of the cases they report). Schnider, Benson, and Scharre (1994) have argued that the splenium is involved only in patients with visual naming problems but who always or almost always are able to demonstrate the use of visually presented objects and who have no difficulty using objects.

Since Freund (1889) published his original observations, there have been a number of documented cases of optic aphasia (for a review see Davidoff & De Bleser, 1993), including patients reported by Coslett and Saffran (1989, 1992), Hillis and Caramazza (1995), Lhermitte and Beauvois (1973), Manning and Campbell (1992), and Riddoch and Humphreys (1987a). Each of these groups of authors has put forward a different hypothesis regarding the underlying deficit in optic aphasia. These include accounts in terms of a disconnection between visual processing and verbal semantic systems (Lhermitte & Beauvois, 1973), a disconnection between visual and verbal semantic systems (Beauvois 1982), a disconnection of the visual processing of object shape from stored functional and associative knowledge (Riddoch & Humphreys, 1987a), impairment in a direct route to naming (Davidoff & De Bleser, 1993), a disconnection between processing in the left and right hemispheres (Coslett & Saffran, 1989, 1992), and, finally, it is suggested that optic aphasia results from two separate impairments: a disconnection between visual analysis and semantic representations, and a disconnection between semantic and phonological representations (Farah, 1990; Manning & Campbell, 1992). I shall review these different accounts, and the case studies that have generated them, plus one more recent proposal concerning visual naming disorders generated by Humphreys, Riddoch, and Price (1997). I will highlight some of the differences between the patients and consider both how gestures to visually presented objects may be generated and whether gesturing performance is diagnostic of intact recognition.

LHERMITTE AND BEAUVOIS' (1973) DISCONNECTION ACCOUNT OF OPTIC APHASIA

Lhermitte and Beauvois' (1973) case description was perhaps the first to provide a detailed analysis of optic aphasia. Their patient, J.F., had suffered brain damage as a result of stenosis of the left posterior cerebral artery. As a result he had disturbances of memory and optic aphasia. Critically, he was impaired in his ability to name objects or pictures of objects. Visual perception was thought to be intact as he was able to produce accurate drawings from memory of objects that he had just seen. In addition, his ability to name objects in response to a verbal definition, or on the basis of tactile or auditory cues, was relatively unimpaired. J.F. was also able to point to named objects. Lhermitte and Beauvois (1973) argued that visual recognition was intact because J.F. was able to pantomime correctly the use of objects that he could not name.

Lhermitte and Beauvois performed a detailed analysis of J.F.'s naming errors both to visually presented objects (he named 77% of the items correctly) and to pictures (he named 72% of the items correctly). Most errors (63% of the total error corpus) were classed as "horizontal semantic errors" (taken to reflect a semantic relationship between the stimulus and the incorrect name). This category of errors included semantic errors (34%, e.g. shoe → hat), and mixed visual and semantic errors (20%, e.g. orange → lemon). Visual errors were also included in this category (i.e. 9% of the total error corpus, e.g. coffee beans → hazel nuts). In addition, a large number of errors (29% of the total error corpus) were described as "vertical errors" on the basis of whether they showed some perseverative effect of an earlier presented item. In general, J.F.'s responses were nearly always characterised by the presence of semantic features belonging to the object shown in the picture. On the basis of this last behaviour in particular, Lhermitte and Beauvois argued that the fundamental disorder was "one which disturbed the naming of correctly perceived and recognised objects and pictures of objects . . ." (Lhermitte & Beauvois, 1973, p. 708).

On a small number of occasions, J.F. produced detailed confabulations in response to a pictured object. The confabulations appeared to be directed towards particular visual features of the target picture. J.F. tended to elaborate on the initial response, and as this process continued, he would sometimes produce the correct name for the item. For instance, to the picture of a window blind he said: "a parasol, metallic curtain rods . . . the cloth roof . . . surrounding sails . . . (de la voilure autour . . .) it could be a parasol . . . there are rods, but isn't it a shelter? A window blind . . . not a window blind, the window blind is rolled up, there is no device to roll, a sunshade ('par soleil') . . . it should be a window-blind which does not roll." (page 706; Lhermitte & Beauvois, 1973). In these instances, Lhermitte and Beauvois argued that J.F.'s performance resembled that of an agnosic patient and this led them to query whether in fact visual recognition was entirely normal or whether J.F. in fact was suffering from a mild form of visual agnosia which became apparent when more complex visual stimuli were used. They attempted to assess this hypothesis experimentally by contrasting J.F.'s a ability to name coloured pictures (stimulus items included fruit, vegetables, clothes, "round objects" and "various pictures") with his ability to name black-and-white line drawings (thought to be more perceptually complex) (stimulus items included animals, "long objects", and "various drawings"). J.F. produced significantly more errors with the black-and-white line drawings (the increased errors were of the "horizontal semantic error" type). Lhermitte and Beauvois used these data to support the idea that perceptual complexity had a significant effect on J.F.'s naming. Unfortunately, since the types of item were not balanced in the two modes of stimulus presentation, any conclusions must be cautious. Hillis and Caramazza (1995) performed the same experiment in a more controlled way with their patient D.H.Y. and found that colour had no effect on naming. Hillis and Caramazza also contrasted D.H.Y.'s ability to name items in isolation or in context and found her to be reliably better at naming items in context (i.e. she could name an iron if she was shown a picture of somebody ironing, but she could not name an iron if it was presented in isolation; similar effects have reported by Manning & Campbell, 1992). On the basis of their investigations, Lhermitte and Beauvois concluded that J.F. was suffering from a mild form of visual agnosia, the effects of which were particularly apparent when more demands were placed on visual processing. This mild visual impairment generated problems in accessing verbal semantic knowledge and name information. Some years later, Beauvois (1982) re-evaluated this position and argued that, in the case of J.F., visual recognition was intact. She proposed that, rather than a mild form of visual agnosia, optic aphasia represents a disconnection between visual and verbal semantic systems.

RE-EVALUATION BY BEAUVOIS (1982) OF HER ORIGINAL ACCOUNT: DISCONNECTION ACCORDING TO MODALITY

Beauvois reconsidered the pattern of results shown by J.F. She proposed that visual recognition was in fact intact since even when J.F. misnamed items, he was able to pantomime their use correctly. She also argued that visual semantics were intact since the patient often produced spontaneous drawings from long-term memory of complex scenes. J.F. had been shown to operate verbally to a high level (speech output and semantic processing were shown to be intact). Rather than attributing J.F.'s impaired performance to a mild form of agnosia, Beauvois proposed that it resulted from a disruption of the processes linking visual and verbal processing; that is, visual processes up to and including recognition (access to a visual semantic system) are disconnected from verbal semantic and naming processes (Beauvois, 1982). The verbalisations produced by the patient (see above) were not the result of a "minimal agnosia" but instead represented attempts by the patient to provide himself with "additional auditory verbal information". Often this strategy would result in the correct response. Beauvois argued that a visual–verbal disconnection would particularly affect tasks which required processing by both visual and verbal semantic systems. The evidence used to support this position came from some of J.F.'s drawings. As part of the procedure when J.F. was originally tested, he was asked to draw misnamed pictures from memory. Usually he was able to produce good representations of the target stimulus. On a few occasions however, J.F. started to draw the correct item (due to intact visual imagery), but then added features belonging to the erroneous verbal response. For example, he named an outline drawing of a tree as a leaf, and his resultant drawing from memory represented an amalgam of the correct item (the tree) and the error (the leaf). This behaviour was thought to represent the independent working of visual and verbal semantic systems. Normally, the functioning of one system would be complemented by the other; J.F.'s lesion was thought to have caused a disconnection between the two so that "cross-talk" was not possible (Beauvois, 1982; Beauvois & Saillant, 1985). Confabulation of this sort facilitated J.F.'s performance on some occasions (as when he was asked to name the window blind, see above), but interfered on others (as in his drawing of a tree).

There have been other reports of patients in the literature who have shown similar interference effects of one modality on another (Geschwind & Fusillo, 1966; Marin & Saffran, 1975). Indeed, Geschwind and Fusillo (1966) have argued that most cases of apparent visual agnosia represent a "confabulatory" visual anomia which interferes with otherwise intact recognition capacities (again thought to result from a left splenio-occipital lesion causing disruption of visual input to the receptive language areas of the left hemisphere). The patient reported by Marin and Saffran (1975) provides a striking example of the effects of confabulation on performance. This patient had had a head injury as a result of a fall which resulted in a haematoma in the left anterior temporal lobe. Post-surgical neuropsychological assessment included the Wechsler Adult Intelligence Scale (WAIS: Wechsler, 1955). When presented with the elephant puzzle (a subtest from the WAIS), it was clear from the patient's gestures that he understood the figure to be an elephant, though he could not produce its name. The patient had fluent speech and was allowed to verbalise freely during testing. At one point (when the puzzle was half complete) he called the trunk a mouth. He then began to rearrange the pieces so that a mouth would form part of the object. Consequently, he was not able to finish the puzzle. If verbalisation was prevented (e.g. by asking the patient to count at the same time he was performing another visual task) the task was performed speedily and correctly. This example can be used to support Beauvois' (1982) contention that normal performance requires intact visual and verbal processing together with intact links between the two systems. Patients with optic aphasia will perform poorly on tasks requiring both visual and verbal processing (such as visual naming) if the links between the two processing systems are impaired.

When producing verbal responses, J.F. seemed to focus on the visual properties of objects (Lhermitte and Beauvois, 1973). Thus to the picture of a wastepaper basket he said ". . . made of cane, of osier, a basket." (Lhermitte & Beauvois, 1973, p. 706). In contrast, J.B., an optic aphasic patient reported by Riddoch and Humphreys (1987a) used speech in conjunction with gesture when asked to name visually presented objects. Rather than describing the visual features of the objects, J.B. focused on its functional aspects. For instance, in response to a flat, zipper topped briefcase, J.B. said "Everybody's got one." He gestured unzipping the top and putting something into the case. He then said "You'd put stuff in and carry it around . . . it's a plastic bag." J.B. never used the visual features of the object in his confabulations, but always discussed the object in terms of what action could be performed with it. For example, when presented with a fork he said "I can imagine myself picking it up by the handle and using it. . . . there's one in every bathroom". In this instance, it is possible that the visual features of the object (such as the handle and prongs of the fork) allowed J.B. to guess the appropriate grasp of the item, however, in this instance, they were not sufficient to specify the correct use of the object. Some of the items that J.B. was asked to name had no distinguishing features. For example, on one occasion J.B. was presented with a necktie. This was draped on the table in front of him. To all intents and purposes, a necktie is a strip of cloth, and it is difficult to conceive that as such it might directly "afford" a specific action. Looking at it, J.B. said "I can imagine myself putting one on, but I can't think what it is for." He then gestured the appropriate action of lacing the tie around his neck and making the specific movements with each hand which were appropriate to the tying of the knot. These actions were repeated as J.B. said: "You put it round your neck, and it hangs down there . . ." The actions were repeated again, and J.B. finally produced the name. Was he naming the object, or was he naming the gesture? Even on occasions when he appeared to recognise the object, he would produce the gesture first. Thus when presented with a pair of glasses he said "Oh yes, it's . . ." and then performed the appropriate gesture of arms of the glasses behind each ear before he said "glasses". It appeared as though the gesture facilitated the name of the object.

It may be that confabulation simply represents a strategy used to facilitate impaired naming, as Beauvois (1982) suggested. In some instances the emphasis during confabulation is on the visual features of the object (Beauvois, 1982), in some instances it relates to the function of the object (Riddoch & Humphreys, 1987a), and in others there appears to be a mixture of visual features and functional aspects of the to-be-named object (Peña-Casanova, Roig-Rovira, Bermudez, & Tolosa-Sarro, 1985). Whatever the case, such verbalisations can be seen as an attempt to raise thresholds of activation for a given item, whether the system where sub-threshold activation is achieved is a verbal semantic system as suggested by Beauvois (1982), or an amodal semantic system, the position adopted by Riddoch and Humphreys (1987a) (see below).

ARE VISUAL SEMANTICS INTACT IN OPTIC APHASIA? DISCONNECTION WITHIN MODALITY

Critical to Beauvois' (1982) argument is the claim that visual access to semantic knowledge is intact in optic aphasia. Shortly after the publication of Beauvois' influential account, a patient, J.B., was referred to me and Glyn Humphreys and appeared to exhibit all the classic signs of optic aphasia. J.B.'s ability to name visually presented objects was impaired relative to tactile naming of the same objects and he was usually able to pantomime the use of objects that he was unable to name (Riddoch & Humphreys, 1987a). J.B. had been involved in a road traffic accident which had resulted in fracture of the skull, brain contusion and haematoma. The CT report indicated a large extradural collection which extended into the posterior fossa. The lesion affected the left parieto-occipital lobes. Surgery was necessary in order to evacuate the haematoma. Our investigations with J.B. commenced six months post lesion. There was no evidence of any dysphasia. J.B. had no word-finding difficulties and his spontaneous speech was well formed and grammatical.

Our preliminary investigations were aimed at confirming a diagnosis of optic aphasia. Like J.F., J.B. performed poorly when asked to name visually presented objects (scoring 45.5% correct, indicating a greater impairment than that shown by J.F.); although when asked to name the same objects presented tactilely and with vision excluded he performed at a higher level (scoring 75% correct; J.F. scored 91% correct on a similar task). When asked to name the same objects given an auditory definition of the item, J.B. performed at ceiling. A striking feature of his performance with visually presented objects was his spontaneous tendency to pantomime the use of the object. In many instances he continued to repeat the gesture over and over again, as though by doing so, it would help him to retrieve the name of the object. Indeed, although able to name only 45.5% of visually presented objects, he produced the correct gestures for 45.8% (11/24) of the objects that he had named incorrectly.[1] The gestures made were remarkably object-specific (it was possible to distinguish between his gestures for a knife and a fork according to the hand used for the response). On the basis of this preliminary testing, a diagnosis of optic aphasia was made. J.B. had a modality-specific naming problem (impaired visual naming, intact auditory and tactile naming); his ability to gesture the use of objects he could not name suggested that visual recognition was intact. Our further investigations focused on the extent of J.B.'s ability to process visually presented stimuli, and in particular to determine whether J.B. was able to access semantic information from visually presented stimuli.

Early visual processing in J.B.

Our investigations of J.B. were very much driven by the zeitgeist of the time. An influential functional model of visual processing had recently been proposed by Marr (1982), and we used this model as a basis for understanding the case, devising tests to assess performance at the different visual processing levels specified. Marr (1982) had identified three major representations: the primal sketch (a two-dimensional (2D) view-centred description of the main light-intensity changes in the visual array including information about edges, contours and blobs); the $2\frac{1}{2}$D sketch (view-centred like the primal sketch, but including a description of the depth and orientation of visible surfaces of objects); and the three dimensional sketch (a view-independent 3D description of the shapes of objects and the relative positions of their parts). According to Marr, these representations are encoded hierarchically, and are necessary before recognition systems (stored knowledge) can be tapped.

The ability to copy objects can be taken as a crude assessment of the ability to derive shape information from vision. J.B. was able to copy reasonably well, suggesting that low-level, viewpoint dependent visual processing was intact. Another characteristic of normal visual recognition is that it can occur irrespective of the viewpoint of the target object. We assessed the ability to derive view-independent representations by testing the matching of different views of the same object (see Humphreys & Riddoch, 1984; Warrington, 1982; Warrington & Taylor, 1973, 1978). While J.B. was frequently unable to name the individual items used in the test, his matching performance was at the same level as that of the controls; that is, he appeared to be able to derive a 3D sketch. On the basis of these tests we argued that pre-semantic visual processing was normal in J.B.

---

[1] J.F. (Lhermitte & Beauvois, 1973) was always able to gesture the use of objects that he was unable to name.

Ability to access stored structural and/or associative knowledge from vision

Stored knowledge of object shape and colour.   There are different forms of stored knowledge about objects, built from contrasting experiences. Associative and functional knowledge about objects may be derived on the basis of everyday experience with objects or through learning via reading and/or schooling. Repeated exposure to objects also allows us to store information about visual characteristics such as their typical shape, colour and/or texture. Our tests with J.B. distinguished between assessment of stored visual knowledge (e.g. shape and colour) and stored functional/associative knowledge.

To assess knowledge of object shape we used a series of line drawings which either had a familiar shape (i.e. line drawings of real objects) or an unfamiliar shape (i.e. line drawings of non-objects). Non-objects were created by replacing one part of a line drawing with part of another line drawing (e.g. a kangaroo's tail was replaced by a human foot). J.B. was presented with equal numbers of familiar and unfamiliar line drawings in a mixed pack and was asked to sort them into two piles, one representing familiar and the other unfamiliar objects. J.B. had no difficulty with this task, but since the unfamiliar shapes were derived from items from different categories it may have been easy to differentiate real from unreal objects on the basis of some general visual property (e.g. goodness of shape). We therefore devised another test where non-objects were created by combining the parts of two objects coming from the same category (e.g. replac-ing the head of the kangaroo with the head of a giraffe). In this case, both the real objects and the non-objects had a global outline that could be construed as belonging to the same parent category (e.g. animal). We proposed that, with the new object decision test, access to stored knowledge of object shape was neces-sary in order to distinguish real objects and the non-objects. However, J.B. still performed the task within the control range, allowing us to conclude that he was able to access stored knowledge of object shape from vision.

As well as a characteristic shape, many objects (in particular, natural objects) have a characteristic colour. While knowledge of object shape is likely to be derived principally from vision, knowledge of colour may be derived on the basis of verbal learning as well as from visual input. We performed a number of different tests to assess J.B.'s ability to access colour information, and found that visual tasks in particular were performed very poorly (i.e. unlike J.F., J.B. did not appear to conform to Beauvois' 1982 hypothesis that visual semantics are intact in optic aphasia at least in so far as stored knowledge of colour was concerned). When asked to pick the correctly coloured line drawing given five identical line drawings four of which were coloured incorrectly, J.B. scored only 52.5% correct. Similarly, on a colour decision task where he had to indicate when an item was the correct or incorrect colour he scored at chance (50% correct) (Riddoch & Humphreys, 1987a; see also Price & Humphreys, 1989).

Performance was not much better in "visuo-verbal" tasks. For instance, when asked to name the characteristic colour of a pictured object (a task involving verbal output following visual input) he scored 29.2% correct; he performed only slightly better (but not significantly so) when asked the characteristic colour of an object given its name (47.9% correct) (a task involving verbal input and output but also visualisation of the object; see Beauvois, 1982). Thus, J.B. performed poorly in all tests where he had to access stored visual knowledge of colour. On the other hand, when asked to provide verbal colour associations to a named word (e.g. what colour is associated with jealousy?) he performed well (93% correct).

Since J.B. performed well on tests where items were distinguished on the basis of shape, but poorly on tests assessing colour knowledge, we suggested that knowledge of object colour and shape may be represented independently in the brain, and that these representations may be impaired selectively as a result of brain damage. A similar argument had been made previously. For instance, Lewandowsky's classic case of a patient with object-colour agnosia has been cited as evidence for the separate representation of colour and object shape in the brain (see Davidoff, 1996; Davidoff & De Bleser, 1993). Lewandowsky's patient (originally described in 1908) was unable to categorise and name colours, and was unable to recognise or recall the colours associated with specific objects; nonetheless, his recognition of objects (and his ability to image them, as assessed by drawing from memory) was good.

Our further investigations with J.B. focused on determining what forms of stored knowledge concerning objects attributes J.B. was able to access.

Stored functional and associative knowledge.   We assessed access to stored functional and associative knowledge using two different tasks: a cued definitions task and a semantic matching task. In the cued definitions task J.B. was presented either with a line drawing of an object or its auditorily presented name and was then asked a series of probe questions about that particular object. This approach was a modification of one originally employed by Warrington (1975). Our questions were designed to assess specific information about each individual item, including functional knowledge (what the item might be used for), associative knowledge (what other items might be linked with or related to the target object), and visual knowledge (the items' colour or distinctive features of shape). J.B. performed quite well at answering general questions about objects (such as how the object might be classified) irrespective of whether he was given the name or the picture of the item, but he did not do so well with the more specific questions. He was particularly impaired when the questions were directed at the picture as opposed to the name of the item. From this result we can conclude that either J.B. was impaired at accessing stored associative and functional knowledge from vision, or that he was not able to link the auditory question with the picture in front of him.

In a further test, we tried to contrast performance on a purely visual recognition task with that on a similar purely verbal recognition task. On each trial J.B. was presented with three items, these were either three real objects or the names that corresponded with the three objects. In each instance J.B. was to indicate which two of the three items were more closely related. There were two levels of difficulty. Initially superordinate knowledge was tested (i.e. J.B. had to indicate which two of the three items belonged to the same category), then coordinate information was assessed (here all three items could belong to the same superordinate category, and J.B. had to indicate which two of the three were associated with each other or were used together). When tested with real objects J.B. was asked to point to the matching items, and after the decision had been made, to name all the three items that were present. We found that J.B.'s superordinate knowledge was relatively intact and there was no difference in his performance when presented with real objects or object names. There was also no relationship between J.B.'s ability to name the item and his ability to perform the correct superordinate match. In contrast, in the coordinate task J.B. did very well when presented with the names of objects (scoring 100%), but he made many errors when presented with real objects. On subsequent data analysis, it was apparent that J.B. made correct coordinate matches primarily when he named the objects correctly. J.B.'s performance indicated an impaired ability to access detailed semantic knowledge with visually presented objects, relative to when he had to make judgements on the basis of their names. Nevertheless, he remained able to access broad category knowledge about objects from vision.

J.B. showed a striking contrast in his ability to access from vision—stored knowledge of object shape (which was intact) and stored functional and associative knowledge about objects and stored colour knowledge (all of which were impaired). We took these data to be supportive of models which propose that stored knowledge of object structure is distinct from stored associative and functional knowledge (Humphreys, Riddoch, & Quinlan, 1988; Morton, 1979; Morton & Patterson, 1985). On the basis of our investigations with J.B. we concluded that he was impaired at accessing semantic knowledge about objects from vision, but that semantic knowledge itself was intact, when accessed from other modalities. Also, the disorder in accessing semantic knowledge from vision arose after successful access to stored knowledge about the shape of objects (i.e. after access to stored structural descriptions; see Humphreys et al., 1988).

Recently, Hillis and Caramazza (1995) have published the report of a patient (D.H.Y.) whose performance was similar in many respects to that of J.B.. D.H.Y. suffered two separate strokes, the area of infarction resulting from the first stroke included the corona radiata, the posterior limb of the internal capsule and possibly the superior aspect of the thalamus. The second stroke affected the distribution of the left posterior cerebral artery and particularly the left occipital lobe. Picture naming was poor (25.4% correct); performance was worse than that of J.B., whose errors were largely semantically related to the target, and often showed perseverative features. Tactile naming and naming to definition were intact. Like J.B., D.H.Y. performed well on tests assessing low-level visual processing (delayed copying and matching tasks); she also performed well on tests assessing access to stored structural descriptions (including difficult object decisions). Visual imagery was good (assessed by drawing items from memory). Hillis and Caramazza assessed D.H.Y. on a number of tests of semantics, and argued that while she performed well on many of the tests that have been used in previous studies to assess semantics (e.g. sorting items by category, sorting items by function, picture association, miming etc.) she tended to make errors on tasks which required more specific semantic information for distinguishing among semantically related items (e.g. when she was asked to distinguish between edible vs nonedible animals, or cats vs dogs etc.). Hillis and Caramazza concluded that D.H.Y. (like J.B.) did not have completely intact access to semantic information from vision.

The functional framework used by Hillis and Caramazza to account for the dysfunction shown by patients with optic aphasia is essentially the same as that proposed by Riddoch and Humphreys (1987a). This account, in terms of impaired access to semantic knowledge from vision, can explain many of the performance characteristics of patients with optic aphasia. For instance, patients with optic aphasia (unlike those with visual agnosia) make a high proportion of semantic errors in visual naming tasks. These could reflect the activation of a number of semantically related representations when specific access to a specific representation is precluded. General as opposed to specific access to semantic knowledge would be sufficient to class items according to category (animals vs plants), but specific semantic knowledge is necessary to distinguish between within-category exemplars (airedale vs alsatian dogs). Hillis and Caramazza also argue that incomplete access to semantic knowledge may be sufficient to support gesturing. However, if this was the case, semantic errors may be expected (i.e. gesturing the use of a semantically related item such as a knife for a fork). We shall discuss the issue of gesturing in more detail later in this chapter; at this stage it is relevant to note that J.B. and D.H.Y. (unlike J.F., Lhermitte & Beauvois, 1973) were not always successful in gesturing the use of visually presented objects. However, semantic errors in gesturing were not reported for either patient.

The essence of the Riddoch and Humphreys position was that J.B. did not show intact visual recognition of the items he was unable to name, although his ability to gesture the use of objects appeared to suggest otherwise. This position was therefore closer to the one originally proposed by Lhermitte and Beauvois (1973) than that proposed by Freund (1889) and Beauvois (1982) (who assumed intact visual recognition in optic aphasia); in particular, Riddoch and Humphreys (1987a) regarded both visual agnosia and optic aphasia as impairments of visual recognition. However, we attempted to be more specific than Lhermitte and Beauvois in that we identified the level of visual processing at which the deficit occurred; for J.B., we suggested that the deficit reflected poor access to stored

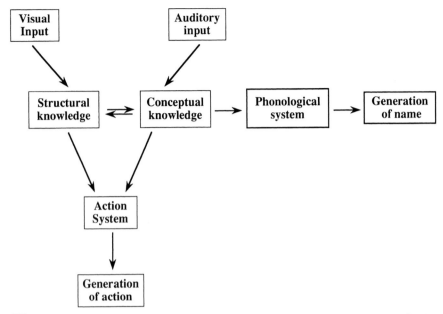

FIG. 7.1   Illustrating the model devised by Riddoch and Humphreys (1987a) to account for the functional locus of J.B.'s lesion. J.B. was able to access structural knowledge from vision (he was able to perform object decision tests) but was impaired in accessing conceptual knowledge from vision (he could not decide which two of three visually presented objects—such as a corkscrew, a bottle and a saucepan—were associatively related). As a result, he was impaired at naming visually presented objects. While J.B. was able to access conceptual knowledge from auditory input, he was impaired at drawing items from memory and in describing the appearance of objects (both of these abilities draw on knowledge of object structure). Riddoch and Humphreys therefore concluded that the functional locus of J.B.'s lesion was in the links between conceptual and structural knowledge. They argued that his ability to gesture the use of objects he could not name resulted from intact processing via the links between the action system and structural knowledge.

functional and associative knowledge from vision following intact access to stored knowledge of object shape. The functional locus of this lesion, in terms of the model proposed by Riddoch and Humphreys (1987a), is illustrated in Fig. 7.1.

The recognition deficit shown by patients with visual agnosia can result from damage affecting one or more functional levels in the object recognition system including processes prior to access to stored visual knowledge. However, where the lesion affects those visual processes *after* access to stored visual knowledge about objects, optic aphasia may result because stored visual knowledge may support gesturing performance (see below). It is also likely to be the case that damage can affect access to different degrees to different functional levels post stored visual knowledge, and that there may therefore be a continuum of deficits collectively described as optic aphasia, with some patients having more access to semantic information than others.

Since 1987, when Riddoch and Humphreys put forward their theoretical perspective regarding the status of optic aphasia, several further positions have been proposed, including: the direct route to naming account; the right hemisphere hypothesis; and the superadditive account. Of these three, the right hemisphere hypothesis is the closest to Freund's original conception of optic aphasia (in particular, in its assumption that visual recognition is intact in such patients).

THE DIRECT ROUTE TO NAMING ACCOUNT

Davidoff and De Bleser (1993), on the basis of a review of cases of visual agnosia and optic aphasia, propose that optic aphasia results from impairment to a direct route for visual naming; this "direct" route would pass from the object's structural description to the phonological output lexicon without access to associative or functional knowledge. A similar proposal, which was not elaborated in any detail, had been made by Ratcliff and Newcombe (1982), although Davidoff and De Bleser also suggested that the "direct" route passes from the structural description through object-colour knowledge to phonology. Impairment in the direct route will result in reliance on "indirect routes" to visual naming, via functional and associative knowledge. Davidoff and De Bleser argue that use of the indirect routes, without the support of the direct route, will result in semantic errors when naming visual stimuli.

In order to assess this proposal, Davidoff and De Bleser conducted a retrospective review of (some) cases of patients with either (i) visual agnosia or (ii) optic aphasia. In particular, they attempted to contrast the performance of the two groups of patients on tapping colour knowledge from visual and verbal inputs. In the visual tasks, patients had to recognise either an incorrectly coloured pictured item (i.e. the task was to decide whether the object was coloured correctly or not), or they had to colour in a line drawing; in the verbal tasks, the patient was asked questions of the type "What colour is a banana?".[2] The patients included in Davidoff and De Bleser's (1993) review all had impairments of naming which were specific to the visual modality (i.e. tactile naming and naming to description were unimpaired). The cases were divided into two groups on the basis of whether stimulus quality affected recognition (i.e. the patients were better at naming 3D objects than pictures). Despite the difficulties of categorising patients studied by different investigators (with no congruity of tests or test materials), Davidoff and De Bleser argue that definite consistencies of performance are apparent over the two patient groups. For instance, the errors made by the patients in the first group (where stimulus quality affected performance) were rarely semantic and there was limited ability to gesture the use of

---

[2] Although note that, according to Beauvois (1982) this last task should require activation of stored visual knowledge by the objects name.

items that could not be named. In addition, the patients usually had difficulties in face recognition (prosopagnosia), there was no clear relation between their reading ability and their object naming, and imagery was poor.[3] For patients in the second group (where stimulus quality did not affect performance) predominantly semantic errors were made in naming, patients had no prosopagnosia, and there was an accompanying alexia. It is unfortunate that Davidoff and De Bleser did not perform direct comparisons of the two groups. For instance, gesturing ability (or rather the lack of it) is one of the characteristics of the first group, but Davidoff and De Bleser do not discuss gesturing ability for the second group (possibly because there is a large degree of variability across the different patients; see below). The second group are also not homogeneous in other respects. For instance, as I outline below, the degree of visual access to semantic knowledge varies over different patients. Imagery abilities are also not uniform across the group. J.F. (described by Lhermitte & Beauvois, 1973) showed good visual imagery (on the whole) while visual imagery was very impaired in J.B. (Riddoch & Humphreys, 1987a). Given the variability in the patient groups, Davidoff and De Bleser's (1993) attempts to provide a unitary explanation for optic aphasia must be suspect. One might also question the proposal for a direct visual route to naming on theoretical grounds. Optic aphasic patients usually make semantic errors in visual naming. If their problem were solely in a direct route to naming from a structural description system, this would imply that visually accessed semantics are not normally sufficient to generate a correct name for an object. However, were that the case, then it is unclear how objects can be named from a verbal (semantic) description or how, in everyday life, we are able to generate speech without a referent being directly present. Also when normal subjects are forced to generate errors by making them name to a deadline, they produce names that are both visually and semantically related to the target objects and only small proportions of visual errors occur (Humphreys, Lloyd-Jones, & Fias, 1995; Vitkovitch, Humphreys, & Lloyd-Jones, 1993). On a direct route account, a high proportion of visual errors might be expected (from the direct route). The high proportions of visual semantic errors suggest that naming is semantically mediated, although the semantic information that is accessed is tightly constrained by the visual properties of objects.

---

[3] The fact that Davidoff and De Bleser (1993) report imagery ability in the first group of patients to be poor is not borne out by the data they present. The ability to perform imagery related tasks is not reported for 6 of the 16 cases, and for a further 3 (not including J.B., the patient studied by Riddoch and Humphreys, 1987a) it is reported to be "fair". The imagery in the case of the agnosic patient (H.J.A.) reported by Riddoch and Humphreys (1987b) was also classed as "fair", when it was in fact generally good, and undoubtedly better than that of J.B. (e.g. as assessed by tasks such as drawing from memory). However, H.J.A. was placed in the first group of patients and J.B. in the second, by virtue of their differential sensitivity to stimulus quality. In fact, only 5 of the 16 patients in the first group are reported to have impaired visual imagery.

THE RIGHT HEMISPHERE HYPOTHESIS:
AN ANATOMICAL DISCONNECTION

The right hemisphere hypothesis was originally proposed by McCormick and Levine (1983) to account for the performance of a patient with a left posterior-occipital lesion. The patient was impaired at naming common objects (50% correct), but she could always describe the use of the item or pantomime how it might be used. Tactile naming was intact. The patient rejected incorrect names when they were offered for the object, and she was always able to select the correct name from a number of alternatives. She could not name colours, but could select the correct colour given the name. She also could not read, although she could identify letters when presented individually; unlike her performance with objects, she was unable to match written and spoken words. Writing skills were normal. McCormick and Levine suggest that the poor spoken–written word matching occurred as a result of an interruption in the pathways between the right visual association area and the left angular gyrus (written words being processed in the language areas of the left hemisphere; Petersen, Fox, Posner, Mintun, & Raichle, 1988, 1989; Petersen, Fox, Snyder, & Raichle, 1990; Price, Wise, Watson, Patterson, Howard, & Frackowiak, 1994). In order to account for good spoken name–visual object matching, McCormick and Levine propose either that (1) auditory words are recognised in the left hemisphere, and the semantic information so derived is transmitted across the anterior portions of the corpus callosum to be matched with object recognition processing in the right hemisphere (presumably the transfer could only operate in one direction other-wise information could pass from right to left hemisphere allowing object naming to take place), or (2) auditory words are recognised in the right hemisphere and matched to right hemisphere object recognition processes.

A similar argument has been made by Coslett and Saffran on the basis of detailed studies of two patients with optic aphasia (Coslett & Saffran, 1989, 1992). The first patient suffered a stroke affecting the left occipital lobe, and the left forceps major, extending into the posterior limb of the internal capsule (Coslett & Saffran, 1989). The second patient also suffered a stroke affecting the left occipital lobe and the left posterior, inferior temporal lobe (Coslett & Saffran, 1992). The first patient was very impaired at naming visually presented objects and pictures (0% correct) while tactile naming was relatively intact (92% correct). Naming to verbal definition was correct for 11/15 items. The ability to gesture the use of visually presented objects was less good, being around 50% correct (Coslett & Saffran, 1989). A similar pattern of performance was shown by the second patient, although, in a number of respects, the impairment was not so severe. Object naming was not quite so poor (21% correct), but was impaired relative to naming to description (68% correct), or tactile naming (68% correct). This patient was able to gesture the use of all objects that he could not name

(Coslett & Saffran, 1992). Different tests were used to assess object recognition in the two cases. The first patient was able to access stored structural descriptions (judged by performance on object decision tasks) and to perform unusual view matches (Coslett & Saffran, 1989); similar tests were not reported for the second patient (Coslett & Saffran, 1992). The first patient was able to (i) categorise pictures (e.g. animals vs inanimate objects, edible vs inedible objects, and matching physically dissimilar exemplars of the same object), (ii) determine which two of three pictures subserved the same function, and (iii) determine which two of three objects were related associatively (Coslett & Saffran, 1989). The second patient was able to match a word to one of four semantically unrelated pictures, and was able to select which two of three pictures were related in terms of function (Coslett & Saffran, 1992). Both of these patients appear to have better access to semantic knowledge from vision than J.B. (Riddoch & Humphreys, 1987a).

For both cases Coslett and Saffran reported the results of a number of reading tests. Neither patient was able to read words aloud; however, both performed lexical decision tests relatively well. Both patients were also able to sort words according to category (e.g. the names of edible items—grape vs visually similar words—graph), and were able to perform picture-word match tests. However, other data indicated that the extent of lexical processing was limited. Coslett and Saffran's (1989) patient was unable to match spoken functors and nonwords to written words or nonwords (although he was able to match nouns), he was insensitive to the appropriateness of affixes, and he made significantly more errors on within-category as opposed to across-category written word to picture matching tasks. The results of the latter tests suggest that the patient was not able to process words to a high semantic or linguistic level. In addition, Coslett and Saffran's (1992) patient was unable to make rhyme judgements. Coslett and Saffran argue that rhyme judgement, nonword processing and the processing of function words are normally conducted by the language centres in the left hemisphere. The impairments to these processes in the patients are consistent with a left hemisphere deficit and right hemisphere processes being used.

Coslett and Saffran suggest that right hemisphere processing can account for the patterns of performance shown for both the cases they report. They proposed that visual processing of objects can occur to a high level in the right hemisphere (including access to semantics; although see Hillis & Caramazza, 1995 as discussed in the next paragraph), along with some processing of words (including a limited degree of semantic processing). However, the right hemisphere cannot support linguistic or phonological processing and when tasks make more stringent demands in this respect, the performance of both patients deteriorated (with function words and with nonwords). Coslett and Saffran (1989, 1992) conclude that the best account for the patterns of performance shown by the two patients is in terms of a disconnection of the right hemisphere from the left hemisphere processing systems. A straightforward visual–verbal disconnection account of optic aphasia does not seem appropriate for these patients since they were able to perform well on some tasks requiring visual and verbal information to be integrated. For instance, the patient described by Coslett and Saffran (1989) was able to answer questions such as what colour is a lime, in which an auditory word needs to be processed so that it can be used to retrieve stored visual knowledge about a stimulus (cf. Beauvois, 1982). Both the patients were also able to point to named objects (this is also true for other patients who have been classified as having optic aphasia: see Larrabee, Levin, Huff, Kay & Guinto, 1985; Manning & Campbell, 1992; Peña-Casanova et al., 1985). Coslett and Saffran (1989, 1992) argue that the failure to name pictures and words occurred as a result of failure to access to the phonological output lexicon in the left hemisphere as a result of their neurological deficit. The naming errors produced by the patients demonstrated no clear relationship with the target object. Indeed, a striking characteristic of both patients performance was that they would frequently deny seeing visually presented stimuli. Coslett and Saffran note that similar effects have been reported when stimuli have been presented to the right hemisphere of patients who have undergone transection of the corpus callosum (Gazzaniga & Sperry, 1967; Sperry, Gazzaniga & Bogen, 1969).

Hillis and Caramazza (1995) questioned whether Coslett and Saffran's patients were in fact able to access high-level semantics from vision. For instance, Coslett and Saffran (1989) report that their patient was successful in semantic association tasks. Thus, the patient was required to group two of three objects on the basis of semantic relatedness (example objects used were a pencil, paper and a knife), and was able to perform the task at ceiling. Hillis and Caramazza (1995) argue that since the distractor item was from a different category to the target items it may have been possible to perform the task on the basis of partial semantic information; indeed, their patient D.H.Y. also performed at ceiling on a similar task. However, when Hillis and Caramazza constructed a new task requiring finer semantic discriminations (e.g. selecting the two most closely associated items from a light switch, a light bulb and a traffic light) D.H.Y. made a large number of errors (58% correct).

Hillis and Caramazza (1995) have argued against Coslett and Saffran's (1989, 1992) account in other ways. For instance, if there was a complete disconnection between recognition systems in the two hemispheres then naming errors should be unrelated to the target stimulus (as has been shown in the data of 'split-brain' patients). The presence of semantic errors, however, suggests that incomplete semantic information is passed onto the phonological representation for naming. Both of the patients described by Coslett and Saffran made semantic errors; with the first patient these only represented a small percentage of the error corpus (18%) (Coslett & Saffran, 1989), but with the second patient all the errors were semantically related to the target item (Coslett & Saffran, 1992). Semantic errors are also a characteristic feature of the performance of other optic aphasic patients.

For instance, of D.H.Y.'s errors, 75% were classified as semantic (Hillis & Caramazza, 1995). As we have indicated above, the errors made by Lhermitte and Beauvois' patient J.F. were also largely semantic (63% of the total error corpus)(Lhermitte & Beauvois, 1973). In Riddoch and Humphreys analysis of their patient's naming errors across a number of the experiments (e.g. naming real objects, or naming items in photographs), there was a relatively high proportion of complete failures to respond (43.3% of the total error corpus), along with several distinct groupings of which the majority were semantic and/or visual. There were also small numbers of either visually related errors and/or errors related by a similar gesture to the target (e.g. cigarette → toothbrush, after gesturing to his mouth). In their review article, Iorio et al. state that the majority of errors produced by optic aphasic patients are semantically related to the target (see Iorio et al., 1992) (see also Davidoff & De Bleser, 1993). Hillis and Caramazza (1995) proposed a partial disconnection account, similar to the arguments made first by Riddoch and Humphreys (1987a), could best accommodate the data. According to this account, incomplete semantic information is used to access phonological representations in object naming tasks. Hillis and Caramazza also argue that tests presented in previous reports of optic aphasia are not stringent enough to demonstrate complete access to semantic information from vision. In two closely studied patients D.H.Y. (Hillis & Caramazza, 1995) and J.B. (Riddoch & Humphreys, 1987a) some impairment in accessing specific semantic information from vision was apparent. Such a partial functional disconnection may also be underscored by a neurological disconnection, of course, in which right hemisphere perceptual processes provide impoverished input into left hemisphere semantic processes.

SUPERADDITIVE EFFECTS OF TWO OR MORE MILD DEFICITS

Farah (1990) presented a somewhat different account of optic aphasia, arguing that it results from two separate deficits: one affecting the route between visual perceptual processing and a semantic representation, and the other affecting a route between semantic processing and output phonology. Manning and Campbell (1992) proposed that the first impairment may be apparent on imagery tasks, while the second may be apparent on verbal fluency tasks. Manning and Campbell used this account to accommodate the pattern of deficits shown by a further optic aphasic patient: A.G.. A.G. had a left occipital lesion as a result of an infarction. He was unable to read. Naming of visually presented objects was poor (39% correct), but he was frequently able to gesture their use (75% correct). Naming to definition or on tactile presentation was good. A.G.'s ability to access semantics from vision also appeared to be good: he was able to categorise pictures, his performance at answering probe questions was at a similar level for pictures and words, and his ability to name pictured actions was good.[4] However, A.G. was impaired on tests of verbal fluency, such as generating spoken words to a category or to a phonological cue, causing Manning and Campbell to suggest that he had a mild impairment in the connections between semantic and phonological representations. Manning and Campbell (1992) also found that A.G.'s performance on tests of visual imagery was impaired only when he had to derive an image from a picture (e.g. when asked to determine whether an animal had a long or short tail from a tail-occluded picture). As a result, they proposed that such a deficit in image generation may relate to optic aphasia; in particular, they offer the tentative suggestion that intact image generation is necessary to support the naming of visually presented objects.

Imagery processes appear to be intact in some patients with optic aphasia, but impaired in others. For instance, although formal testing of visual imagery was not carried out by Lhermitte and Beauvois (1973) with patient J.F., his drawing of items from memory was good. He was asked to draw 31 items from memory corresponding to the correct names for pictures he had misnamed. J.F. was always able to draw correctly the object that he had misnamed in the pictorial representation; he was also always able to draw the object corresponding to the incorrect name he had given to a pictorial representation. Lhermitte and Beauvois state that "The graphic quality of most of the drawings was excellent . . ." (page 700, Lhermitte & Beauvois, 1973). Hillis and Caramazza's (1995) patient also had intact visual imagery as assessed by the ability to draw from memory. In contrast, J.B. (Riddoch & Humphreys, 1987a) showed marked impairments in his ability to draw items from memory. Typically, he would comment "I know what it is, but I just can't picture it" (Riddoch & Humphreys, 1987a, p. 148). Riddoch and Humphreys (1987a) tried to assess J.B.'s visualisation abilities in two further tests. In the first he was asked to select which one of four depicted heads corresponded to the body of an animal or an object (presented on the same card, below the four heads). J.B. performed poorly, well outside the control range. It was also interesting to note that even on the few occasions that he was able to name the "body", he was still unable to match it to the appropriate head. In the second test, J.B. was asked to complete an incomplete drawing of an object. Again he performed very poorly (relative to control performance). Visual imagery abilities were not reported in Coslett and Saffran's (1989, 1992) patients. Given the heterogeneity of imagery abilities in this small group of optic aphasic patients, it seems unlikely that impaired imagery is a contributory factor. In addition, it seems doubtful that a naming impairment normally plays a substantial part; for instance naming to auditory definition in most optic aphasics is very good. There is little direct evidence for a deficit in accessing phonology from semantic knowledge. Indeed, the tests of verbal fluency, used by Manning

---

[4] Given the more recent arguments by Hillis and Caramazza (1995), authors need to be cautious in arguing that patients have completely intact access to semantic knowledge from vision in the absence of rigorous testing.

and Campbell (1992) to assess phonological retrieval, likely involves a number of factors, perhaps even including interrogation of visual knowledge, which may be poor in their patient.

GESTURING ABILITY AS AN INDICATOR OF VISUAL RECOGNITION

As we indicated in the Introduction, the presence of intact gesturing is often taken to signify that visual recognition is intact in optic aphasia (Farah, 1990; Hodges, 1994), and clearly the ability to make a reliably more correct gesture relative to naming responses from vision is at least crucial for defining the syndrome. However, it has also been argued that gestures are a relatively imprecise method of assessing visual recognition. For instance, Ratcliff and Newcombe (1982) point out that similar gestures could be produced for a SHOE and a SOCK; however, if the name SOCK was given to a picture of a SHOE, the response would be classed as an error. How good a measure of recognition do gesture responses provide, and how consistent are the data across patients?

The advantage for gesturing over visual naming varies to a considerable degree over the reported cases of optic aphasia. Some cases are at ceiling in their gesturing performance (Gil, Pluchon, Toullat, Michenau, Rogez, & Levevre, 1985; Lhermitte & Beauvois, 1973), while others show some impairment. As previously noted, J.B. (Riddoch & Humphreys, 1987a) scored 75% correct in gesturing the use of visually presented objects, and was able to make the correct gesture to 46% of objects that had been named incorrectly. A.G. (Manning & Campbell, 1992) also scored 75% correct in gesturing the use of visually presented objects (the relationship between correct gesturing to misnamed objects was not made explicit, but A.G. was able to name only 38.7% of pictured items correctly). The patients reported by Coslett and Saffran (1989, 1992) scored 50% (0% correct naming) and 15% (21% correct naming) correct respectively in gesturing the use of visually presented objects. D.H.Y. (Hillis & Caramazza, 1995) scored 30% correct in the ability to gesture the use of visually presented objects (in this case the ability to name visually presented objects was not reported, although the ability to name line drawings was very impaired).

Notwithstanding the variability in gesturing performance of the patients, does correct gesturing indicate intact recognition? Data from patients with dementia indicates that correct gesturing can occur even when visual recognition appears to be severely compromised. A clear account of the abilities of a patient with a progressive dementing illness is given by Schwartz, Marin, and Saffran (1979). W.L.P. was impaired on matching-to-sample tasks whether the stimuli were words or pictures (Schwartz et al., 1979). On a simple picture naming task, W.L.P. was only able to name one of 70 household objects. She was also impaired in the ability to select the correct written name for a pictured item from five alternatives (the target item, and four distractor items which were semantically,

phonologically or unrelated to the target). Nonetheless, she "... was consistently able, through her gestures, to demonstrate that she recognised the objects.
Indeed her miming was so precise that a naive observer was able to differentiate,
for example, her 'use' of the spoon as distinct from the fork (for the former she
employed a scooping and stirring motion; for the latter, a gesture of spearing;
cigarette vs pipe (by hand position); pants vs skirt etc. ..." (Schwartz et al.,
1979) pp. 283–4). These data suggest that an intact visual recognition system is
not a prerequisite for gesturing ability. In studies of optic aphasia, the contrast
that can occur between relatively spared gesturing and poor semantic matching,
shown by patients such as J.B. (Riddoch & Humphreys, 1987a), also indicates that
correct gestures should not be taken as evidence for intact object recognition.

More recently, Sirigu, Duhamel, and Poncet (1991) have described a patient,
F.B., with bilateral temporal lobe lesions and with severe visual multimodal
recognition impairments. F.B. had difficulty in identifying both real and pictured objects; in addition, tactile naming, and identification of sounds were also
impaired. The problem was due to impaired recognition and not just impaired
naming since F.G. was not able to match visually presented objects on the basis
of functional or contextual links, he was impaired at sound–picture matching
tasks, and he was poor at gesturing the use of tactilely presented objects. Interestingly, F.B. was able to demonstrate (in action) and describe in explicit detail
how most visually presented objects might be used, but he still reported functional information incorrectly. For instance, when presented with an iron he
said: "You hold it in one hand, and move it backwards and forwards horizontally
(mimes action). Maybe you can spread glue evenly with it." Thus, despite good
descriptions of actions appropriate to visually presented objects, identification of
the function of those objects was poor. Sirigu et al. propose that the spontaneous
gestures used by F.B. represented "a self-cueing kinaesthetic strategy helping
the patient to generate certain hypotheses about the function of objects ... it
may be that in many cases semantic representations are not activated directly
from vision, but indirectly through the representation of the pattern of actions
that a particular object specifically affords" (Sirigu et al., 1991, p. 2570). Direct
activation of gestures may thus facilitate object naming. Gesture may also boost
performance in other tasks. For instance, Sirigu et al. (1991) observed that F.B.
would often use gesture as a facilitator for his drawings. They offer the following example: "... while the patient was drawing the guitar, he often paused and
mimed the act of playing, as if the kinaesthetic cues helped him shape his
representation ..." (p. 2563).

It is of course a fact that objects may be used for a purpose other than the
ones they were designed for (e.g. a shoe may be used to hammer a nail into the
wall). This form of usage is not arbitrary, however. It occurs when the structural
characteristics of the object are congruent with the intended action. This is one
of the tenets of Gibson's ecological approach to perception (Gibson, 1979).
According to this approach, the crucial aspect of perceptual processing is not

the development of some internal concept (or percept) but rather the direct links between perceptual processing, action, and correlated environmental characteristics (i.e. affordances). The affordance of environmental stimuli may be defined in terms of what is offered to the organism; for instance, if a surface is flat, reasonably substantial and of an appropriate height, it will "afford" sitting on whether it has been specifically designed for this purpose (e.g. a stool), or happens to be available in the environment (e.g. a tree stump). Gibson argued that affordances are perceived directly without the need for mediation by cognitive processes. Riddoch and Humphreys (1987a) proposed that their patient J.B.'s gestures were based either on affordances (which would not be contingent on access to stored knowledge), or on associated links to action from the stored structural descriptions of objects (which they showed to be accessed from vision in this patient). For instance, when presented with a tray, J.B. misnamed it as a chair, the naming error possibly being driven by the "affordance" offered by the tray's flat surface. However, in other instances it was apparent that an explanation in terms of affordances was not sufficient to account for the specificity of J.B.'s gestural performance. For example, consider a hand razor. In Gibson's terms, it can be argued that the handle of the razor affords "holding" and that the head affords "scraping"; but there is nothing in this affordance that determines where the scraping will take place (i.e. the face rather than the table top). Nonetheless, J.B.'s gesture when presented with a hand razor was explicitly directed towards his chin, suggesting that something more than the processing of visual affordances was responsible for his explicit gestural ability in some instances.

Recently, Goodale, Jakobson, and Keillor have examined the differences in the visual control of pantomimed and natural grasping movements (Goodale, Jakobson, & Keillor, 1994) and have shown that the kinematics of pantomimed actions are distinctly different from the kinematics of natural, target directed actions. For instance, the grasp aperture of the hand may be significantly smaller when subjects mime the action appropriate for a given object relative to when they actually perform the action with the object. Similar effects obtain whether the subject is asked to pantomime the use of an object that is physically absent, or to perform the action *beside* an object (in contrast to grasping the object directly). Goodale et al. argue that normal visuomotor programmes are not implemented during pantomimed grasping movements; instead, pantomimes are driven by actively constructing a stored percept of the object. Data from an agnosic patient, D.F., has been used to support this hypothesis. D.F. sustained diffuse brain damage as a result of carbon monoxide poisoning leading to bilateral occipital damage, and also suffered damage bilaterally in the globus pallidus. On standard tests of perception, D.F. performed poorly, being unable to discriminate between objects using properties such as object shape, size, reflectance and orientation. However, despite such poor perceptual performance, D.F. was able to reach and grasp objects normally and she showed sensitivity to object

orientation and size in her grasping responses. Such a dissociation in performance has led Goodale and his colleagues to suggest that the visual processing
underlying perceptual judgements operates separately from that underlying
visuomotor procedures used in reaching and grasping (Goodale, Milner, Jakobson,
& Carey, 1991; Milner & Goodale, 1995; Milner, Perrett, Johnston, Benson,
Jordan, Heeley et al., 1991). "On-line" reaching and grasping uses visual information coded in the dorsal visual system, which is intact in D.F. Object recognition
uses visual information coded in the ventral visual system which is severely
impaired in this patient. It is of interest that, in contrast to her good "on-line"
reaching and grasping of objects, D.F. was poor at pantomiming the same response when the object was withdrawn and at making the response to the side of
real objects (Goodale et al., 1994). This is consistent with such pantomimed
responses being determined by the ventral visual system (impaired in D.F.).

D.F. differs from patients with optic aphasia in that she seemed unable to
construct a visual percept; such percepts may be used as cues to access, from
stored visual knowledge, the overlearned and very familiar gestures which are
associated with objects that are in everyday use. These are the very gestures that
are made by optic aphasic patients. It follows that the gestures made by optic
aphasics are based on at least residual activation of the ventral object recognition
system, and, where highly specific gestures are made, there seems to be access
to item-specific stored knowledge. A highly likely candidate for this is some
form of direct (non-semantic) route from the structural description system to the
action system controlling gesturing. Nevertheless, such specific gestures would
still not necessarily indicate that full access to semantic information was achieved
from vision.

SUMMARY TO DATE

The critical feature that distinguishes optic aphasia from anomia is its modality
specificity. This is not a contentious issue, and all reported cases of optic aphasia
demonstrate better tactile naming and naming to definition than naming visually
presented objects. The critical feature that distinguishes optic aphasia from visual
agnosia is whether visual recognition is intact. This is more controversial. Current definitions of optic aphasia use the ability of such patients to gesture to
visual objects as an indicator of intact visual recognition (Farah, 1990; Hodges,
1994), but as I have indicated here, there is both large variability in gesturing
performance in reported patients and intact gesturing performance can co-exist
with impaired visual access to semantic information (Riddoch & Humphreys,
1987a; Schwartz et al., 1979). If gesture is not to be considered diagnostic
of intact visual recognition, then other assessments are necessary, including
semantic matching.

In anatomical terms, Coslett and Saffran's right hemisphere hypothesis has
an intuitive appeal considering the nature of the lesions of patients with optic

aphasia (generally speaking, left unilateral infero-temporal-occipital lesions, see Iorio et al., 1992). However, the semantic errors observed in patients with optic aphasia are not characteristic of the errors observed when the right hemisphere of split brain patients is probed. Against this, it is important to note that Coslett and Saffran's patients frequently denied seeing visual stimuli, an effect that is reported in split brain patients but has not been an aspect of performance that has been observed in other optic aphasics. It is certainly possible that residual perceptual processes in the right hemisphere can access partial semantic information from objects, but fail to narrow down the semantic field to allow precise naming to take place. Importantly, as shown by Riddoch and Humphreys (1987a) and Hillis and Caramazza (1995), this failure to narrow down a semantic field occurs after intact access to stored knowledge of the structure of objects. In view of the last proposal, crucial to naming is the ability to narrow down a field of semantic competitors; it is useful to note a final account of visual naming disorders that links optic aphasia to constraints on the way visual object naming is normally achieved.

A CODA

Humphreys et al. (1997) have recently proposed an account of object naming disorders that offers a role for top-down interrogation of perceptual knowledge in identification, rather than naming being seen as a purely bottom-up process. Humphreys et al. suggest that, normally, object naming is based on the continuous transmission of information from the structural description system to the semantic system and from the semantic system to stored representations of object names. This can lead to the activation of a broad semantic field during object naming, and consequent competition for name selection. The problem may be less severe for other modalities, if such stimuli do not activate as large a set of competitors. In normal subjects, naming may be facilitated by top-down activation of perceptual knowledge, to help differentiate a target object from its competitors. This is supported by PET (Positron Emission Tomography) studies showing enhanced activation of visual processing areas in the brain when identification is required over and above the structural encoding of objects (Martin, Wiggs, Ungeleider, & Haxby, 1996; Price, Moore, Humphreys, Frackowiak, & Friston, 1996).

On such an account, object naming disorders could arise not only from impairments to late processes in naming, operating after semantic access, but also to earlier processes including activation of the structural description system and the transmission of information from the structural description system to the semantic system. Impairments in these earlier processes can lead either to more competitors being activated than normal, or to problems in top-down interrogation which then fails to differentiate between targets from competing items. Since competition is more severe for visual naming than for accessing semantic information, and since top-down interrogation is needed more for naming too, the result may be an impairment in naming (more severe than in recognition) that is most severe for visual stimuli. The specificity of any semantic information accessed by patients would itself depend on the magnitude of the impairment to earlier processing mechanisms, but it is possible that a mild impairment early on affects naming (e.g. by blocking top-down interrogation) whilst having minimal consequences on access to semantics. Such an account places an emphasis on the access of stored knowledge over time rather than on the involvement of different processing routes (direct vs semantically mediated; visual vs verbal), and may provide a parsimonious way to account for a wide range of naming disorders.

ACKNOWLEDGEMENTS

I would like to thank Glyn Humphreys for his helpful comments on an earlier draft of this chapter. This work was supported by the Medical Research Council.

REFERENCES

Beauvois, M.-F. (1982). Optic aphasia: A process of interaction between vision and language. *Philosophical Transactions of the Royal Society, B289*, 35–47.

Beauvois, M.-F., & Saillant, B. (1985). Optic aphasia for colours and colour agnosia: A distinction between visual and visuo-verbal impairments in the processing of colours. *Cognitive Neuropsychology, 2*, 1–48.

Coslett, H.B., & Saffran, E.M. (1989). Preserved object recognition and reading comprehension in optic aphasia. *Brain*, 1091–110.

Coslett, H.M., & Saffran, E.M. (1992). Optic aphasia and the right hemisphere: A replication and extension. *Brain and Language, 43*, 148–61.

Davidoff, J. (1996). Classic cases in neuropsychology. In C. Case, W. C-W., Y. Joanette and A. Roth (Eds), *Classic cases in neuropsychology*. Hove: Psychology Press.

Davidoff, J., & De Bleser, R. (1993). Optic aphasia: A review of past studies and a reappraisal. *Aphasiology, 7*, 135–54.

Farah, M.J. (1990). *Visual Agnosia*. Cambridge: MIT Press.

Freund, C.S. (1889). Über optische Aphasie und Seelenblindheit. *Archiv für Psychiatrie und Nervenkrankheiten, 20*, 371–416.

Gazzaniga, M.S., & Sperry, R.W. (1967). Language after section of the cerebral commissures. *Brain, 90*, 131–48.

Geschwind, N., & Fusillo, M. (1966). Color-naming deficits in association with alexia. *Archives of Neurology, 15*, 137–46.

Gibson, J.J. (1979). *The ecological approach to visual perception*. Boston: Houghton Mifflin.

Gil, R., Pluchon, C., Toullat, G., Michenau, D., Rogez, R., & Levevre, J.P. (1985). Disconnexion visuo-verbale (aphasie optique) pour les objets, les images, les couleurs et les visages avec alexie "abstractive". *Neuropsychologia, 23*, 333–49.

Goodale, M.A., Jakobson, L.S., & Keillor, J.M. (1994). Differences in the visual control of pantomimed and natural grasping movements. *Neuropsychologia, 32*, 1159–78.

Goodale, M.A., Milner, A.D., Jakobson, L.S., & Carey, D.P. (1991). A neurological dissociation between perceiving objects and grasping them. *Nature, 349*, 154–6.

Hillis, A.E., & Caramazza, A. (1995). Cognitive and neural mechanisms underlying visual and semantic processing: Implications from "Optic Aphasia". *Journal of Cognitive Neuroscience, 7*, 457–78.

Hodges, J.R. (1994). *Cognitive assessment for clinicians*. Oxford: Oxford University Press.

Humphreys, G.W., Lloyd-Jones, T.J., & Fias, W. (1995). Semantic interference effects on naming using a postcue procedure: Tapping the links between semantics and phonology with pictures and words. *Journal of Experimental Psychology: Learning, Memory and Cognition, 21*, 961–80.

Humphreys, G.W., & Riddoch, M.J. (1984). Routes to object constancy: Implications from neuro-logical impairments of object constancy. *Quarterly Journal of Experimental Psychology, 36A*, 385–415.

Humphreys, G.W., Riddoch, M.J., & Price, C.J. (1997). Top-down processes in object identification: Evidence from experimental psychology, neuropsychology and functional anatomy. *Philosophical Transactions of the Royal Society, Series B, 352*, 1275–82.

Humphreys, G.W., Riddoch, M.J., & Quinlan, P.T. (1988). Cascade processes in picture identifica-tion. *Cognitive Neuropsychology, 5*, 67–103.

Iorio, L., Falanga, A., Fragassi, N.A., & Grossi, D. (1992). Visual associative agnosia and optic aphasia. A single case study and a review of the syndromes. *Cortex, 28*, 23–37.

Larrabee, G.L., Levin, H.S., Huff, F.J., Kay, M.C., & Guinto, F.G. (1985). Visual agnosia con-trasted with visual-verbal disconnection. *Neuropsychologia, 23*, 1–12.

Lhermitte, F., & Beauvois, M.F. (1973). A visual-speech disconnection syndrome. Report of a case with optic aphasia. *Brain, 96*, 695–714.

McCormick, G.F., & Levine, D.A. (1983). Visual anomia: A unidirectional disconnection. *Neurology, 33*, 664–6.

Manning, L., & Campbell, R. (1992). Optic aphasia with spared action naming: A description and possible loci of impairment. *Neuropsychologia, 30*, 587–92.

Marin, O.S.M., & Saffran, E.M. (1975). Agnosic behaviour in anomia: A case of pathological verbal dominance. *Cortex, 11*, 83–9.

Marr, D. (1982). *Vision*. San Francisco: W.H. Freeman.

Martin, A., Wiggs, C.L., Ungeleider, L.G., & Haxby, J.V. (1996). Neural correlates of category-specific knowledge. *Nature, 379*, 649–52.

Milner, A.D., & Goodale, M.A. (1995). *The visual brain in action*. Oxford: Oxford University Press.

Milner, A.D., Perrett, D.I., Johnston, R.S., Benson, P.J., Jordan, T.R., Heeley, D.W., Bettuci, D., Motara, F., Mutani, R., Terazzi, E., & Davidson, D.L.W. (1991). Perception and action in "visual form agnosia". *Brain, 114*, 405–28.

Morton, J. (1979). Facilitation in word recognition: Experiments causing change in the logogen model. In P.A. Kohlers, M.E. Wrolstad and H. Bouma (Eds), *Processing of visible language 1*. New York: Plenum Press.

Morton, J., & Patterson, K. (1985). A new attempt at an interpretation, or, an attempt at a new interpretation. In M. Coltheart, K. Patterson, and J.C. Marshall (Eds), *Deep dyslexia*, London: Routledge and Kegan Paul.

Peña-Casanova, J., Roig-Rovira, T., Bermudez, A., & Tolosa-Sarro, E. (1985). Optic aphasia, optic apraxia and loss of dreaming. *Brain and Language, 26*, 63–71.

Petersen, S.E., Fox, P.T., Posner, M.I., Mintun, M., & Raichle, M.E. (1988). Positron emission tomographic studies of the cortical anatomy of single word processing. *Nature, 331*, 585–9.

Petersen, S.E., Fox, P.T., Posner, M.I., Mintun, M., & Raichle, M.E. (1989). Positron emission tomographic studies of the processing of single words. *Journal of Cognitive Neuroscience, 1*, 153–70.

Petersen, S.E., Fox, P.T., Snyder, A., & Raichle, M.E. (1990). Activation of extrastriate and frontal cortical areas by visual words and word-like stimuli. *Science, 249*, 1041–4.

Price, C.J., & Humphreys, G.W. (1989). The effects of surface detail on object categorisation and naming. *The Quarterly Journal of Experimental Psychology, 41A*, 797–828.

Price, C.J., Moore, C.J., Humphreys, G.W., Frackowiak, R.S.J., & Friston, K.J. (1996). The neural regions sustaining object recognition and naming. *Proceedings of the Royal Society(B263)*, 1501–7.

Price, C., Wise, R., Watson, J., Patterson, K., Howard, D., & Frackowiak, R. (1994). Brain activity during reading: The effects of task and exposure duration. *Brain, 117*, 1255–69.

Ratcliff, G., & Newcombe, F. (1982). Object recognition: Some deductions from clinical evidence. In A.W. Ellis (Eds), *Normality and pathology in cognitive function*, pp. 147–71. London: Academic Press.

Riddoch, M.J., & Humphreys, G.W. (1987a). Visual object processing in optic aphasia: A case of semantic access agnosia. *Cognitive Neuropsychology, 4*, 131–85.

Riddoch, M.J., & Humphreys, G.W. (1987b). A case of integrative agnosia. *Brain, 110*, 1431–62.

Schnider, A., Benson, D.F., & Scharre, D.W. (1994). Visual agnosia and optic aphasia: Are they anatomically distinct? *Cortex, 30*, 445–57.

Schwartz, M.F., Marin, O.S.M., & Saffran, E.M. (1979). Dissociations of language function in dementia: A case study. *Brain, 7*, 277–306.

Sirigu, A., Duhamel, J.-R., & Poncet, M. (1991). The role of sensorimotor experience in object recognition. *Brain, 114*, 2555–73.

Sperry, R.W., Gazzaniga, M.S., & Bogen, J.E. (1969). Interhemispheric relationships: the neocortical commissures; syndromes of language disconnection. In P.J. Vinken and G.W. Bruyn (Eds), *Handbook of clinical neurology*. Amsterdam: North-Holland.

Vitkovitch, M., Humphreys, G.W., & Lloyd-Jones, T.J. (1993). On naming a giraffe a zebra: Picture naming errors across object categories. *Journal of Experimental Psychology: Learning, Memory and Cognition, 19*, 243–59.

Warrington, E.K. (1975). The selective impairment of semantic memory. *Quarterly Journal of Experimental Psychology, 27*, 635–57.

Warrington, E.K. (1982). Neuropsychological studies of object recognition. *Philosophical Transactions of the Royal Society of London, Series B., 298*, 15–33.

Warrington, E.K., & Taylor, A. (1973). The contribution of the right parietal lobe to object recognition. *Cortex, 9*, 152–64.

Warrington, E.K., & Taylor, A. (1978). Two categorical stages of object recognition. *Perception, 9*, 152–64.

Wechsler, D. (1955). *Wechsler Adult Intelligence Scale. Manual*. New York: Psychological Corporation.

CHAPTER EIGHT

Covert recognition and anosognosia in prosopagnosic patients

Edward H.F. De Haan
Psychological Laboratory, Utrecht University, The Netherlands

> ... the disease first settled in the head, went on to affect every
> part of the body in turn, and even when people escaped its worst
> effects, it still left its traces on them by fastening upon the extrem-
> ities of the body. It affected the genitals, the fingers, and the toes,
> and many of those who recovered lost the use of these members;
> some, too, went blind. There were some also who, when they first
> began to get better, suffered from a total loss of memory, not
> knowing who they were themselves and **being unable to recognise
> their friends**.
>
> Thucydides. *The History of the Peloponnesian War.*
> *Book II, 49, 153.*

Studying the effects of brain injury is not something particular to modern times
as this quote from the Greek general Thucydides indicates. It would be strange
if it were otherwise given the unusual and intriguing behaviour which can be
observed after damage to the central nervous system. However, the main reason
to quote Thucydides here is that he appears to have made the important observation that identification of others is a specific and important human ability, which
can be disrupted by (brain) disease. This observation was repeated in a more
scientific manner only 50 years ago. The German neurologist Bodamer described
in a report (Bodamer, 1947) how some patients experience a particularly selective
difficulty in recognising faces.

Bodamer named the condition "prosopagnosia" with reference to the Greek *prosopon* (face) and *a-gnosis* (without knowledge). As far as we know now, all prosopagnosic patients know when they are looking at a face, and they can identify and describe separate features such as the eyes and mouth. Therefore, they clearly know that they are looking at a human face. However, the face has lost its value as a cue for identification of a person. In severe cases, even the faces of family members and close friends and sometimes the patient's own face seen in a mirror (Pallis, 1955) remain unrecognised. Not even a vague feeling of familiarity when the patient is looking at a known face survives. At this point, it is useful to point out that there are patients who still experience a sense of familiarity when seeing a known face but who are unable to recall any information pertaining to that person (like his or her occupation or name). This condition, where recognition of familiarity is intact but identification of the person in terms of knowing "who (s)he is" (De Haan, Young, & Newcombe, 1991a), is arguably better classified as an impairment of autobiographical memory than prosopagnosia.

Bodamer (1947) argued very strongly for the selectivity of the impairment, suggesting that other types of visual stimuli (text, objects, etc.) could still be recognised in a normal fashion by prosopagnosic patients. Consequently, he argued for a specific face recognition system in the brain. This claim has remained controversial ever since, as it cannot be tested in a straightforward manner. The ability to recognise faces is probably the most difficult visual recognition task we are able to perform, despite the subjective ease with which we do it. In a lifetime, we learn thousands of faces, most of which we are able to recognise relatively unaffected by changes due to age and variable additions such as spectacles and facial hair. These faces, however, only differ very slightly in visual appearance. This point is well illustrated by the general experience that faces from another race than one's own are difficult to remember; to black people, all whites look the same. The question is then whether face recognition deficits can be selective, because the extent of a general visual recognition deficit is such that only the most demanding recognition (faces) is affected, or because a dedicated face recognition system is disrupted.

It is clear from the literature, on the one hand, that very selective face recognition impairments do occur in patients with neurological disease. De Renzi (1986), for instance, has described prosopagnosic patients who were able to perform visual recognition tasks which resemble face recognition in terms of "task demands". The recognition of one's own motor in a car park, for example, requires the identification of a personally familiar item from an array with many visually similar items. A patient studied by De Renzi was able to recognise his own car in the car park, his own wallet from an array of similar wallets, and his own handwriting amidst that of others. Moreover, selectivity is even possible within the realm of information which can be "read" from faces (Young, Newcombe, De Haan, Small, & Hay, 1993). In addition to deriving the identity of a person, we use faces to infer the emotional state of a person from his or her expression, and we are reasonably proficient in establishing gender and age from the face. It has been shown that some prosopagnosic patients remain able to determine age, gender, and expression (Shuttleworth, Syring, & Allen, 1982; De Renzi, 1986).

It is clear from the literature that, on the one hand, very selective face recognition impairments do occur in patients with neurological disease. De Renzi (1986), for instance, has described prosopagnosic patients who were able to perform other visual recognition tasks that resemble face recognition in terms of "task demands". The recognition of one's own car in a car-park or your own wallet from an array of similar wallets requires the identification of a personally familiar item from an array with many visually similar items.

Until recently, the controversy about a dedicated face recognition system continued, as the other half of the necessary double dissociation (Teuber, 1968) was still lacking, although there are a number of clinical reports that describe a statistical trend towards relatively more severe problems in recognising objects than faces (Feinberg et al., 1994; McCarthy & Warrington, 1986). However, Moscovitch et al. (1997) recently investigated a patient who performs normally on face recognition tasks while being severely impaired in the recognition of common objects. Therefore, the available evidence now strongly supports the notion of separate processes dedicated to the recognition of faces. Indirect evidence for a specific face recognition system—such as the ability of neonates to recognise their mother after a very short interval (Maurer & Barrera, 1981; Roder et al., 1992), the discovery of cells in the macaque monkey brain which are selectively responsive to the face of one individual (Perrett et al., 1982), and the clinical phenomenon of "Metamorphopsia" where the patient sees faces, and only faces, in a distorted manner (Whiteley & Warrington, 1997)—gives further support to this position.

Selectivity has now also been demonstrated within the realm of information which can be "read" from faces (Young et al., 1993). In addition to deriving the identity of a person, we use faces to infer the emotional state of a person from his or her expression, and we are reasonably proficient in establishing gender and age from the face. It has been shown that some prosopagnosic patients remain able to determine age, gender and expression (De Renzi, 1986; Shuttleworth et al., 1982).

Regarding the anatomy, the bilateral left and the right occipito-temporal junctions have traditionally been identified as the substrate for face recognition. Most patients with prosopagnosia (and all patients who have come to post-mortem investigation) had lesions in those areas. A number of reports have more recently claimed that a unilateral right hemisphere lesion might be sufficient to cause prosopagnosia (Landis, Cummings, Christen, Bogen, & Imhof, 1986), but the status of these demonstrations remains somewhat unclear as long as they depend on neurosurgical reports and neuro-imaging instead of post-mortem findings.

In addition to acquired cases of prosopagnosia, there are a number of reports indicating that developmental cases also exist (McConachie, 1976; De Haan & Campbell, 1991).

At the time when our studies on prosopagnosia commenced, the most influential theoretical model (see Fig. 8.1) describing the separate processing stages involved in face recognition was that proposed by Bruce and Young (1986). This component model was designed to provide an adequate description of the phenomenology of neuropsychological patients with face-processing problems and experimental data from studies with normal subjects. Apart from postulating different processing routes for the analysis of facial expression (Kurucz & Feldmar, 1979), the perceptual scrutiny of faces for short-term recollection of unfamiliar faces (Malone, Morris, Kay, & Levin, 1982; McNeil & Warrington, 1991), and the perception of the movements of lips and tongue (lipreading) in

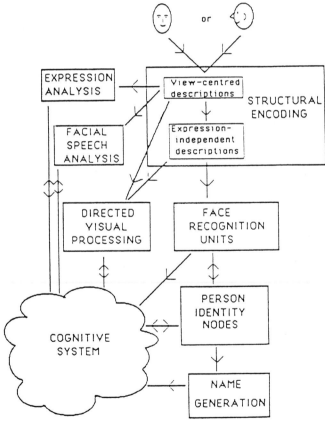

FIG. 8.1   The model put forward by Bruce & Young (1986) for describing the parallel and serial arranged processing stages involved in perceiving and recognising faces.

order to enhance the understanding of spoken language (Campbell, Landis, & Regard, 1986; Campbell, Brooks, De Haan, & Roberts, 1996), the model distinguishes a number of sequentially arranged processing stages for the recognition of faces. In short, one needs to create an internal representation of the face. Here one can discern two levels. First, a more or less one-to-one representation is created reflecting the particular view under which the face is perceived. Next, in order to allow for recognition of the face under many different viewing conditions, a more abstract representation is created. These two representations are comparable to the ideas put forward by Marr (1982) regarding $2\frac{1}{2}$D and 3D representations. The latter representation is subsequently matched to a stored representation, and when successful, a "hit" is signalled in the form of recognition that a familiar face has been encountered. Subsequently, the retrieval of autobiographical information about the particular person can be instigated, and this in turn could lead to accessing the name.

As was mentioned earlier, although face recognition is objectively a very demanding task, subjectively it appears to be instantaneous and effortless. To put it another way, if the different processing stages which are postulated in the model of Bruce and Young (1986) are real, then we are not consciously aware of them. As far as our introspection regarding the processes involved in face recognition is concerned, it appears that we have little insight into the underlying mechanisms. Furthermore, it is questionable to what degree face recognition is under voluntary control. At least it does *not* seem to be possible to instruct oneself *not* to recognise any faces for the next 10 min. The main goal of this chapter is to attempt to demonstrate, by presenting a number of case studies, that face recognition is carried out by "automatic" processes, which are not open to introspective insight, which are not under conscious control, and which can continue to function in the absence of conscious knowledge of its output.

It was a study by Bauer (1984) which was the impetus for our research on face recognition and awareness. He investigated a patient who had become prosopagnosic after a severe closed head injury. First, he asked his patient to select the correct name from five alternatives to match a photograph of a familiar face. As expected, the patient performed at chance level. However, skin conductance responses (a sensitive measure of autonomic nervous system activity), recorded during the experiment, occurred significantly more often and with higher amplitude to the correct name than to the other four foils. Similarly, Tranel and Damasio (1985) recorded significantly increased autonomic responses when their prosopagnosic patients looked at slides of familiar faces embedded among those of unknown people. On the basis of this psychophysiological evidence, and careful analysis of the possible underlying anatomy and the particular lesion sites of his patient, Bauer (1984, 1986) suggested that an autonomic route to face recognition can be selectively preserved, while the route to overt recognition is damaged. Drawing on the work by Bear (1983) and Ungerleider and Mishkin (1982), Bauer suggested that conscious recognition was subserved by the ventral occipito-temporal pathway while "autonomic" recognition was carried out by a system consisting of a dorsal pathway connected to the limbic system. Further psychophysiological evidence for covert face recognition was, subsequently, produced in studies using visual evoked potentials (Renault, Signoret, DeBruille, Breton, & Bolgert, 1989) and eye movements (Rizzo, Hurtig, & Damasio, 1987).

One important implication of Bauer's hypothesis is that there are two recognition systems with two sets of stored representations. To us, this seemed a rather expensive way of trying to explain the data. Therefore, our working hypothesis was that the autonomic recognition effects observed by Bauer and others were in fact derived from the same system that underlies overt recognition. Thus, the first question we addressed was whether we could find cognitive (as compared with autonomic) evidence of covert knowledge.

In 1982, at the age of 19, P.H. was involved in a road traffic accident in which he sustained a severe closed head injury. The physical, ophthalmological, and neuropsychological sequelae have been described in detail by De Haan, Young, and Newcombe (1987a), and only the essential points will be reiterated here. On examination in 1985 his intellectual abilities were reduced on the performance subtests, but were in the average range on the verbal subtests of the Revised Wechsler Adult Intelligence Scale. Language functions were relatively preserved, and he could read without difficulty. P.H.'s short-term memory was intact with verbal and visual material, but long-term memory was severely reduced in both domains. He was unable to recall any items from two short paragraphs of prose (Wechsler memory scale) read to him an hour earlier, and his delayed (45 min) reproduction of the complex Rey–Osterrieth line drawing was very meagre. It was noted that this pronounced anterograde memory deficit on formal tests was not generally reflected in his everyday life. He was well oriented and could give a coherent account of his daily activities.

P.H. had a variety of problems in visual and spatial perception. For instance, contrast sensitivity for the middle and high spatial frequencies was reduced, and he had problems perceiving the three-dimensional structure in a line drawing of a block model in order to count the number of blocks that touch a particular block. In contrast, he could read very small print, and had no colour perception problems. Faces were recognised as such, and easily distinguished from animal faces. Matching of photographs of unfamiliar faces (Benton & van Allen, 1973), recognition of emotional facial expressions, and race and gender discriminations were all moderately impaired. Recognition of familiar faces was nearly always unsuccessful, but people whose faces remained unidentified were easily recognised from the name or the voice. P.H.'s visual recognition problems were not confined to faces. Other types of within-class recognition (Damasio, Damasio, & Van Hoesen, 1982), such as for cars or flowers, were very poor, and on object-naming tasks he would demonstrate a (very) mild degree of object agnosia.

The severity of P.H.'s face recognition problem is striking. During the last eight years that we have been working with him, he has only occasionally recognised a face. For example, he has sometimes recognised Margaret Thatcher from photographs, but he has failed to recognise her on other occasions. This is remarkable given the limited number of photographs of celebrities we have been using during so many testing sessions. An MRI scan showed bilateral abnormal signal in the temporo-occipital junction, mainly in the inferior surface.

The studies started with demonstrating the extent of his face recognition problem. He was shown a series of individually presented faces, half of which were of famous people and the other half unknown, and he was asked to indicate whether the face appeared familiar or not. His performance on this task was at chance level. However, this demonstration is open to the criticism that the patient might have had some vestigial awareness of the familiar face but was too lacking in confidence to acknowledge familiarity. This was checked with a new task employing a forced-choice procedure. He was presented, over a large number of trials, with two faces: one familiar and the other unfamiliar. He was explicitly instructed that on each trial one of the faces was familiar, and asked to point to the face that appeared familiar and to *guess* if he was unsure. In this set-up, response bias can no longer influence the result of the task. P.H. was correct on 51% (see Table 8.1) of the trials—a chance performance. Thus, we concluded that P.H. was unable to extract any information regarding identity from photographs of familiar faces.

Next, in seeking to demonstrate covert knowledge, we exploited experiments (borrowed from experimental psychology) that had been shown to be sensitive to knowledge of face familiarity in normal, uninjured people but which do not require an overt identification of the famous faces used as experimental stimuli. Such experiments used the procedures of matching, interference, associative priming, and paired associate learning.

In the matching experiment, subjects are required to decide whether two simultaneously presented photographs of faces are taken from the same person or two different people. Two different views of the face are used to avoid the possibility of visual pattern matching rather than a matching strategy which involves the identity of the person shown in the two pictures. Note that this

TABLE 8.1
Number of correct choices by P.H. and control subjects
on the forced-choice familiarity decision task

		Faces	*Names*
PH		65	118
Normal subjects	mean	125.50	127.50
	SD	3.33	0.84

procedure does not call for conscious recognition of the face per se. Studies with normal, uninjured subjects had shown that they are faster to match photographs of familiar than unfamiliar people. Thus, we are quicker to decide that two photographs are taken from the same people (or not) if we know the people. P.H. showed exactly the same effect of faster matching of familiar faces as the control subjects, yet he was unable to identify any of the faces used (De Haan et al., 1987a).

The "interference" experiment (see Fig. 8.2) was also based on normal studies. Subjects are shown a series of photographs of faces, each with a printed name in a cartoon-like speech bubble. The printed name is that of the person in the photograph, a person in a related occupation (e.g. the name of Francois Mitterand with a photograph of Helmut Kohl), or was entirely unrelated (e.g. the name of Boris Becker with a photograph of Francois Mitterand). Ostensibly, the subject's task is to say as quickly as possible whether the printed *name* is that of a politician or not. Control subjects are nevertheless influenced by the accompany-

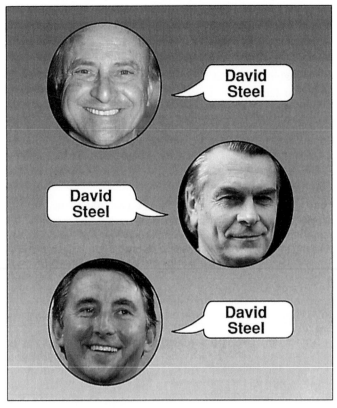

FIG. 8.2   Examples of stimuli used in the face–name interference experiment (© 1991, *New Scientist/* Rex.)

TABLE 8.2
Mean reaction times in milliseconds for P.H. on the face–name
interference experiment

| | *Type of face distractor* | | |
	Same person	*Related*	*Unrelated*
Politicians' names	1008	1106	1256
Non-politicians' names	1110	1139	1212
Overall	1059	1122	1234

ing face photograph to the extent that they take somewhat longer to respond correctly when the printed name is attached to an unrelated face. P.H., who has no difficulty in judging correctly whether a printed name, presented on its own, is that of a politician or not, was nevertheless influenced when face photographs were simultaneously presented with printed names. He showed (see Table 8.2) the same interference effect as normals: he was faster to respond correctly to the printed name when it was attached to the correct or a related face compared to when the face was *un*related (De Haan, Young, & Newcombe, 1987b).

Covert processing can also be demonstrated in "associative priming" experiments (see Fig. 8.3). Such experiments show the influence of previously presented stimuli on a subsequent response. In this particular case, the response explicitly required of subjects is to decide whether the targets (i.e. written names of familiar and unfamiliar people) were familiar or not. The responses of control subjects are influenced by the presentation of a "prime" stimulus (e.g. a face) shortly before the target appears. If there is a strong association between the prime stimulus (e.g. a photograph of Prince Charles) and the target (e.g. the name of Princess Diana), the subject responds faster than when the prime is

Priming experiment

	Related	Neutral	Unrelated
Prime:	face or name	face or name	face or name
	Ronald Reagan	unfamiliar	David Niven

	Target:	George Bush	John Medcalf

| Response: | | "Familiar" | "Unfamiliar" |

FIG. 8.3   A schematic outline of the associative priming experiment.

either the face of an unfamiliar person or that of a familiar person who is not closely associated with the target (e.g. the face of Prince Charles followed by the name of George Bush).

The patient, P.H., shows this type of priming effect from faces that he does not overtly recognise. Moreover, we were able to compare the size of the priming effect with that triggered by *name* primes (which P.H. recognises without difficulty). The effects are equivalent: overt recognition of name primes makes no additional contribution to the associative priming effect (see Table 8.3). This suggests that P.H. not only covertly recognises faces, but that his recognition is "normal" in the amount of associative priming that it produces (Young, Hellawell, & De Haan, 1988). It might, of course, be argued that these experimental effects were derived from weak degrees of overt face recognition which were enhanced by the particular manipulations. In our study, this objection was overridden by the demonstration that, even in forced-choice experiments where the patient had to guess which of two face photographs were familiar, no such weak traces of recognition emerged (Young & De Haan, 1988).

To warrant the conclusion that Bauer's original explanation of two face recognition systems had become less plausible, it was thought prudent to verify whether we had been talking about the same phenomenon. Therefore, De Haan, Bauer, and Greve (1992) investigated the possibility of covert face recognition using behavioural tasks in the patient L.F. who had been the subject in the original studies by Bauer using autonomic indices. Using a similar task as the priming experiment described above, we were able to demonstrate covert face recognition on a behavioural measure in this patient. The conclusion was reached that autonomic and behavioural manifestations of covert recognition presumably reflect the same underlying phenomenon. However, it was also stressed that this particular association did not preclude the possibility of an association.

Another useful method to demonstrate covert recognition was an adaptation of an experiment carried out by Bruyer, Laterre, Seron, Feyereisen, Strypstein, et al. (1983). This requires the patient to learn to attach printed names to faces along the lines of the traditional paired associate learning experiments used in studies of memory. On half the trials, the name belonged to the person depicted on the photograph; on the other half, an incorrect name was used belonging to

TABLE 8.3
Mean reaction times in milliseconds for P.H. on the associative priming experiment

	Familiar targets			Unfamiliar targets
	Related	*Neutral*	*Unrelated*	
Face primes	1016	1080	1117	1480
Name primes	945	1032	1048	1265

another celebrity. Covert face recognition is indicated when a patient is better at learning the correct than the incorrect face–name pairings.

Two findings are worth mentioning here which were demonstrated using this procedure of paired-associate learning. The first concerns the boundaries of the knowledge which can be accessed covertly. For instance, one could ask whether the fact that P.H. finds it easier to learn the correct names to the faces indicates that he covertly accesses the name from seeing the face. We tested this possibility by trying to teach him correct and incorrect Christian names to photographs of famous faces. The idea behind this task is that Christian names (e.g. "John") do not identify a particular person. Therefore, correct face–christian name combinations could only be learned faster if the full name is accessed covertly from the face. In this task there was no difference between P.H.'s performance on the correct and the incorrect pairings. Having demonstrated that P.H. does not get to the name covertly, the next question was whether he does have access to autobiographical information concerning the people. An identical task was devised but this time he was taught to link correct and incorrect sports to photographs of famous sports people. For example, John McEnroe was "cricketer" (not true) and Ruud Gullit a "football player" (true). Again, there was no evidence for a better learning performance on the correct pairings. This indicates that P.H.'s covert processing of familiar faces proceeds at least up to the level of successful matching with stored representations but not much further. He does not covertly access the name or autobiographical information from the face. The second question we addressed using the paired associate learning paradigm was whether P.H. continues to learn new faces despite the absence of awareness. One group of people he had never met before his accident was the staff at the research institute. To our surprise, but in accordance with the idea of a recognition system which continues to operate, he has learned to recognise us covertly.

The most convincing demonstrations of covert recognition in P.H. (and other cases reported in the literature) appear to depend on experiments in which both the names and the faces of familiar faces are employed. The effect of covert face recognition is apparent on a response to the name in the interference, the priming and the paired-associate learning paradigm. In addition, De Haan, Young, and Newcombe (1991b) showed that P.H. showed some covert recognition effect on a binary-choice task where he had to choose the correct familiar name to match a photograph of a familiar face. This suggests that covert face recognition effects are derived from the interconnections between the face and other person-identification systems, such as name recognition.

It should be noted that covert recognition effects are not invariably found in agnosias. Another patient, M.S., was investigated with the tasks described above. M.S. was first examined in 1971 and has been studied at regular intervals thereafter (e.g. Young et al., 1989; Heywood & Cowey, ibid.). The clinical history is therefore only briefly summarised. In 1970, at the age of 21, M.S. sustained a presumptive herpes encephalitis. The permanent neurological and clinical features include a left-sided homonymous hemianopia, central achromatopsia, amnesia, and agnosia (for both faces and objects). He has never presented with sensorimotor loss, aphasia, or apraxia. His verbal IQ (WAIS and WAIS-R) has remained in the average range and he is a regular reader of a daily newspaper. His visual acuity is excellent on clinical examination. Now, at the age of forty-two, he is still able to read, uncorrected, with either left or right eye. His difficulty in recognising objects and faces is very severe and has not changed significantly on formal testing since 1971. Over the years he has identified only seven to eleven of the 36 Oldfield–Wingfield line-drawings of objects (Newcombe, Oldfield, Ratcliff, & Wingfield, 1971), and seven from a sample of 72 of the Snodgrass and Vanderwart (1980) set of object line-drawings. An MRI scan revealed extensive bilateral temporo-occipital damage.

When we presented M.S. with the forced-choice face familiarity task (see Fig. 8.2) where he had to decide which of two faces appeared familiar his performance was, like P.H., at chance level. Thus, he also shows no sign of overt face recognition. Subsequently, we employed the priming experiment with face and name primes. The fact that this task allows a direct within-subject comparison of the possible priming effects from names, which can be recognised, and faces which can not be recognised, makes this in our view the strongest test for covert face recognition. From Table 8.4, it is clear that he does show priming from names (demonstrating that the test is appropriate in his case), but there is no hint of any priming from the faces. It was, therefore, concluded that there is no evidence for covert face recognition in M.S. A similar finding was made while testing the possibility of covert object recognition using a priming experiment. In this experiment, two sorts of picture primes were used, pictures of objects that he consistently recognised and objects that he consistently failed to recognise. The results showed a priming effect only from the objects that he can recognise (Newcombe, Young, & De Haan, 1989). The overall conclusion seems warranted that, in the case of M.S., there is no evidence for covert recognition. A similar observation has been made by Bauer (1986) using an autonomic index for covert face recognition.

The fact that by no means all patients show these covert effects has led to the suggestion that indirect recognition tasks may help in identifying different

TABLE 8.4

Mean reaction times in milliseconds for M.S. on the associative priming experiment

	Familiar targets			Unfamiliar targets
	Related	Neutral	Unrelated	
Face primes	1260	1276	1264	1810
Name primes	1178	1370	1439	1872

types of face recognition impairment. It might thus be possible to expand the taxonomy which was suggested by the model of Bruce and Young (1986).

In March 1982, at the age of 25, N.R. was involved in a head-on motorcar collision in which he suffered a severe closed head injury. A penetrating wound to the left eye reduced his visual acuity in that eye to 6/60. His corrected visual acuity was 6/6 in the right eye, he had full visual fields on confrontation, and he could read small print. His intellectual abilities fell into the "below average" range on verbal subtests and his performance abilities were "inferior". Pre-morbid history and the pattern of subtests suggested a severe reduction of general abilities, especially in nonverbal domains. His speech was hampered by word-finding problems. Short-term memory was normal but he had severe problems in storing and retrieving new information.

Colour perception was moderately impaired, and visuo-spatial perception was poor. Visual perception of facial stimuli was very defective. N.R. was rarely able to perceive accurately the age and sex of faces in Mooney's stimuli. Simultaneous matching and immediate recognition of unfamiliar faces was essentially at chance level (Benton & van Allen, 1973), and matching of facial expressions (De Haan, Young, & Newcombe, 1992) was performed at the lower end of the normal range. Identification of familiar faces, whether by naming them or giving appropriate semantic information, was virtually impossible. On the faces line-up task (Young, De Haan, & Newcombe, 1990), he failed to recognise any of the familiar faces. He also performed at chance level on a task where he had to decide whether a face looked familiar or not, but was within the normal range on a parallel version of this task which used written names as stimuli (De Haan et al., 1987b). In short, in clinical terms N.R. was completely prosopagnosic. CT scans carried out in April and May 1982 showed a shallow extra-cerebral collection of blood and cerebro-spinal fluid over the convexity of the *right* parietal lobe. A repeat scan in June 1983 revealed an area of infarction in the *left* parieto-temporal region of the brain.

On the forced-choice familiarity task (see Table 8.5) where subjects have to decide which one of two simultaneously presented faces appear familiar, N.R. performed at an above-chance level (approx. 75% correct). Although N.R. maintained to be guessing continuously, his performance on the forced-choice task

TABLE 8.5
Number of correct choices by N.R. and control subjects
on the forced-choice familiarity decision task

		Faces	*Names*
N.R.		96	122
Normal subjects	mean	125.50	127.50
	SD	3.33	0.84

indicated a degree of familiar face recognition. Surprisingly, the priming experiment with face and name primes showed a performance comparable to that of M.S.; there was a clear facilitation from name primes (which he could recognise overtly) but no effect from face primes. This discrepancy between a degree of rudimentary overt recognition and absence of covert effects on the priming task was addressed using a newly constructed priming experiment. This examined separately the possibility of preserved recognition for faces which N.R. consistently chose correctly in a forced-choice familiarity decision, and those on which he performed at chance level in this type of task. Priming effects were apparent only for the faces that were consistently chosen as "familiar" in forced-choice (see Table 8.6). We suggested that N.R.'s stored representations of familiar faces are degraded, so that face recognition is possible through a limited set of relatively preserved representations able to support a rudimentary form of overt recognition and to facilitate performance in matching and priming tasks (De Haan et al., 1992).

Farah (1994) and Burton, Bruce and Johnston (1990) have suggested that overt face recognition phenomena can be modelled using neural-network simulations. The idea is that in a "degraded" network reduced or partial activation at the intermediate processing levels results in failure to reach threshold activation at the output level. There is, however, enough activation at the intermediate level to influence the weights of connected nodes, thereby influencing the working of the network in a way that resembles covert recognition. This is an elegant explanation of the data, and it is in accordance with the observation that in certain specific experimental conditions overt recognition can be provoked in patients with covert recognition. When presented with photographs of faces from a small number of highly connected celebrities (actors in the TV soap series "Eastenders"), P.H. first recognised the category ("They are all Eastenders") and subsequently started to identify some of the faces (De Haan et al., 1991b). This "provoked overt recognition" does, however, not generalise over time, and has in the case of P.H. only been observed once. Farah's theoretical suggestions have, however, also met with criticism (e.g. Hezewijk & De Haan, 1994). One

TABLE 8.6

Mean reaction times in milliseconds for N.R. on the priming experiment with face primes which were and those which were not consistently recognised in a forced-choice familiarity task

	Familiar name targets			Unfamiliar name targets
	Same person	Neutral	Unrelated	
Face primes recognised in pre-test	1852	2224	2190	2285
Face primes not recognised in pre-test	2273	2101	2250	

of the main problems is that it is an inherently post-hoc explanation. The case of P.H. poses a more specific problem for this explanation. The priming study showed not only that he covertly recognised the familiar faces, but in addition indicated that the amount of priming from unrecognised faces was not significantly reduced in comparison to the priming from names. The partial activation model of Farah would predict a reduced priming effect.

It is clear that these observations of covert recognition impose constraints on theoretical models of visual recognition and, perhaps more importantly, awareness. Similar observations of "knowledge without awareness" have now been demonstrated in a variety of cognitive domains, for instance, in patients with reading problems. Patients who are no longer able to read words "at a glance" and have to adopt a slow and painful strategy of sounding out individual letters can nevertheless respond to words that were presented for such short times that reading was impossible. The patient studied by Shallice and Saffran (1986) was able to tell whether the stimulus was a word or a nonsense letter string and, even more surprisingly, whether a printed name was that of an author or a politician. The close parallel between preserved abilities on implicit tests and those aspects of recognition that seem to operate automatically for normal people are impressive. In other words, covert processing can be seen as a disconnection of the *output* of an otherwise adequately functioning recognition system from whatever processes are needed to support awareness of recognition. The result is a curious disorder of awareness, in which there is no global disturbance of consciousness, but one specific aspect (overt recognition of familiar faces) is lost.

> You know that Harpastes, my wife's fatuous companion, has remained in my home as an inherited burden. . . . This foolish woman has suddenly lost her sight. Incredibly as it might appear, what I am going to tell you is true: she does not know she is blind. Therefore, again and again she asks her guardian to take her elsewhere. She claims that my home is dark.
>
> (Citation from a letter of Seneca to his friend Lucilius.
> Seneca, L.A. *Liber V, Epistula IX*)

Preserved cognitive processing in the absence of acknowledged awareness is arguably not the only manner in which neurological disease can affect consciousness. One of the most striking forms of neuropsychological deficit involves patients who are unaware of their impairments. The term "anosognosia" was coined by Von Monakov (1885), and one of the first seminal writings on this topic was from the hand of Anton (1899), who described patients who were unaware of their blindness or deafness. Anosognosia has been described for a number of different disorders, such as hemiplegia (Babinski, 1914), hemianopia (Critchley, 1949; Warrington, 1962), aphasia (Wernicke, 1874; Lebrun, 1987) and amnesia (Korsakoff, 1889; Talland, 1965). In a review, McGlynn and Schacter (1989) provide evidence against suggestions that the problem can be explained as resulting from intellectual deterioration or general disorientation or confusion.

In addition, they counter the proposal that unawareness would be related to severity of impairment. In particular, in the realm of memory this would be a possible way explaining the problem: severe memory problems would prevent a patient from remembering the occasions when his or her memory had failed. Although other explanations have been offered for specific instances of anosognosia, such as that problems in body-schema would cause unawareness of hemiplegia, a number of authors have recently advanced the idea of anosognosia as a problem in conscious awareness (e.g. Schacter, McAndrews, & Moscovitch, 1988). One observation supporting this idea is the selectivity of anosognosia. Patients with multiple impairments, like hemiplegia and hemianopia, often deny one problem while being painfully aware of the other (Bisiach, Vallar, Perani, Papagno, & Berti, 1986). These investigators conclude (p. 480): "monitoring of the internal working is not secured in the nervous system by a general superordinate organ, but it is decentralized and appointed to the different blocks to which it refers."

S.P. was a 52 year old woman when she suffered a sub-arachnoid haemorrhage from a right middle cerebral artery aneurysm. The chronic sequelae consisted of a left hemiparesis, a left homonymous hemianopia and severe amnesia for verbal and nonverbal material. It was only during routine neuropsychological assessment that we "discovered" that she was severely impaired in recognising familiar faces, as she had never mentioned any subjective problems in this domain. This was particularly surprising since she was clearly very aware of and actively tried to compensate for her other deficits. More detailed investigations revealed that S.P. suffers from rather generalised face perception and recognition impairments. She encounters difficulties in perceiving faces ("closure"), matching unfamiliar faces (Benton & Van Allen, 1973), recognising facial expressions and identifying familiar faces. Moreover, repeated testing has shown that these deficits have remained stable over at least two years (Young et al., 1990). Neither the failings in everyday life nor the demonstrations in our laboratory over the years have managed to instill even a remote sense of her problems in recognising familiar faces. Her anosognosia was perhaps most poignant when her husband took some photographs of paintings she had made before her stroke. She had obviously been an accomplished portrait painter, and this particular set of photographs depicted portraits of close family members. Although she remembered having made the paintings, she was very poor at identifying her relatives. This demonstration, which seemed rather painful and confrontational to us, did not appear to affect her in any way. When queried whether she thought she might have some problems recognising faces, she just seemed puzzled by the question.

This complete lack of insight for prosopagnosia was starkly contrasted by her good insight in the other cognitive and physical disabilities. This led to the conclusion that S.P. suffered from a *deficit-specific anosognosia*. Like Bisiach et al. (1986), it is argued here that such a deficit-specific anosognosia reflects the existence of the need to monitor our own performance. This monitoring might be especially important when it concerns cognitive abilities, like face recognition, which are carried out automatically and do not rely on conscious control. As a consequence, there is no introspection possible into the processes underlying this type of ability. This raises the question about reliability of information: "is that really the face of X?" or "that face looks very similar to that of X but actually it is not." This is exactly the sort of information a monitoring device would supply. Dysfunction of this monitoring device could produce a selective problem in detecting the fact that the recognition of familiar faces has become difficult. It was in this context that we looked for—and found—evidence for covert face recognition in S.P. This last result points to the (very) hypothetical explanation that the face recognition system monitoring process continues to signal that all is well, because at the level at which it is monitoring all is well. Obviously, this cannot be the whole story as this would suggest that every patient with covert face recognition would also show anosognosia. This is obviously not the case. Therefore, one has to assume that the monitor itself it is not functioning properly either. At any rate, the opposite hypothesis, that covert processing is a prerequisite for anosognosia, is intriguing and warrants further investigation.

In summary, neuropsychological evidence demonstrates that awareness can break down in a number of different ways. In contrast to earlier suggestions, it is clearly not necessary for these patients to suffer from a global loss of consciousness. Instead, the loss of awareness in the cases presented above is highly *specific*, i.e. unawareness of preserved processing versus unawareness of (overt) impairment. In addition, the problems presented have been highly *selective* in the sense of confined to one cognitive ability, in this case familiar face recognition. Therefore, on the basis of clinical data the same conclusion is reached that conscious awareness is *not* a unitary concept (Young & De Haan, 1990). To put it more boldly, it appears to have *levels* and *domains*, and if this idea is taken seriously, the concept of awareness has been drawn well into the realm of cognitive processing. Or, as Anton suggested as early as 1899 in the context of denial of blindness and deafness: "the problem of anosognosia for an impaired function results from a disturbance at the highest level of organisation of that particular function."

ACKNOWLEDGEMENTS

The experimental work reported in this chapter was carried out in collaboration with Freda Newcombe, Andrew W. Young and Russell Bauer, and supported by MRC grant G8804850 to Freda Newcombe and Andrew Young and MRC grant G9114877N to Edward De Haan, Freda Newcombe and Richard Kerr.

REFERENCES

Anton, G. (1899). Ueber die Selbstwahrnemung der Herderkrankungen des Gehirns durch den Kranken bei Rindenblindheit und Rindentaubheit. *Archiv für Psychiatrie und Nervenkrankheiten*, *32*, 86–127.

Babinski, M.J. (1914). Contribution à l'étude des troubles mentaux dans l'hemiplégie organique cérébrale (Anosognosie). *Revue Neurologique, 12*, 845–8.

Bauer, R.M. (1984). Autonomic recognition of names and faces in prosopagnosia: a neuropsychological application of the guilty knowledge test. *Neuropsychologia, 22*, 457–69.

Bauer, R.M. (1986). The cognitive psychophysiology of prosopagnosia. In H.D. Ellis, M.A. Jeeves, F. Newcombe, & A. Young (Eds), *Aspects of face processing*, pp. 253–67. Dordrecht: Martinus Nijhoff.

Bear, D.M. (1983). Hemispheric specialization and the neurology of emotion. *Archives of Neurology, 40*, 195.

Benton, A.L., & Van Allen, M.W. (1973). *Manual: Test of facial recognition*. Neurosensory Center Publication No. 287. Department of Neurology, University Hospitals, Iowa City, Iowa.

Bisiach, E., Vallar, G., Perani, D., Papagno, C., & Berti, A. (1986). Unawareness of disease following lesions of the right hemisphere: anosognosia for hemiplegia and anosognosia for hemianopia. *Neuropsychologia, 24*, 471–82.

Bodamer, J. (1947). Die Prosop-Agnosie. *Archiv für Psychiatrie und Nervenkrankheiten, 179*, 6–53.

Bruce, V., & Young, A.W. (1986). Understanding face recognition. *British Journal of Psychology, 77*, 305–327.

Bruyer, R., Laterre, C., Seron, X., Feyereisen, P., Strypstein, E., Pierrard, E., & Rectem, D. (1983). A case of prosopagnosia with some preserved covert remembrance of familiar faces. *Brain and Cognition, 2*, 257–84.

Burton, A.M., Bruce, V., & Johnston, R.A. (1990). Understanding face recognition with an interactive activation model. *British Journal of Psychology, 81*, 361–80.

Campbell, R., Brooks, B., De Haan, E.H.F., & Roberts, A. (1996). Dissociated face processing skills: Reaction time evidence on seen speech, expression and identity matching from photographs. *Quarterly Journal of Experimental Psychology, 49*, 295–314.

Campbell, R., Landis, T., & Regard, M. (1986). Face recognition and lipreading: a neurological dissociation. *Brain, 109*, 509–21.

Critchley, M. (1949). The problem of awareness or non-awareness of hemianopic field defects. *Transactions of the Ophthalmological Society of the UK, 69*, 95–109.

Damasio, A.R., Damasio, H., & Van Hoesen, G.W. (1982). Prosopagnosia: anatomic basis and behavioral mechanisms. *Neurology, 32*, 331–41.

De Haan, E.H.F., Bauer, R.M., & Greve, K.W. (1992). Behavioural and physiological evidence for covert face recognition in a prosopagnosic patient. *Cortex, 28*, 77–95.

De Haan, E.H.F., & Campbell, R. (1991). A fifteen year follow-up of a case of developmental prosopagnosia. *Cortex, 27*, 489–509.

De Haan, E.H.F., Young, A., & Newcombe, F. (1987a). Face recognition without awareness. *Cognitive Neuropsychology, 4*, 385–415.

De Haan, E.H.F., Young, A., & Newcombe, F. (1987b). Faces interfere with name classification in a prosopagnosic patient. *Cortex, 23*, 309–16.

De Haan, E.H.F., Young, A.W., & Newcombe, F. (1991a). A dissociation between the sense of familiarity and access to semantic information concerning familiar people. *European Journal of Cognitive Psychology, 3*, 51–67.

De Haan, E.H.F., Young, A.W., & Newcombe, F. (1991b). Covert and overt recognition in prosopagnosia. *Brain, 114*, 2575–91.

De Haan, E.H.F., Young, A.W., & Newcombe, F. (1992). Neuropsychological impairments of face recognition units. *Quarterly Journal of Experimental Psychology, 44A*, 141–75.

De Renzi, E. (1986). Current issues in prosopagnosia. In H.D. Ellis, M.A. Jeeves, F. Newcombe, & A. Young (Eds), *Aspects of face processing*, pp. 243–52. Dordrecht: Martinus Nijhoff.

Farah, M. (1994). Neuropsychological interference with an interactive brain: a critique of the "locality" assumption. *Behavioral and Brain Sciences, 17*, 43–104.

Feinberg, T.E., Schindler, R.J., Ochoa, E., & Kwan, P.C. (1994). Associative visual agnosia and alexia without prosopagnosia. *Cortex, 30*, 395–412.

Hezewijk, R. Van, & De Haan, E.H.F. (1994). The symbolic brain or the invisible hand. *Behavioral and Brain Sciences*, *17*, 85–6.

Korsakoff, S.S. (1889). Etude médico-psychologique sur une forme des maladies de la mémoire. *Revue Philosophique*, *28*, 501–30.

Kurucz, J., & Feldmar, G. (1979). Prosopo-affective agnosia as a symptom of cerebral organic disease. *Journal of the American Geriatrics Society*, *27*, 225–30.

Landis, T., Cummings, J.L., Christen, L., Bogen, J.E., & Imhof, H-G (1986). Are unilateral right posterior cerebral lesions sufficient to cause prosopagnosia? Clinical and radiological findings in 6 additional patients *Cortex*, *22*, 243–52.

Lebrun, Y. (1987). Anosognosia in aphasics. *Cortex*, *23*, 251–63.

McCarthy, R.A., & Warrington, E.K. (1986). Visual associative agnosia: a clinico-anatomical study of a single case. *Journal of Neurology, Neurosurgery and Psychiatry*, *49*, 1233–40.

McConachie, H.R. (1976). Developmental prosopagnosia. A single case report. *Cortex*, *12*, 76–82.

McGlynn, S., & Schacter, D.L. (1989). Unawareness of deficits in neuropsychological syndromes. *Journal of Clinical and Experimental Neuropsychology*, *11*, 143–205.

McNeil, J.A., & Warrington, E.K. (1991). Prosopagnosia: a reclassification. *Quarterly Journal of Experimental Psychology*, *43A*, 267–87.

Malone, D.R., Morris, H.H., Kay, M.C., & Levin, H.S. (1982). Prosopagnosia: a double dissociation between the recognition of familiar and unfamiliar faces. *Journal of Neurology, Neurosurgery and Psychiatry*, *45*, 820–22.

Marr, D. (1982). *Vision*. San Francisco, CA: Freeman.

Maurer, D., & Barrera, M-E. (1981). Infants' perception of natural and distorted arrangements of a schematic face. *Child Development*, *52*, 196–202.

Moscovitch, M., Winocur, G., & Behrmann, M. (1997). What is special about faces? Nineteen experiments on a person with visual object agnosia and dyslexia but normal face recognition. *Journal of Cognitive Neuroscience*, *9*, 555–604.

Newcombe, F., Oldfield, R.C., Ratcliff, G.G., & Wingfield, A. (1971). Recognition and naming of object-drawings by men with focal brain wounds. *Journal of Neurology, Neurosurgery and Psychiatry*, *34*, 329–40.

Newcombe, F., Young, A.W., & De Haan, E.H.F. (1989). Prosopagnosia and object agnosia without covert recognition. *Neuropsychologia*, *27*, 179–91.

Pallis, C.A. (1955). Impaired identification of faces and places with agnosia for colours. *Journal of Neurology, Neurosurgery and Psychiatry*, *18*, 218–24.

Perrett, D.I., Rolls, E.T., & Caan, W. (1982). Visual neurons responsive to faces in the monkey temporal cortex. *Experimental Brain Research*, *47*, 329–42.

Renault, B., Signoret, J.L., DeBruille, B., Breton, F., & Bolgert, F. (1989). Brain potentials reveal covert facial recognition in prosopagnosia. *Neuropsychologia*, *27*, 905–12.

Rizzo, M., Hurtig, R., & Damasio, A.R. (1987). The role of scanpaths in facial recognition and learning. *Annals of Neurology*, *22*, 41–5.

Roder, B., Bates, C., Crowell, S., & Schilling, Th. (1992). The perception of identity by $6\frac{1}{2}$ month old infants. *Journal of Experimental Child Psychology*, *54*, 57–73.

Schacter, D.L., McAndrews, M.P., & Moscovitch, M. (1988). Access to consciousness: dissociations between implicit and explicit knowledge in neuropsychological syndromes. In L. Weiskrantz (Ed.), *Thought without language*, pp. 242–78. Oxford: Oxford University Press.

Shallice, T., & Saffran, E. (1986). Lexical processing in the absence of explicit word identification: evidence from a letter-by-letter reader. *Cognitive Neuropsychology*, *3*, 429–58.

Shuttleworth, E.C., Syring, V., & Allen, N. (1982). Further observations on the nature of prosopagnosia. *Brain and Cognition*, *1*, 302–32.

Snodgrass, J.G., & Vanderwart, M. (1980). A standardized set of 260 pictures: norms for name agreement, image agreement, familiarity, and visual complexity. *Journal of Experimental Psychology: Human Learning and Memory*, *6*, 174–215.

Talland, G.A. (1965). *Deranged memory*. New York: Academic Press.

Teuber, H-L. (1955). Physiological psychology. *Annual Review of Psychology, 6,* 267–96.

Teuber, H-L. (1968). Alteration of perception and memory in man. In L. Weiskrantz (Ed.), *Analysis of behaviour change.* New York: Harper and Row.

Tranel, D., & Damasio, A.R. (1985). Knowledge without awareness: an autonomic index of facial recognition by prosopagnosics. *Science, 228,* 1453–4.

Ungerleider, L.G., & Mishkin, M. (1982). Two cortical systems. In D.J. Ingle, M.A. Goodale and R.J.W. Mansfield (Eds), pp. 549–86. *Analysis of visual behavior.* Cambridge, MA.: MIT press.

Von Monakow, C. (1885). Experimentelle und pathologisch-anatomische Untersuchungen über die Beziehungen der sogenannten Sehsphäre zu den infracorticalen Opticuscentren und zum N. opticus. *Archiv für Psychiatrie und Nervenkrankheiten, 16,* 151–99.

Warrington, E.K. (1962). The completion of visual forms across hemianopic field defects. *Journal of Neurology, Neurosurgery and Psychiatry, 25,* 208–17.

Wernicke, C. (1874). *Der aphatische Symptomencomplex.* Breslau: Cohn und Weigert.

Whiteley, A.M., & Warrington, E.K. (1977). Prosopagnosia; a clinical, psychological and anatomical study of three patients. *Journal of Neurology, Neurosurgery and Psychiatry, 40,* 395–403.

Young, A.W., & De Haan, E.H.F. (1988). Boundaries of covert recognition in prosopagnosia. *Cognitive Neuropsychology, 5,* 317–36.

Young, A.W., & De Haan, E.H.F. (1990). Impairments of visual awareness. *Mind and Language, 5,* 29–48.

Young, A.W., De Haan, E.H.F., & Newcombe, F. (1990). Unawareness of impaired face recognition. *Brain and Cognition, 14,* 1–18.

Young, A.W., Hellawell, D., & De Haan, E.H.F. (1988). Cross-domain semantic priming in normal subjects and a prosopagnosic patient. *Quarterly Journal of Experimental Psychology, 40A,* 561–80.

Young, A.W., Newcombe, F., De Haan, E.H.F., Small, M., & Hay, D.C. (1993). Face perception after brain injury: selective impairments affecting identity and expression. *Brain, 116,* 941–59.

Young, A.W., Newcombe, F., Hellawell, D., & De Haan, E.H.F. (1989). Implicit access to semantic information. *Brain and Cognition, 11,* 186–209.

CHAPTER NINE

Relations among the agnosias

Martha J. Farah
Department of Psychology, University of Pennsylvania, USA

Visual agnosia is the impairment of visual object recognition in people who possess sufficiently preserved visual fields, acuity and other elementary forms of visual ability to enable object recognition, and in whom the object recognition impairment cannot be attributed to dementia or loss of knowledge about objects. Thus agnosics can describe at least some visual attributes of the objects they cannot recognise, and they can generally recognise these same objects when encountered through hearing or touch. Their impairment is one of visual recognition rather than naming, and is therefore manifest on naming and nonverbal tasks alike. For example, they will be impaired at sorting objects according to their uses, such as putting an orange together with a banana, separate from a tennis ball.

Neuropsychologists disagree on how much grouping versus fractionating of cases should be done when discussing cognitive impairments following brain damage. Some traditional categories such as Broca's aphasia or neglect may well be heterogeneous, and correct scientific generalisations may be possible only after finer subdivision (e.g. Caramazza, 1984). Nevertheless, there are instances in which differences in surface manifestation do not necessarily signal different underlying disorders (e.g. see Behrmann, Moscovitch, Black, & Mozer, 1990). The different presentations of visual agnosia are sufficiently varied that no one would be tempted to propose a single category for theorising about disorders of visual object recognition. However, just how finely the agnosias should be subdivided, and along what lines, has been a matter of debate. Before discussing the relations among the agnosias as I have delineated them, I will briefly review other taxonomies.

TAXONOMIES OF VISUAL AGNOSIA

The first explicit taxonomy of visual agnosia came from Lissauer (1890), who suggested that visual object recognition could break down two ways: Either perception of objects could be impaired, or the perception of objects could be normal but the process of associating the object percept with associated knowledge in memory could be impaired. Although all forms of agnosia by definition exclude elementary visual deficits, Lissauer pointed out that object perception requires more than the local registration of elements of brightness, colour or contour, and he termed this higher level of perception "apperception". The resulting two types of agonsia were therefore called apperceptive and associative agnosia. Lissauer's distinction between these two categories of agnosia has been extremely influential in the history of theorising about agnosia. Many subsequent authors have retained this distinction or a similar one. Indeed, the best-known cases of what have come to be called "apperceptive" and "associative" agnosia were described by authors writing decades later; Lissauer had drawn the distinction in the abstract and did not present clear-cut cases of either.

Nielsen (1936) proposed a detailed taxonomy of agnosias based on the types of visual stimuli affected and associated lesion sites, with relatively little specification of the status of perception per se. His clinical experience led him to distinguish patients with impaired recognition of living things, nonliving things, printed words, printed symbols, and so forth. He believed that these were distinct disorders that had localising value for the neurologist. Some decades later, Konorski (1967) proposed a similarly generous number of distinct visual agnosias for different stimulus categories. He was less concerned with the localisation of these agnosias than with the organising principles giving rise to the stimulus categories that the agnosias revealed. For example, he proposed that agnosia for small manipulable objects and large stable objects were dissociable, and explained this in terms of the different conditions under which the relevant visual knowledge could be obtained. In one case, the entire object is visible at a glance and has associated tactile knowledge, whereas in the other several different views must be integrated and there are no associated manual sensations. The empirical evidence for the large number of stimulus-specific visual agnosias proposed by Neilsen and Konorski was largely anecdotal, and when included the case reports were sketchy. Perhaps for this reason, more recent authors have ignored most of the distinctions embodied in these taxonomies, and have returned to an emphasis on the status of visual perception as a basis for delineating different agnosias.

Warrington (e.g. 1985) distinguishes between apperceptive and associative visual agnosia, as well as what she terms "pseudoagnosia". In her taxonomy, apperceptive agnosia is a failure of shape constancy that is revealed when patients view objects from unusual perspectives or under unusual patterns of illumination (see Chapter 4). Under normal viewing conditions, these same patients are able to recognise objects. Associative agnosia results when object perception is essentially intact but semantic knowledge about objects is destroyed or inaccessible to visual stimuli. When only the most elementary forms of visual perception are intact, such as brightness perception, colour perception and acuity, but shape perception is impaired under normal viewing conditions, Warrington labels the impairment "pseudognosia". Orthogonal to the dimension of percep-tual preservation, Warrington also classifies agnosias by the category of stimuli affected, distinguishing between agnosia for faces, and agnosia for objects (e.g. McNeil & Warrington, 1993).

Kertesz (1987) proposes three major categories of agnosia, which are further elaborated or subdivided by virtue of their co-occurrence with a list of ten associated disorders. The first of the three major categories is apperceptive agnosia. By this term Kertesz refers to loss of shape perception with relative sparing of elementary perceptual capabilities such as colour and brightness perception and acuity. Note that this is the same disorder that Warrington refers to as pseudoagnosia. Kertesz's second major category is associative agnosia, within which he includes patients whose perception is sufficiently intact to copy or match pictures of objects, but who nevertheless fail to recognise them. He sug-gests that associative agnosics may have impaired access to semantics from vision, or a subtle impairment of perception, thus encompassing patients whom Warrington would exclude. The third of Kertesz's major categories in optic aphasia, a disorder of naming specific to visual stimuli, which Kertesz suggests may simply be a mild form of associative visual agnosia (see Chapter 7). These disorders may occur in conjunction with colour vision deficits, alexia (printed word recognition deficits), prosopagnosia, confabulation, loss of visual imagery, amnesia, denial of visual impairment, Balint's syndrome (a complex of dis-ordered reaching, attention and eye movements directed towards visual stimuli), static agnosia (in which moving stimuli are perceived better than static) and simultanagnosia (defined by Kertesz as an impairment in perceiving multiple parts of a complex stimulus simultaneously).

Humphreys and Riddoch (1987) proposed a seven-part taxonomy of visual agnosia, guided jointly by empirical and theoretical considerations. Their "impaired shape processing" corresponds to Warrington's pseudoagnosia and to what Kertesz and many other contemporary authors call apperceptive agnosia. Their "impaired transformation processes" corresponds to Warrington's apper-ceptive agnosia. "Impaired integration processes" encompasses patients who have good perception as assessed by conventional tests such as copying, but in whom certain subtle perceptual impairments can be demonstrated with more sensitive tests, including those probing the integration of shape information. Thus, some patients whom others would have called associative agnosics fall into this category (see Chapter 3). "Loss of stereoscopic vision" is a relatively self-explanatory category, which Humphreys and Riddoch suggest might in principle lead to impairments of object and especially face recognition because of the usefulness of binocular depth perception in representing shape. In "impaired access to form knowledge", patients' perception is normal but their access to stored visual memories of object shape is blocked due to damage or disconnection. "Impaired access to semantics" encompasses patients who can recognise objects in the sense of deriving a normal shape representation and matching it with a stored shape representation in memory, but who cannot use that visual representation to access semantic information about the object. The example they cite is a patient who would traditionally be called an optic aphasic, for example in Kertesz' taxonomy. Their final category, "impaired semantic knowledge", is also self-explanatory, and corresponds to Warrington's associative agnosia.

Bauer (1993) recently offered a taxonomy of agnosia consisting of five main categories: apperceptive agnosia, associative agnosia, optic aphasia, colour agnosia, prosopagnosia, and category-specific agnosia. Within apperceptive agnosia, Bauer follows me (Farah, 1990) in distinguishing four types of apperceptive agnosia. The first is apperceptive agnosia in the narrow sense, referring to the impairment of shape perception in the absence of elementary visual sensory impairments. This corresponds to the most common use of the term, for example by Kertesz. However, the term "apperceptive agnosia" has also been extended by some to encompass two distinct forms of so-called simultanagnosia, as well as the distinct disorder referred to by Warrington as apperceptive agnosia. The relations among these categories of impairment will be discussed in the next section. Bauer delineates associative agnosia and optic aphasia in the traditional ways, with associative agnosics by definition impaired at all tasks requiring visual recognition and optic aphasics impaired only at naming. Colour agnosia is included in his taxonomy and further subdivided, although this category will not be discussed here because the emphasis of the present chapter is on object recognition. Prosopagnosia ranks as a distinct disorder in Bauer's taxonomy, although he interprets it not as a face-specific disorder but as an impairment in distinguishing visually similar members of a category. Category-specific agnosia refers to impaired recognition of objects from a specific semantic category, most often living things (animals, plants) or man-made objects. At least some patients in this category would be classified in Warrington's taxonomy as associative agnosics.

This small sample of taxonomies for agnosia gives some indication of the range of systems that have been proposed. Although some of the differences between taxonomies are purely a matter of labelling, others are more substantive and concern the relations among different agnosias and agnosia-like disorders. For example, do disorders such as prosopagnosia and object agnosia, or object agnosia and optic aphasia, differ in degree or in kind? Ought disorders of depth perception or colour perception be considered object recognition disorders?

Different answers to these questions correspond to assumptions about the distinct and therefore separately lesionable components of visual object recognition, and the dimensions of vision that play a central as opposed to a peripheral role in object recognition. These assumptions in effect form a theory of object recognition implicit in each taxonomy. For this reason, taxonomies of agnosia are of theoretical importance. They reflect our assumptions about the underlying nature of object recognition and its disorders, and they constrain our attempts at further understanding by making certain theoretically relevant commonalities and distinctions more or less salient.

I have proposed a taxonomy of visual agnosia in which cases are grouped using criteria that are as purely empirical as possible (Farah, 1990). My motivation was to let the natural category structure of the data first "speak for itself", and then use that structure to test theories of visual object recognition. The resulting taxonomy was, reassuringly, not radically different from that of previous authors, although some new distinctions were introduced and some old distinctions were collapsed. Like many other authors, I retain the apperceptive– associative distinction, but view it as a purely empirical distinction between those agnosics with and without gross, obvious perceptual impairments rather than as a distinction between underlying mechanisms of a perceptual and associative nature. I also distinguish two forms of associative agnosia, as a function of the types of stimuli most affected. In the next two sections, I will review two classic case studies of agnosia, one of the apperceptive variety and one of the associative. In each section I will highlight the cardinal signs of these disorders and the relations between them and other forms of visual disorder with which they are sometimes categorised. In the final two sections, I will describe two forms of associative agnosia that I classify separately within my taxonomy, and which I hypothesise reflect impairments of different underlying forms of shape representation. For one of these forms, prosopagnosia, I will also provide a case study.

APPERCEPTIVE AGNOSIA

One of the classic case studies of *apperceptive agnosia* was written by Benson and Greenberg (1969). Their patient was a young man who had suffered carbon monoxide poisoning, resulting in a profound apperceptive visual agnosia. They write (pp. 83–5):

> Visual acuity could not be measured with a Snellen eye chart, as he could neither identify letters of the alphabet nor describe their configuration. He was able to indicate the orientation of a letter "E", however, and could detect movement of a

small object at standard distance. He could identify some familiar numbers if they were slowly drawn in small size on a screen. He could readily maintain optic fixation during fundoscopic examination, and optokinetic nystagmus was elicited bilaterally with fine, $\frac{1}{8}$ inch marks on a tape . . . Visual fields were normal to 10mm and 3mm white objects, and showed only minimal inferior constriction bilaterally to 3mm red and green objects . . .

The patient was able to distinguish small differences in the luminance (0.1log unit) and wavelength (7–10mu) of a test aperture subtending a visual angle of approximately 2 degrees. While he could detect these differences in luminance, wavelength, and area, and could respond to small movements of objects before him, he was unable to distinguish between two objects of the same luminance, wavelength, and area when the only difference between them was shape.

Recent and remote memory, spontaneous speech, comprehension of spoken language, and repetition were intact. He could name colours, but was unable to name objects, pictures of objects, body parts, letters, numbers, or geometrical figures on visual confrontation. Yet he could readily identify and name objects from tactile, olfactory or auditory cues. Confabulatory responses in visual identification utilized color and size cues (a safety pin was "silver and shiny like a watch or a nail clipper" and a rubber eraser was "a small ball"). He identified a photograph of a white typewritten letter on a blue background as "a beach scene", pointing to the blue background as "the ocean", the stationary as "the beach", and the small typewritten print as "people seen on the beach from an airplane".

He consistently failed to identify or to match block letters; occasionally he "read" straight line numbers, but never those with curved parts. He could clumsily write only a few letters (X, L) and numbers (1, 4, 7), but often inverted or reversed these. Although he could consistently identify Os or Xs as they were slowly drawn, or if the paper containing them was moved slowly before him, he was unable to identify the very same letters afterwards on the motionless page. He was totally unable to copy letters or simple figures, and he could neither describe nor trace the outline of common objects . . .

He was unable to select his doctor or family members from a group until they spoke and was unable to identify family members from photographs. At one time he identified his own face in a mirror as his doctor's face. He did identify his own photograph, but only by the colour of his military uniform. After closely inspecting a scantily attired magazine "cover girl", he surmised that she was a woman because "there is no hair on her arms". That this surmise was based on flesh color identification was evident when he failed to identify any body parts. For example, when asked to locate her eyes he pointed to her breasts . . .

In this description we see the essential features of apperceptive agnosia, which can be found in a number of other cases in the literature (Adler, 1944; Alexander & Albert, 1983; Campion & Latto, 1985; Gelb & Goldstein, 1918; Landis, Graves, Benson, & Hebben, 1982; Milner, Perrett, Johnston, Benson et al., 1991). Elementary visual functions including visual fields, acuity, colour and depth perception appear sufficient for object recognition. Despite this, the patient is extremely impaired at naming, copying and matching even simple

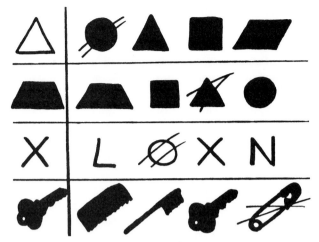

FIG. 9.1   Sample trials from the shape matching task that Benson and Greenberg (1969) adminis-tered to their apperceptive agnosic subject, along with the subject's responses.

shapes. Figure 9.1 shows the shape matching task that Benson and Greenberg's subject failed, with his erroneous choices. Recognition of real objects may be somewhat better than recognition of geometric shapes, although this appears to be due to the availability of cues such as size, and surface properties such as color, texture and specularity, rather than object shape. Facilitation of shape perception by motion has been noted in several cases of apperceptive agnosia. In this as in most cases of apperceptive agnosia, the brain damage is diffuse.

One way of interpreting apperceptive agnosia is in terms of a disorder of grouping processes that normally operate over the array of local features representing contour, colour, depth and so on (Farah, 1990). Outside of their field defects, apperceptive agnosics have surprisingly good perception of local visual properties. They fail when they must extract more global structure from the image. Motion is helpful because it provides another cue to global structure, in the form of correlated local motions. The perception of structure from motion may also have different neural substrates from the perception of structure from static contour (e.g. Marcar & Cowey, 1992) and this may contribute to its sparing in apperceptive agnosia.

Relations to other disorders. Some authors have grouped two types of simultanagnosic patients with the ones cited here as cases of apperceptive agnosia (e.g. Alexander & Albert, 1983; Rubens & Bauer, 1985). In addition, Warrington (e.g. 1985) has used the term apperceptive agnosia to denote yet another distinct disorder. The relations among these different disorders will be reviewed briefly here (see Farah, 1990, Chapter 2 for more detail).

Simultanagnosia is a term used to describe an impairment in perception of multielement or multipart visual displays. When shown a complex picture with multiple objects or people, simultanagnosics typically describe them in a piecemeal manner, sometimes omitting much of the material entirely and therefore failing to interpret the overall nature of the scene being depicted.

In *dorsal simultanagnosia*, patients have an attentional limitation which prevents them from seeing more than one object at a time. Occasionally their attention may be captured by just one part of an object, leading to misidentification of the object and the appearance of perception confined to relatively local image features. The similarity to apperceptive agnosia is limited, however. Once they can attend to an object, dorsal simultanagnosics recognise it quickly and accurately, and even their "local" errors encompass much more global shape information than is available to apperceptive agnosics. Their lesions are typically in the posterior parietal cortex bilaterally.

Ventral simultanagnosics can recognise whole objects, but are limited in how many objects can be recognised in a given period of time. Their descriptions of complex scenes are slow and piecemeal, but unlike apperceptive agnosics their perception of single shapes is not obviously impaired. This impairment is most apparent when reading, because the individual letters of words are recognised in an abnormally slow and generally serial manner. Unlike dorsal simultanagnosics, their detection of multiple stimuli appears normal; the bottleneck is in recognition per se. Unlike apperceptive agnosics, they perceive individual shapes reasonably well. In fact, the perceptual disorder of these patients is mild in comparison to both dorsal simultanagnosics and apperceptive agnosics, and for this reason it may be more sensible to consider them to have a form of associative agnosia. Indeed, they will be discussed further below, in the context of associative agnosia. Their lesions are typically in the left inferior temporo-occipital cortex.

Perceptual categorisation deficit is a final category of impairment whose relation to apperceptive agnosia should be made clear. It is equivalent to the impairment that Warrington (1985) terms apperceptive agnosia (see also Chapter 4), but is quite distinct from what I and most other writers mean by the term. The hallmark of perceptual categorisation deficit is poor performance at recognising or matching objects seen from unusual views or illuminated in unusual ways so as to produce confusing shadows. This impairment has been interpreted as a breakdown in the mechanisms of object shape constancy, that is, the visual mechanisms that allow us to appreciate the equivalence of an object's three-dimensional shape across different views and under different lighting conditions. Two considerations suggest that we should be cautious before accepting this interpretation. First, the impairment has been demonstrated only with unusual views, in which major axes are foreshortened or salient features occluded, whereas a true loss of shape constancy would affect the matching of any views that differ from one another, whether or not they are unusual. Second, the impairment is often seen in patients who have no problems with everyday object recognition. Thus, perceptual categorisation deficit may represent a loss of a certain type of visual problem-solving ability, rather than of an essential component of object recognition.

ASSOCIATIVE AGNOSIA

A classic case of *associative visual agnosia* was reported by Rubens and Benson (1971). Their subject was a middle-aged physician who became agnosic following an acute hypotensive episode. They report (pp. 308–9) that:

> For the first three weeks in the hospital, the patient could not identify common objects presented visually, and did not know what was on his plate until he tasted it. He identified objects immediately on touching them. When shown a stethoscope, he described it as "a long cord with a round thing at the end", and asked if it could be a watch. He identified a can opener as "could be a key." Asked to name a cigarette lighter, he said, "I don't know" but named it after the examiner lit it. He said he was "not sure" when shown a toothbrush. Asked to identify a comb, he said, "I don't know." When shown a large matchbook, he said, "It could be a container for keys." He correctly identified a glass. For a pipe, he said, "Some type of utensil, I'm not sure." Shown a key, he said, "I don't know what that is; perhaps a file or a tool of some sort."
>
> He was never able to describe or demonstrate the use of an object if he could not name it. If he misnamed an object his demonstration of its use would correspond to the mistaken identification. Identification improved very slightly when given the category of the object (e.g., "something to eat") or when asked to point to a named object instead of being required to give the name. When told the correct name of an object, he usually responded with a quick nod and said, "Yes, I see it now." Then, often he could point out various parts of the previously unrecognized object as readily as a normal subject (e.g., the stem and bowl of a pipe, and the laces, sole and heel of a shoe). However, if asked by the examiner "Suppose I told you that the last object was not really a pipe, what would you say?" He would reply, "I would take your word for it. Perhaps it's not really a pipe." Similar vacillation never occurred with tactilely or aurally identified objects.
>
> After three weeks on the ward, object naming ability had improved so that he could name many common objects, but this was variable; he might correctly name an object one time and misname it later. Performance deteriorated severely if any part of the object was covered by the examiner. He could match identical objects but not group objects by categories (clothing, food). He could draw outlines of objects (key, spoon, etc.) which he could not identify. He was unable to recognize members of his family, the hospital staff, or even his own face in the mirror . . . Sometimes he had difficulty distinguishing a line drawing of an animal's face from a man's face, but he always recognized it as a face.
>
> Ability to recognize pictures of objects was greatly impaired, and after repeated testing he could name only one or two out of ten line drawings. He was always able to name geometrical forms (circle, square, triangle, cube). Remarkably, he could make excellent copies of line drawings and still fail to name the subject . . . He

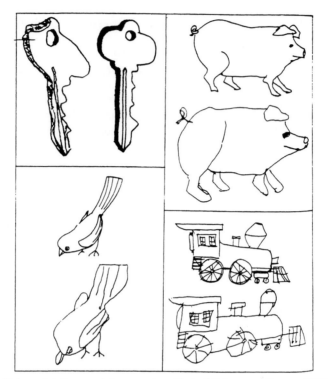

FIG. 9.2   Pictures that the associative agnosic subject of Rubens and Benson (1971) could not recognise, along with the subject's copies of the pictures.

easily matched drawings of objects that he could not identify, and had no difficulty discriminating between complex nonrepresentational patterns differing from each other only subtly. He occasionally failed in discriminating because he included imperfections in the paper or in the printer's ink. He could never group drawings by class unless he could first name the subject.

Reading, both aloud and for comprehension, was greatly limited. He could read, hesitantly, most printed letters, but often misread "K" as "R" and "L" as "T" and vice versa . . . He was able to read words slowly by spelling them aloud.

In this case we see all the elements of associative agnosia: Impaired recognition of visually presented objects, demonstrated verbally and nonverbally, in a patient with apparently adequate visual perception. Recognition of objects through other modalities is intact, and copying and matching ability appear remarkably preserved. Figure 9.2 shows four drawings that this patient was unable to recognise, along with his excellent copies. Other well-documented cases of associative agnosia include those reported by Albert, Reches and Silverberg (1975), Bauer (1982), Davidoff and Wilson (1985), Feinberg, Schindler, Ochoa, Kwan and Farah (1994), Levine (1978), Levine and Calvanio (1989), Mack and Boller

(1977), McCarthy and Warrington (1986), Ratcliff and Newcombe (1982) and Riddoch and Humphreys (1987a).

The perceptual abilities of associative agnosics are dramatically superior to those of apperceptive agnosics, and it is hard to resist the conclusion that their perception of objects is truely normal and that their object recognition difficulties emerge downstream of perception. However, on closer inspection, the evidence for normal perception is not terribly strong. Although their copies are normal, their method of copying is not. Brown (1972), who observed the Rubens and Benson's patient, described his copying as "fairly accurate but slavish". The process by which associative agnosics produce their good copies is invariably characterised as slow, slavish, and line-by-line (see Farah, 1990, Chapters 4 and 5, for a review).

Several other observations are consistent with the idea that an impairment in visual perception underlies associative agnosia. Associative agnosic patients are also abnormally sensitive to the visual quality of stimuli, performing best with real objects, next best with photographs, and worst with line drawings, an ordering reflecting increasing impoverishment of the stimulus, and tachistoscopic presentation also impairs performance dramatically. Additional evidence comes from the nature of the recognition errors made by associative agnosics, which are primarily shape-based, for example mistaking a coiled hose for a bracelet. Additional evidence comes from the matching of complex abstract designs, in which post-perceptual or semantic knowledge could not play a role. Recall that Rubens and Benson's patient occasionally mistook flaws in the paper or printer's ink for a part of an abstract design in a matching task, reminiscent of IT-lesioned monkeys' use of local, idiosyncratic features in visual discrimination learning (Plaut & Farah, 1990). Levine (1978) administered a visual discrimination learning task to an associative agnosic, and found her unable to learn a subtle discrimination between two abstract patterns after 30 trials.

In sum, a variety of different observations is consistent with the idea that associative visual agnosics fail to recognise visually presented objects because they fail to represent their shape in a normal way. The extremely slow and slavish copying technique, the visual nature of their errors, and abnormalities in performance at matching abstract designs all point fairly directly to a shape perception impairment.

Relations to other disorders

Associative agnosia is distinct from *optic aphasia*, which is traditionally interpreted as a naming impairment specific to visually presented stimuli. Optic aphasics can convey their recognition of a visual stimulus by gesturing (e.g. a drinking motion when shown a cup) or sorting semantically related stimuli together, and can name stimuli in modalities other than vision. Most authors currently distinguish between associative agnosia and optic aphasia, although patients suffering the latter have sometimes been called associative agnosics (e.g. Ferro & Santos, 1984). The line between the disorders has been further blurred by some authors' suggestions that optic aphasia is a mild version of associative agnosia in which naming is impaired but other manifestations of recognition are preserved (Bauer & Rubens, 1985; Kertesz, 1987). The underlying impairment in optic aphasia is unclear (see Farah, 1990, Chapter 5, for a review of interpretations of optic aphasia). To the extent that optic aphasics are able to derive semantic understanding of visual stimuli, it seems strange that they should be unable to name them. In recent years the preservation of semantic encoding in optic aphasics has been questioned, and sorting tasks designed to test recognition of visual stimuli more stringently have revealed defective performance (Hillis & Caramazza, 1995; Riddoch & Humphreys, 1987b). This suggests that optic aphasia may be a problem of accessing very precise semantic knowledge from vision rather than of accessing language per se. However, optic aphasics can often make extremely specific gestures to identify objects by pantomime that they cannot identify by name. On the face of things, this suggests that semantic knowledge is intact and that the problem is language-specific or at least disproportionate for vision–language coordination. (It has been countered, however, that preserved pantomime reflects the use of direct vision–action associations, not mediated by semantic knowledge; see Riddoch, ibid; Riddoch & Humphreys, 1987b.) In addition, language may help support the representation of fine semantic distinctions in sorting tasks (Luria, 1961), making these alternative interpretations difficult to distinguish empirically.

Associative agnosia, in the sense discussed here, should also be distinguished from *semantic memory impairment*, including category-specific impairments for living or man-made objects. The relation between these two types of impairment is admittedly far from clear at present, particularly when the semantic impairment involves modality-specific visual semantic knowledge (as has been hypothesised when knowledge of living things is impaired, e.g. Warrington & Shallice, 1984; Farah & McClelland, 1991). Nevertheless, the two seem empirically distinct, with some agnosic patients able to answer questions about even the visual attributes of objects from memory (e.g. Behrmann, Winocur, & Moscovitch, 1992) and some semantically impaired patients performing normally on tests of visual perception (e.g. De Renzi & Lucchelli, 1994).

SUBTYPES OF ASSOCIATIVE AGNOSIA

Face–object dissociations

Within associative agnosia, the scope of the impairment varies from patient to patient, with recognition of faces, objects and printed words all pairwise dissociable. When the agnosia is confined to faces or disproportionately severe for faces, it is *prosopagnosia*. There are many cases of profound face recognition impairment, with little or no evident object agnosia, in the literature (e.g. Bornstein & Kidron, 1959; Cole & Perez-Cruet, 1964; De Renzi, 1986; Shuttleworth, Syring, & Allen, 1982; Whiteley & Warrington, 1977). A classic case study of prosopagnosia by Pallis (1955) is excerpted here:

> He was of above average intelligence and his general level of awareness was extremely keen. His memory was remarkable . . . His span of digit retention was 8 forward and 6 backwards. There was no hesitation in his speech and he could obey complex orders. He read smoothly and there was no trouble in understanding and later describing what he had read . . . He promptly recognized, named, and demonstrated the use of a wide variety of test objects . . . The significance of line drawings was immediately apparent to him, and he could accurately describe the content of various pictures he was shown.
>
> He mixed readily with the other patients on the ward, but rarely spoke unless spoken to first. He could not identify his medical attendants. "You must be a doctor because of your white coat, but I don't know which one you are. I'll know if you speak." He failed to identify his wife during visiting hours. She was told one day, without his possible knowledge, to walk right past his bed, but he did not show the least sign of recognition. Repeated attempts were made to "catch him out" but none succeeded. If the disability was a feigned one, it was a performance of quite unbelievable virtuosity and consistency . . . He failed to identify pictures of Mr Churchill, Mr Aneurin Bevan, Hitler, Stalin, Miss Marilyn Monroe, or Mr Groucho Marx. When confronted with such portraits he would proceed deductively, analyzing one feature after another, searching for the "critical detail" which would yield the answer. In human faces, this was rarely forthcoming. There was somewhat less difficulty with animal faces. A goat was eventually recognized by its ears and beard, a giraffe by its neck, a crocodile by its dentition, and a cat by its whiskers . . .
>
> The patient analyzed his difficulty in identifying faces with considerable insight. "I can see the eyes, nose, and mouth quite clearly, but they just don't add up. They all seem chalked in, like on a blackboard . . . I have to tell by the clothes or by the voice whether it is a man or a woman . . . The hair may help a lot, or if there is a mustache . . .
>
> "At the club I saw someone strange staring at me, and asked the steward who it was. You'll laugh at me. I'd been looking at myself in a mirror."

Are faces really disproportionately impaired in prosopagnosia, or does the appearance of a selective deficit result from the need for exceedingly fine discrimination among visually similar members of a single category (e.g. Bauer, 1993; Damasio, 1990)? Phrased in terms of relations among the agnosias, is prosopagnosia distinct from object agnosia, or is it just a mild version of the same? Recent evidence suggests that it is a distinct disorder. McNeil and Warrington (1993) showed that a prosopagnosic patient was better able to recognise individual sheep faces than individual human faces, even though normal subjects find the human faces easier to recognise. Farah, Klein, and Levinson (1995) showed that a prosopagnosic was disproportionately impaired at face recognition relative to common object recognition, taking into account the difficulty of the stimulus sets for normal subjects. This was true even when the common objects were all eyeglass frames, a large and visually homogeneous category. Figure 9.3 shows typical stimuli from this experiment. Farah, Wilson, Drain, and Tanaka (1995) showed that the same subject was impaired at upright face perception relative to inverted face perception, even though normal subjects find the latter harder.

The existence of patients who are more impaired with objects than with faces also supports the independence of prosopagnosia and object agnosia. Moscovitch, Winocur and Behrmann (1997) have examined the face recognition ability of case C.K. in detail, and have shown that it is preserved relative to his object recognition ability. In fact, when given the face and eyeglass recognition task, which we developed for assessing the selectivity of the face recognition impairment in prosopagnosia, C.K.'s results deviated from normalcy in the opposite direction: He was preserved at face recognition, relative to the normal pattern of performance on faces and eyeglasses (unpublished data).

Word–object dissociations

Pure alexics typically read words letter by letter, in a slow and sometimes error-prone manner. Their impairment is called "pure" because they are able to comprehend spoken words, they have no problem writing words, and their recognition of objects and faces seems normal. Although pure alexia is generally discussed in the context of language and reading disorders, it is clearly also an impairment of visual recognition affecting printed words. Furthermore, in all the cases so far examined, the visual recognition impairment is not confined to words, but also affects the processing of nonorthographic stimuli whenever rapid processing of multiple shapes is required, be they letters in words or sets of abstract shapes (Farah & Wallace, 1991; Kinsbourne & Warrington, 1962; Levine & Calvanio, 1978; see Farah & Wallace, 1991 for a discussion of some apparently conflicting data). Although clinical descriptions suggest that in some cases orthographic stimuli may be disproportionately affected, for example relative to numerical stimuli, this can be understood in terms of segregation of representations for orthographic stimuli within a visual area dedicated to rapid encoding of multiple shapes in general. Polk and Farah (1995, 1998) describe and test a mechanism by which such segregation could occur in a self-organising network, based on the statistics of co-ocurrence among letter and nonletter stimuli in the environment.

Just as pure alexia is an impairment of printed word recognition in the absence of obvious impairments of single object recognition, there are cases of object recognition impairment with preserved reading. For example, the case of Gomori and Hawryluk (1984) was impaired at recognising a variety of objects

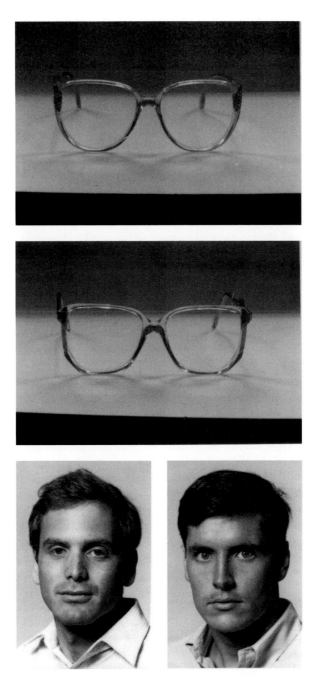

FIG. 9.3 Examples of glasses and face stimuli used in Farah, Klein, and Levinson's (1995) experiments.

and the faces of his friends and family. He nevertheless continued to read with ease, even when interfering lines were drawn across the words. Thus, like prosopagnosia and object agnosia, pure alexia and object agnosia are doubly dissociable.

Relations among prosopagnosia, object agnosia, and pure alexia

Although the pairwise dissociability of agnosia for faces, objects and words might seem to imply that there are three underlying forms of visual recognition ability, I have suggested that there may be only two underlying recognition abilities, based on the patterns of co-occurence among the associative agnosias (Farah, 1991). If there were three forms of visual recognition ability, one would expect to see all three-way combinations of impaired and preserved face, object, and word recognition. However, in a survey of 99 published cases of visual associative agnosia, there were no unambiguous cases of impaired object recognition without either impaired face or word recognition, and no unambigous cases of both impaired face and word recognition without impaired object recognition. This outcome is consistent with just two abilities: One essential for face recognition, used for object recognition, and not used for printed word recognition, and the other essential for printed word recognition, used for object recognition, and not used for face recognition.

This two-part organisation for visual recognition brings out a regularity in the neuropathology of asssociative visual agnosia. Agnosia has been noted after both unilateral left and right hemisphere damage as well as bilateral damage. When the two types of agnosia hypothesised here are considered separately, this wide variability in lesion site is reduced. Agnosic patients presumed to have an impairment of just the first ability (in mild form affecting just faces, in more severe form affecting faces and objects but not words) usually have bilateral inferior lesions, although occasionally unilateral right hemisphere lesions are reported (Farah, 1991). Agnosic patients presumed to have an impairment of just the second ability (in mild form affecting just words, in more severe form affecting words and objects but not faces) generally have unilateral left inferior lesions (Farah, 1991; Feinberg et al., 1994). Agnosic patients presumed to have an impairment in both abilities (affecting faces, objects and words) generally have bilateral lesions.

How do the two hypothesised recognition abilities differ functionally? I have suggested an answer to this question based on the concept of a structural description. In a structural description, shapes are decomposed into parts that are explicitly represented as units of shape in their own right. The first type of visual recognition ability may involve the ability to represent complex units of shape, for objects that undergo little or no part decomposition. The other type may involve the ability to represent numerous units of shape, for objects that undergo extensive part decomposition. There is evidence that face recognition depends on the ability to represent complex shape holistically, that is without part decomposition (Farah, Wilson, Drain, & Tanaka, 1998; Farah, Tanaka, & Drain, 1995; Tanaka & Farah, 1993). There is also evidence that printed word recognition depends on the ability to represent complex shape in terms of parts (Johnston & McClelland, 1980) and that selective impairments in printed word recognition arise from a limitation in the number of shape units that can be apprehended simultaneously (Farah & Wallace, 1991).

The sufficiency of just two underlying recognition abilities for explaining all manifestations of associative agnosia has recently been challenged. Buxbaum, Glosser and Coslett (1996) describe a case in which recognition of all three categories of stimuli were impaired, but the alexia and prosopagnosia were severe in comparison to the object agnosia. As the authors point out, such a case is not easily accommodated by the hypothesis of two underlying abilities, although it can be made to fit with additional assumptions. Potentially more decisive evidence against the hypothesis has been provided by Humphreys, Rumiati, and colleagues in the form of two case studies of patients with impaired object processing in the absence of alexia or prosopagnosia. The published case (Rumiati, Humphreys, Riddoch, & Bateman, 1994) has been critiqued by me on the grounds that the patient's problem was in semantics, especially access to semantics from vision (whether printed words or objects), not visual object representation per se (Farah, 1997a). Of course, this was not the last word on the case (Rumiati & Humphreys, 1997; Farah, 1997b), and another case report is forthcoming (Humphreys & Rumiati, 1998). Further research will undoubtedly clarify the proper interpretation of these cases, and their implications for the underlying architecture of visual object recognition.

ACKNOWLEDGEMENTS

The writing of this chapter was supported by NIH grants RO1 R01 NS34030, R01-AG14082 and K02-AG0056. I thank Glyn Humphreys for his helpful editing of this chapter.

REFERENCES

Adler, A. (1944). Disintegration and restoration of optic recognition in visual agnosia: Analysis of a case. *Archives of Neurology and Psychiatry, 51*, 243–59.

Albert, M.L., Reches, A., & Silverberg, R. (1975). Associative visual agnosia without alexia. *Neurology, 25*, 322–6.

Alexander, M.P., & Albert, M.L. (1983). The anatomical basis of visual agnosia. In A. Kertesz (Ed.), *Localization in neuropsychology*. New York: Academic Press.

Bauer, R.M. (1982). Visual hypoemotionality as a symptom of visual-limbic disconnection in man. *Archives of Neurology, 39*, 702–8.

Bauer, R.M. (1993). Agnosia. In K.M. Heilman & E. Valenstein (Eds), *Clinical neuropsychology, 3rd Edn*. New York: Oxford University Press.

Bauer, R.M., & Rubens, A.B. (1985). Agnosia. In K.M. Heilman & E. Valenstein (Eds), *Clinical neuropsychology*, 2nd edn. New York: Oxford University Press.

Behrmann, M., Moscovitch, M., Black, S., & Mozer, M. (1990). Perceptual and conceptual mechanisms in neglect dyslexia: Two contrasting case studies. *Brain, 113*, 1163–83.

Behrmann, M., Winocur, G., & Moscovitch, M. (1992). Dissociation between mental imagery and object recognition in a brain-damaged patient. *Nature, 359*, 636–7.

Benson, D.F., & Greenberg, J.P. (1969). Visual form agnosia. *Archives of Neurology, 20*, 82–9.

Bornstein, B., & Kidron, D.P. (1959). Prosopagnosia. *Journal of Neurology, Neurosurgery, and Psychiatry, 22*, 124–31.

Brown, J.W. (1972). *Aphasia, apraxia and agnosia: Clinical and theoretical aspects.* Springfield, IL: Charles C. Thomas.

Buxbaum, L.J., Glosser, G., & Coslett, H.B. (1996). Relative sparing of object recognition in alexia-prosopagnosia. *Brain and Cognition, 32*, 202–5.

Campion, J., & Latto, R. (1985). Apperceptive agnosia due to carbon monoxide poisoning: An interpretation based on critical band masking from disseminated lesions. *Behavioral Brain Research, 15*, 227–40.

Caramazza, A. (1984). The logic of neuropsychological research and the problem of patient classification in aphasia. *Brain and Language, 21*, 9–20.

Cole, M., & Perez-Cruet, J. (1964). Prosopagnosia. *Neuropsychologia, 2*, 237–46.

Damasio, A.R. (1990). Synchronous activation in multiple cortical regions: a mechanism for recall. *Seminars in The Neurosciences, 2*, 287–96.

Davidoff, J., & Wilson, B. (1985). A case of visual agnosia showing a disorder of pre-semantic vision classification. *Cortex, 21*, 121–34.

De Renzi, E. (1986). Current issues in prosopagnosia. In H.D. Ellis, M.A. Jeeves, F. Newcome, & A. Young (Eds), *Aspects of face processing.* Dordrecht: Martinus Nijhoff.

De Renzi, E., & Lucchelli, F. (1994). Are semantic systems separately represented in the brain? The case of living category impairment. *Cortex, 30*, 3–25.

Farah, M.J. (1990). *Visual agnosia: Disorders of object recognition and what they tell us about normal vision.* Cambridge, MA: MIT Press/Bradford Books.

Farah, M.J. (1991). Patterns of co-occurrence among the associative agnosias: Implications for visual object representation. *Cognitive Neuropsychology, 8*, 1–19.

Farah, M.J. (1997a). Distinguishing perceptual and semantic impairments affecting visual object recognition. *Visual Cognition, 4*, 199–206.

Farah, M.J. (1997b). Reply to Rumiati and Humphreys. *Visual Cognition, 4*, 219–20.

Farah, M.J., Klein, K.L., & Levinson, K.L. (1995). Face perception and within-category discrimination in prosopagnosia. *Neuropsychologia, 33*, 661–74.

Farah, M.J., & McClelland, J.L. (1991). A computational model of semantic memory impairment: Modality-specificity and emergent category-specificity. *Journal of Experimental Psychology: General, 120*, 339–57.

Farah, M.J., Tanaka, J.W., & Drain, H.M. (1995). What causes the face inversion effect? *Journal of Experimental Psychology: Human Perception and Performance, 21*, 628–34.

Farah, M.J., & Wallace, M.A. (1991). Pure alexia as a visual impairment: A reconsideration. *Cognitive Neuropsychology, 8*, 313–34.

Farah, M.J., Wilson, K.D., Drain, H.M., & Tanaka, J.W. (1995). The inverted inversion effect in prosopagnosia: Evidence for mandatory face-specific processing mechanisms. *Vision Research, 35*, 2089–93.

Farah, M.J., Wilson, K.D., Drain, H.M., & Tanaka, J.W. (1998). What is "special" about face recognition? *Psychological Review, 105*, 482–98.

Feinberg, T.E., Schindler, R.J., Ochoa, E., Kwan, P.C., & Farah, M.J. (1994). Associative visual agnosia and alexia without prosopagnosia. *Cortex, 30*, 395–411.

Ferro, J.M., & Santos, M.E. (1984). Associative visual agnosia: A case study. *Cortex, 20*, 121–34.

Gelb, A., & Goldstein, K. (1918). Analysis of a case of figural blindness. *Neurology and Psychology*, *41*, 1–143.

Gomori, A.J., & Hawryluk, G.A. (1984). Visual agnosia without alexia. *Neurology*, *34*, 947–50.

Hillis, A., & Caramazza, A. (1995). Cognitive and neural mechanisms underlying visual and semantic processing: Implications from "optic aphasia". *Journal of Cognitive Neuroscience*, *7*, 457–78.

Humphreys, G.W., & Riddoch, M.J. (1987). The fractionation of visual agnosia. In G.W. Humphreys, & M.J. Riddoch (Eds), *Visual object processing: A cognitive neuropsychological approach*. London: Lawrence Erlbaum Associates.

Humphreys, G.W., & Rumiati, R.I. (1998). Agnosia without prosopagnosia or alexia: Evidence for stored visual memories specific to objects. *Cognitive Neuropsychology*, *15*, 243–78.

Johnston, J.C., & McClelland, J.C. (1980). Experimental tests of a hierarchical model of word identification. *Journal of Verbal Learning and Verbal Behavior*, *19*, 503–24.

Kertesz, A. (1987). The clinical spectrum and localization of visual agnosia. In G.W. Humphreys, & M.J. Riddoch (Eds), *Visual object processing: A cognitive neuropsychological approach*. London: Lawrence Erlbaum Associates.

Kinsbourne, M., & Warrington, E.K. (1962). A disorder of simultaneous form perception. *Brain*, *85*, 461–86.

Konorski, J. (1967). *Integrative Activity of the Brain*. Chicago: University of Chicago Press.

Landis, T., Graves, R., Benson, F., & Hebben, N. (1982). Visual recognition through kinaesthetic mediation. *Psychological Medicine*, *12*, 515–31.

Levine, D.N. (1978). Prosopagnosia and visual object agnosia: A behavioral study. *Neuropsychologia*, *5*, 341–65.

Levine, D.N., & Calvanio, R. (1978). A study of the visual defect in verbal alexia-simultanagnosia. *Brain*, *101*, 65–81.

Levine, D.N., & Calvanio, R. (1989). Prosopagnosia: A defect in visual configural processing. *Brain and Cognition*, *10*, 149–170.

Lissauer, H. (1890). Ein fall von seelenblindheit nebst einem Beitrage zur Theori derselben. *Archiv für Psychiatrie und Nervenkrankheiten*, *21*, 222–70.

Luria, A.R. (1961). *The role of speech in the regulation of normal and abnormal behavior*. New York: Pergaman Press.

McCarthy, R.A., & Warrington, E.K. (1986). Visual associative agnosia: A clinico-anatomical study of a single case. *Journal of Neurology, Neurosurgery, and Psychiatry*, *49*, 1233–40.

McNeil, J.E., & Warrington, E.K. (1993). Prosopagnosia: A face-specific disorder. *Quarterly Journal of Experimental Psychology*, *46A*, 1–10.

Mack, J.L., & Boller, F. (1977). Associative visual agnosia and its related deficits: The role of the minor hemisphere in assigning meaning to visual perceptions. *Neuropsychologia*, *15*, 345–9.

Marcar, V.L., & Cowey, A. (1992). The effect of removing superior temporal cortical motion areas in the Macaque monkey: II. Motion discriminations using random dot displays. *European Journal of Neuroscience*, *4*, 1228–38.

Milner, A.D., Perrett, D.I., Johnston, R.S., Benson, P.J., Jordan, T.R., Heeley, D.W., Bettucci, D., Mortara, F., Mutani, R., Terrazzi, E., & Davidson, D.L.W. (1991). Perception and action in "visual form agnosia". *Brain*, *114*, 405–28.

Moscovitch, M., Winocur, G., & Behrmann, M. (1997). What is special about face recognition? Nineteen experiments on a person with visual object agnosia and dyslexia but normal face recognition. *Journal of Cognitive Neuroscience*, *9*, 555–604.

Nielsen, J.M. (1936). *Agnosia, apraxia, and aphasia: Their value in cerebral localization*. New York: Paul Hoeber.

Pallis, C.A. (1955). Impaired identification of faces and places with agnosia for colors. *Journal of Neurology, Neurosurgery and Psychiatry*, *18*, 218–24.

Plaut, D.C., & Farah, M.J. (1990). Visual object representation: Interpreting neurophysiological data within a computational framework. *Journal of Cognitive Neuroscience*, *2*, 320–43.

Polk, T.A., & Farah, M.J. (1995). Brain localization for arbitrary stimulus categories: A simple account based on Hebbian learning. *Proceedings of the National Academy of Sciences, 92,* 12370–3.

Polk, T.A., & Farah, M.J. (1998). The neural development and organization of letter recognition: Evidence from functional neuroimaging, computational modeling, and behavioral studies. *Proceedings of the National Academy of Sciences, 95,* 847–52.

Ratcliff, G., & Newcombe, F. (1982). Object recognition: Some deductions from the clinical evidence. In A.W. Ellis (Ed.), *Normality and pathology in cognitive functions.* New York: Academic Press.

Riddoch, M.J., & Humphreys, G.W. (1987a). A case of integrative visual agnosia. *Brain, 110,* 1431–62.

Riddoch, M.J., & Humphreys, G.W. (1987b). Visual object processing in optic aphasia: A case of semantic access agnosia. *Cognitive Neuropsychology, 4,* 131–85.

Rubens, A.B., & Benson, D.F. (1971). Associative visual agnosia. *Archives of Neurology, 24,* 305–16.

Rumiati, R.I., & Humphreys, G.W. (1997). Visual object agnosia without prosopagnosia or alexia: Arguments for separate knowledge stores. *Visual Cognition, 4,* 207–17.

Rumiati, R.I., Humphreys, G.W., Riddoch, M.J., & Bateman, A. (1994). Visual object agnosia without prosopagnosia or alexia: Evidence for hierarchical theories of visual recognition. *Visual Cognition, 1,* 181–226.

Shuttleworth, E.C., Syring, V., & Allen, N. (1982). Further observations on the nature of prosopagnosia. *Brain and Cognition, 1,* 302–32.

Tanaka, J.W., & Farah, M.J. (1993). Parts and wholes in face recognition. *Quarterly Journal of Experimental Psychology, 46A,* 225–45.

Warrington, E.K. (1985). Agnosia: The impairment of object recognition. In P.J. Vinken, G.W. Bruyn, & H.L. Klawans (Eds), *Handbook of clinical neurology.* Amsterdam: Elsevier.

Warrington, E.K., & Shallice, T. (1984). Category specific semantic impairments. *Brain, 107,* 829–54.

Whiteley, A.M., & Warrington, E.K. (1977). Prosopagnosia: A clinical, psychological, and anatomical study of three patients. *Journal of Neurology, Neurosurgery and Psychiatry, 40,* 395–403.

Author index

Subject index